RAINBOWS, RECOLLECTIONS AND REALITY

A Memoir of mid-twentieth Century Britain
(1935-1955)

Wendy and family.

RAINBOWS, RECOLLECTIONS AND REALITY

A Memoir of mid-twentieth Century Britain
(1935-1955)

Wendy M. Stuart

HAYLOFT PUBLISHING LTD.
CUMBRIA

First published by Hayloft Publishing Ltd., 2015

Hayloft Publishing Ltd, South Stainmore,
Kirkby Stephen, Cumbria, CA17 4DJ

tel: 07971 352473
email: books@hayloft.eu
web: www.hayloft.eu

ISBN 978 1 910237 11 3

Designed, printed and bound in the EU

Papers used by Hayloft are natural, recyclable products made from wood grown
in sustainable forests. The manufacturing processes conform to the environmental
regulations of the country of origin.

*For those that I have always loved
and always will*

FOREWORD

Wendy was a member of my Creative Writing classes a couple of years ago and one of the first exercises was to take a childhood memory and to treat it as a piece of creative non-fiction. She read a piece to the class that began with a recollection of playing alongside her sister Jane which developed into an enchanting account of a fond father's magical imagination. I saw the reactions on the faces of the students in the group and knew instantly that Wendy's was a story that was crying out to be written and read.

I asked if there was any more that she could remember. Over the following weeks, then months she wrote the story of twenty years of her life in such painstaking and well-remembered detail that I became absolutely fascinated. There is so much buried treasure to be discovered in each episode that it is just like opening a memory box full of things that we have long forgotten. Wendy's dedication and careful efforts to produce this lovingly re-created memoir have been truly remarkable.

She combines an artist's eye with her own unique writer's voice and this combination allows us to step into the Britain of the 1930s, 1940s and 1950s in the company of an experienced and trusted guide. This is Wendy's third book and to me it is the most extraordinary, because it gives me as a reader something so very special – a look through a door that would have remained permanently closed were it not for this beautiful memoir.

Wendy is a person of a great many talents that she has brought to bear on the making of this book. She has written an intensely personal account. Yet it is a story which will affect everyone who grew up in wartime and post-war Britain, but this is no dry history tome. This is real life and she gives it an intensity and proximity that at times can be quite breathtaking. As she revealed her story week by week, it often reminded me of things my own grandmothers and aunts had told me about their growing up during the same period.

There was an urgency and commitment to the telling of this story which never wavered throughout the time Wendy was writing it and I admired this so much. I watched her piece together all the parts of her life like a jigsaw of the past and I am very proud of being able to say that I was witness to the writing of the first chapter of Wendy's compelling and captivating work.

Susanne Holt, BA Hons, MA(Lit)
Course Leader for Creative Writing,
Runshaw College, Lancashire.

CONTENTS

Part 1, 1935-43

1	The fairies' Rainbows	9
2	Leaving Fairyland	12
3	Victorian Magic	17
4	The Faraway Tree	26
5	The Paintbox	32
6	Bowers House harvest	38
7	Piglet's Great Adventure	43

Part 2, 1943-45

8	Nunk Knowles	49
9	Thunderbolt	56
10	Bailey Bridges	61
11	Hens and Coal Mines	69
12	The Red Fez	75

Part 3, 1945-48

13	Reality Check	82
14	Oddity of Peace	88
15	London Awakes	95
16	Life in Isleworth	103
17	Going Shrimping	112

Part 4, 1948-50

18	Sporting Chance	120
19	Real Red Blood!	130
20	Those men in Blue	137
21	Royalty	142
22	Wisdom of Solomon	148

Part 5, 1950-52

23	Tigerlily	156
24	Sounding Brass	163
25	Ettersgill Farm	169
26	Win Some, lose Some	178
27	Horse Sense	184
28	A Taste of Yorkshire	191

Part 6, 1952-55

29	Banishing Bwana Devils	198
30	Cuckfield Park	207
31	French Connection	217
32	Broom Close and the Bull	225
33	The Shropshire Rat	234
34	Busby Stoop	244
35	An 1854 Wedding Dress	255

Epilogue and Aferword — 262

'Hillbrook', the house at Holywood, near Belfast, Northern Ireland.

THE FAIRIES' RAINBOWS

The bedroom was pretty in pink with rosebud motifs, scattered across the wallpaper. Two beds were placed on either side of a large doll's house, one a normal small bed, and the other a large drop-sided cot, with blankets slung over the barred sides. In the middle of the room was a low round table surrounded by chairs of differing sizes for holding their assorted guests of dollies and teddies, awaiting their afternoon tea. Presiding over this make believe meal was four year old Jane. Her younger two and a half year old sister, myself, had set up another small table, laid out with smaller little plates and mugs, beside which I was happily talking, seemingly to myself.

'Now come and drink your milk or the teddies will have it!' I implored my invisible guests, while continuing to hand out make believe food to the fairy folk.

'You must stop the teddies growling at my fairies!' I called out to my sister, who was engrossed with her own guests of dollies, rabbits and teddy bears, offering them papier-mâché cakes, plaster cast jam tarts and make believe jellies, and real little sweets out of a tiny packet.

'Don't be silly. They don't exist! You cannot see them! You're such a baby!' My sister's reply started me sobbing, 'They do, they do, and Daddy says so!'

The outside world did not intrude into this secret make believe world until tea time. By now the evening became darker and colder, with the sea mists sneaking in unobtrusively among the buildings along the shore. The herring gulls subsided into the night, gradually lessening their eerie calls. Within an hour the street lamps acquired haloes of mist, fading away, and finally disappeared into the deepening fog.

New sounds became apparent; the fog horns in Belfast Loch that were so vital to the safety of the continuous stream of craft in this busy shipping lane. The mournful sounds of foghorns repeated their warnings at regular intervals which seemed louder in the dark.

I put off going to bed, but sat instead on the landing window sill peering out into the mists. I longed for Daddy to return quickly from the Barracks, he who made all things possible for me. I looked wistfully at the old grandfather clock on the landing, which struck every quarter hour with deep melodious chimes, wishing that I knew how to read it. At that age, I thought the foghorns must be sea goblins, and believed that, like many little girls living in Ireland, I was surrounded by the wee folk that I could not see, but knew they were there.

When my father, who was a Major at Holywood Barracks, returned by nightfall, I was in a tearful state, and could not be persuaded to go to bed into my high sided cot. Jane, however, not bothered in the least about foghorns, demanded a bedtime story, whilst Father lifted me into my cot still protesting loudly, 'They are coming here. They are the wailing Banshees!'

I was finally placated into resting by Father, who drew me a handful of exquisite little pictures of fairies, and pinned one of them on the wall, saying, 'The good fairies will protect you, and arrive here down their rainbows, or the sunbeams in fine weather, even when you cannot see them.' He arranged some blankets to hang over the cot sides to create a little cave, promising to bring the fairy queen to visit me the next evening, and finally sang a little song, with the hint of an Irish accent flowing from his twinkling, smiling face. Thus I was lulled to sleep.

The November weather continued to be cold and misty, so the next day my sister and I with Mother took a trip into Belfast to cheer ourselves up, buying warm mitts and woolly pom-pom hats, then returned in the evening dusk, when again the sea mists rolled in and the eerie sounds of the foghorns continued to sound their alerts, in the otherwise silent loch.

Over the water the sounds were magnified, and reverberated round the echoing hills. The different foghorns were pitched at varying levels of sound, and their continual cries seemed to be having an urgent conversation among themselves, the more distant ones being softer in speech. There was a kind of musical rhythm to be heard across the watery expanses, occasionally interspersed with the clangs of the mid-chan-

My father.

nel bells on the buoys, with the herring gulls joining in to this maritime orchestration, like a symphony of the sea, but all the more eerie in the stillness of fog.

Our kindly father, already home before us, greeted us shoppers with cheerful playfulness, admired our purchases, and tried on the pom-pom hats. We sat down for a well anticipated tea in front of the big fire, spearing teacakes on the toasting forks in front of the flames, while Father remarked that the fire sprites danced a merry jig whilst cooking the teacakes, then leapt up the chimney, riding upon the billowing and twisting smoke

'They are watching for the road up to fairyland, for the bright rainbows are their pathways, and the fairies ride along them from place to place. Sometimes they travel on the sunbeams! This is how they visit children everywhere!'

When the subject of bedtime arose, Father said to Jane and I, 'I have a surprise for you. Tonight the Fairy Queen and all her attendants have come to play with you, but will only come out of hiding when you are both in bed!' Hearing this promise, we rushed up the stairs, the wailing foghorns now forgotten in our eagerness to reach the bedroom. Jane was the first into the room, and put on the light, but she could see no changes. Mother and I followed her in, but likewise could see no difference, no fairies. We wondered what we should have expected.

'Where? How? When?' We clamoured for answers, but Father said, 'You haven't fulfilled your part of the bargain yet. You will only see the fairies when both of you are in bed and ready for sleep, with the light off! Then they will surely come out to dance for you all night,' then added, 'quick now and into bed with you!' With that said, we

The family, left to right, my sister Jane, Mother, the author, and Father.

were soon into our beds as he turned off the light.

The transformation was truly magnificent! Accustoming our eyes to the dark, slowly it was possible to see little fairies, and then larger ones, near and far off, flitting in all directions, swooping as if in glee to all corners of the room, dancing and frolicking everywhere. They had large delicate wings, and gossamer dresses that trailed as they flew, perhaps pink, or was it blue? This was all a joy to behold for us both. We stared spellbound at the display quite transfixed with the magic, until our tired heads nodded off to sleep, with the goblin foghorns entirely forgotten.

The next day, with the sunshine streaming into the room, not a fairy could be seen. Nor were they ever seen in the daylight. But they returned each night in the dark to watch over us.

Father was up early the next day, and drove back to the Barracks.

'Morning, Major!' his Staff Sergeant said. 'I've solved the problem of the vehicles driving on the grassy curb sides. I had big stones placed to line the routes, and then painted them with that stuff you ordered, to make them shine. That was what you bought it for, wasn't it?' The Major just smiled.

LEAVING FAIRYLAND

Living in Northern Ireland clearly had an impact on me from an early age – my mind is littered with many early memories, unfortunately very few preceding my second birthday. Some incidents though have remained, for I clearly remember one occasion of being fastened into the High Cross pram with my reins, when I reached up to pull the fringe off the sun canopy. But records show that I was born in a Preston nursing home, taken to Catterick Camp in North Yorkshire, where I was duly christened at Richmond Church, and then taken at about three months old to my father's new posting in Northern Ireland. Being the commanding officer of his regiment, he chose to live, not in the barracks itself, but in a tall, square Victorian house, Mrs Kemp and her family being the other Anglo-Irish occupants, and proved to be great fun for us all. It was not far outside the barracks, in a small pretty village called Holywood, overlooking the sea in Belfast Lough, within striking distance of my father's beloved golf links. He and all his family were keen players.

On the beach at Holywood –
Father, Jane, Miss Robinson and myself.

For those first five years, my memories of life were happy and always seemingly sunny; I thought it would last forever. Father worked at the Barracks much of the time, but took us on long walks across the golf links, carrying me on his shoulders down to the sea, when he felt like going for a swim. Mother had her car there, a little Austin 7, and on fine days we explored the coastal areas, picnicking and swimming on the Strand in Antrim, (long miles of hard sands that could be driven upon), always accompanied by Miss Robinson, our loving, and very Irish, governess, who guarded us children, like a mother duck with her ducklings, while Mother did the practical duties of packing picnic hampers, sorting out swimsuits, sunhats, sand buckets and sun cream.

We took trips to visit relatives in other towns, such as Portadown, Armagh, Stewartstown, and Derry, (or Londonderry as it was called in the 1930s). Father came originally from a well spread out Anglo-Irish family, some of whom seemed to be involved in the army. His two younger brothers, John and Robin, and his father, all initially served in the same regiment. Having been posted to Northern Ireland, it gave us the opportunity of meeting distant relations who lived so far away, aunts and uncles who were hereafter never seen again.

Mother loved driving, and studied the road maps of the locality, planning outings.

Thus we saw the Annual Hill Road Racing (now banned) and another Annual event of the Horse racing on the Strand, and donkey racing too! We loved the "Marching Season", listening to all the local bands, for the crowds were very good humoured and fun, with children joining in all the processions. The darker political significance of these events did not touch us, and whatever the parental religious beliefs were, all the youngsters mixed freely for every occasion in those days.

At other times, in our big garden, my father spent his leisure time in planting vegetables, and

On the beach with mother.

long rows of sweet peas, interspersed with real ones. My sister quickly discovered the peas, ate them raw, and then was thoroughly sick. The cook scolded, my father laughed, and Mother said, 'I have no sympathy for you!' Father was not pleased and hatched a plan. Next day he attached a low volt wire to the supporting frame of the peas. Jane promised to leave the peas alone, but as temptation overcame good sense, she went there again for a little feast, only to recoil in indignation, and floods of tears, saying 'The peas have stung me, they have stung me!'

Seeing the ease with which my sister attracted punishment for her misdeeds, I tended

Paddling on Holywood beach.

to keep quiet, hide when trouble was brewing, and generally speaking, avoided chastisement, but my sister was high spirited, adventurous and sly, and usually liked to get her own way. But I caused my own kind of trouble by wandering off exploring everything, and on one occasion, for ever-after remembered, I walked into a bed of Kingcups (water Marigolds) growing in the centre of the shallow gravelled stream at the bottom of our garden, thinking they grew on solid ground, and when my red wellies sunk without trace into the soft stream bed, I had to scramble out barefoot, and received a severe spanking for my trouble. Minus my boots!

There was a wireless in the kitchen to which the cook listened avidly. She was joined by father's batman, and whilst preparing his equipment, polishing boots,

13

Father with sweetpeas in the garden.

belt, buttons and his 'Sam-Browne' (an officers' shoulder strap for supporting his sword) we heard them talking of strange events; appeasement, Hitler's rise, a coming war, gathering troops, recruitments, then – 'War has been declared!' and other such matters, none of which made any sense to us young eavesdroppers. However, we listened in to long conversations when our names were mentioned, as to where we should be to be safe. Were we not safe here? What did 'moving' mean? Moving other peoples' children into safe areas was discussed, but the significance of parting company with dear Papa had not yet become an issue for us.

We had visitors, army friends, who were cousins of my father, staying with us from Victoria, Vancouver in Canada, and at this uncertain time needed to travel back home in a hurry. They were going to follow his uncle, Sir Richard Stuart-Lake, the Lt. Governor of Saskatchewan, on the next ship to Canada, to help furthering his work with the Red Cross. Sir Richard had taken a berth on the *SS Athenia*. 'If you like, we will take Jane and Wendy back with us to Vancouver for the duration' they suggested.

So it was agreed that we should go for a 'holiday' with them, until the 'European situation had become clear,' and after much discussions, my mother promised to follow the Canadian relatives, with her girls, but first we were to go to our maternal grandfather's house in England, before embarking on our cross-Atlantic journey.

But this plan was quickly and firmly abandoned the first week in September, when the horrifying news of the sinking of the *SS Athenia*, a passenger ship with 1,103 people, including the Sir Richard on board. It was the first passenger ship, travelling to Montreal, to be torpedoed by a German submarine in September 1939, despite the Geneva Conventions demanding immunity for civilian ships .

Frantic with worry, and several telephone calls later, it was discovered that Sir Richard was amongst the survivors of about a thousand, and he was taken back to England to recover, our cousins met him and organised his recuperation. Some years later, very welcome food parcels arrived for us via the Red Cross system from Vancouver, and little children's gifts appeared occasionally. We were told to remember our Canadian cousins in our bedtime prayers, and I knew exactly whose safety we were praying for.

Father was soon to move with his regiment, so the house in Ireland was put up for sale. Packing up our household goods was done with a minimum of fuss and the help of the willing cook, father's batman, and another soldier, for all our belongings were to be shipped to Lancashire to my grandfather's property. By now, I felt very unsettled,

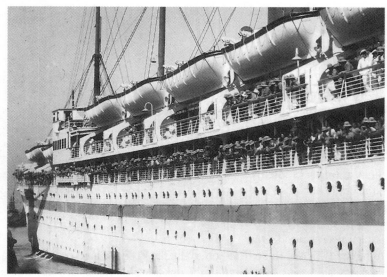

Leaving Belfast.

especially when I found out Miss Robinson was staying behind, and asked, 'What about the fairies? Will they fly to England too? We will need them!' I knew we were to cross the sea to travel to a place, somewhere a long way off. My young mind still strongly believed in their powers, but my wise father had anticipated my wishes.

'I have drawn paintings of the fairies to take with you, and the little ones are tucked up in this trunk drawn in the corner of the picture. Fairies do not like the sea, so will be much happier travelling in the dark in your suitcase.' Then he added, 'If you cannot see them, they are always with you, protecting you, and secretly flying around, riding on the rainbows.' So I believed my father implicitly – the fairies lived within the paintings and could fly out at will when I needed them!

The day of our move arrived, and the car, complete with all our crates, were taken to the docks in Belfast. We travelled in a staff car, for Father was to see us off, and then return to the barracks to oversee the regimental move. The docks, with the strong aroma of the sea, fish, and diesel, was heaving with people, a noisy busy hub of continual activity, with fishing vessels, crates of fish, and commandeered troop ships vying for space next to our small ship. There were railway lines along the docks to step over, many moving trucks to avoid, and trundles of suitcases and trunks, being made into stacks all along the quayside with large nets around them. All these stacks slowly disappeared into the holds of one ship or another, by means of the dock cranes, that hooked onto the net fastenings. The huge bundles were swung aloft and placed in the open holds with the stevedores, who rode them to guide into place, and fasten them securely against bad weather. I could not take my fascinated eyes off this activity. Eventually they shut down the hatches of our ship, having loaded our possessions and those of the other passengers.

'What about our car?' I suddenly shouted, and was given the reply, 'All five cars go on the deck!' Private cars were a rarity at that time, with no real provision for carrying many of them across the sea, and there were five of them waiting on the quayside to be loaded. Large canvas straps were placed around the first car, which had been driven onto a wooden pallet, with much packing to avoid scratching. Chains were then attached at the four corners of the pallet to the great hooks from the crane, and then heaved aloft slowly, as the main chain took the strain. One man, as usual, rode with the load, to guide the positioning of each car in turn onto the deck, where he securely fastened the platform and car with deck straps, to avoid any movement in rolling seas, finally releasing the crane hooks so that the crane driver could lift it away.

Belfast docks.

The first car was secured. Our car was to be the fifth one to be lifted on to the deck, so we said our tearful farewells to Father beside the ship, with much fear of the unknown on my part, and with many promises from him, to see us soon at my unknown grandfather's house across the sea, and a whispered 'Your fairies are in your suitcase! Now don't forget. They will keep you safe!'

We went up the gang plank, and were shown our cabin, but soon we returned to the rails of the passenger deck, to watch the outside activities again. Suddenly I witnessed an accident like a slow motion horror film, to be replayed in my mind over and over again, during the coming weeks. Another car was receiving the same treatment as the first, a bigger one with a different shape. When it had the four corner hooks of its pallet attached to the crane hook, the stevedore riding the hoist shouted 'Away! Up!' and the crane duly lifted the car way up high and began to swing it inwards.

Suddenly there was a cracking sound, and as the load was half way over the rails, it appeared to break asunder, spilling the car out onto the deck below. It landed on the Taff rail with a thunderous crashing sound, splitting the car in two. The broken piece of car that was overhanging the rail, fell into the water with a great splash. The man riding the load had also landed on the deck below, but lay motionless in a contorted position, with blood trickling out from beneath him. Instantly, men appeared, running all over the ship, carrying a stretcher to the man, picking up wreckage on the deck, and organising clearance and rescue of the portion of the car that landed in the water in front of the bow of the ship, as quickly as they could manage. Due to my tender age, the fate of the unfortunate man I never knew, and the seriousness of the accident did not register with me.

Since the declaration of war, it was vital that ships in Belfast harbour were turned around with great speed. Our ship was due to depart on the evening tide, and was holding up the safe departure of other more important vessels. Jane and I were both quite frightened by the tremendous commotion, frantic activities and hammering noises caused by the imminent departure, and remains a vivid memory. I shall never forget it. Mother pulled us away from the scene, to the dining room for some supper, before putting us both to bed in our cabin, and the last I saw of my Irish fairyland in reality, was the fading outline of the coast, seen in the gloom of the evening through the porthole, as we sailed away to England.

VICTORIAN MAGIC

We sailed into Heysham Harbour in northern Lancashire, in the early hours of the morning through sea fog, accompanied by the ever present noisy, squabbling, herring gulls. As we arrived my first memories of England were the feeling of extreme cold and the smell of damp air and fishing trawlers. I knew that it smelled differently from the home territory which I had recently left behind. Smells are very evocative of past times, and on this occasion it was one of those memories that stayed with me for some years.

We were met by grandfather's chauffeur in a big grey car, a Lanchester. Soon we were tucked in on the back seat with a red tartan rug whilst Mother organised luggage with the chauffeur. Jane and I were both thirsty but as it was about 5.30 in the morning the only drink to be had was milk from an early milkman, whose horse ambled resignedly from house to house, not requiring orders to stop and go as he worked along his well-known route. We were given square waxed cartons of milk with round press-openers for a straw. Quickly we were under way, drinking our milk whilst peering into the endless foggy spaces ahead of us, with trees looming up unexpectedly like grey spiders, intertwining with the next spider, through the mist. We suddenly spotted the tall electric pylons, which mystically disappeared into the clouds, making me think of a ladder to a weird witches' castle. My overactive imagination required rest, so I hid my head in the blanket, and soon settled down to sleep.

Bowerswood near Garstang, Lancashire, in 1939.

However, I woke up when we arrived at Grandfather's house. We were met by him, and also great-aunt Caroline, Janet, our new governess, and various staff. They helped Mother unload ourselves and our belongings; after lunch, we were hastened up to our bedroom for an afternoon sleep. We had finally arrived at our new home, a large, well-run Victorian country house with a variety of servants, to ensure the smooth running of day-to-day matters and according to Grandfather's wishes.

Unaware of it when we first arrived from Heysham, the journey from the docks to Grandfather's house was on a pretty route (a minor road off the A6 towards Knott End), which always created feelings of anticipation when arriving home again after visiting Garstang for shopping – we often cycled there and back from Bowerswood on this well-remembered road.

If we had arrived at the house first during full daylight, we would have noted the farming activities, passing various farms at regular intervals along the route, their gates opening upon timeless buildings – cow byres, milking parlours, barns, tractor sheds, and flat fields enclosing occasional flocks of sheep, but many more cows, for this was, and still is, dairy country. The muddy tracks issuing from the gated fields were evidence of the daily passage of these herds to and from their pastures for milking.

About two miles along this tree-lined road there suddenly appeared on the right hand side, a pair of large five-barred white gates supported by carved stone pillars, behind which lay a Victorian gatehouse. Opposite the gatehouse the sounds of the activities of a working farm could be heard, the clatter of milking, with the cows communicating to the farmer or the herd, whilst farm hands moved the churns onto the roadside platforms for daily collection by milk lorries.

Through these large gates one entered a mile long driveway, lined with woodland and edged with a small hawthorn hedge. Within this woodland nettles freely grew along with tall grasses and cow-parsley, all reaching for the light and their survival. The drive eventually divided into two entrances, the right hand continuing to the home farm, Bowers House, run by Farmer Jackson. This was a seventeenth century farmhouse with many outbuildings for milking herds, barns for hay and storage for the cattle provender.

Front view of Bowerswood in 1941.

To the left, was another stone built gated entrance, similar to the earlier one, and beyond this wound a yellow gravel driveway bordered with evergreens, pine trees and ornamental shrubs. The orange Montbretias in the late summer also lined the foreground, delineating the sweep of the drive. Suddenly this canopy opened out to reveal an extensive view, with the driveway surrounding a large grass circle, enclosing a big weeping ash, which stood majestically in front of the red brick Victorian house of imposing proportions, with its tall French windows, and taller chimneys. This was my grandfather's house named Bowerswood.

This was to be my home for the next ten years, to which I kept returning wherever I was, for my holidays, interspersed by the term times of school, so my memories are very seasonal – a month at Christmas, the same at Easter, and the long summer holidays, of two and a half months, somewhat longer than more recent times. The introduction of double summertime to help the war efforts in the factories, made them seem even longer.

Part of the frontage of the house was covered with Virginia creeper, which, during the advancing seasons, changed from yellow, to pink, red and purple until, its life cycle spent, the leaves all carpeted the ground. The two lone pine trees, stood in stately splendour amidst their cones on the front lawn, through which could be seen the white painted railings, fencing the parkland in front of the house. Here I often stood silently for a moment of contemplation, to breathe in the unique country perfumes of this spot, while listening to the skylarks high above, and watch the horses picking their way to tasty areas of grass in the field, where they circled round a small spinney of tall trees. I could see patches of field mushrooms unattended, to be gathered later in the day.

Whenever I entered that white painted porch, which was lined with a curved seat around it, and cushioned for comfort, I knew that I had arrived home again. The beautiful patterned Victorian tiles on the floor welcomed me; the smell of the interior white paint peeling off, caused by years of strong sunshine blistering it, evoked strong feelings of my homecomings. Whenever I finally opened the inner door with its coloured glass panel, and stepped up into the dim hall, with furniture thoroughly bees-waxed, I remember gazing upon beautifully arranged bowls of flowers, lovingly produced by my artistic Aunt Coco (Caroline). I would sit down in the King Charles' chair beside the hall table, looking at the pile of post to be taken, or visitors' cards, which were casually thrown on a silver tray, and placed next to my grandfather's beloved *Bradshaw's Almanac*.

A few words here about this remarkable man will help to create a picture of the very Victorian household in which we found ourselves. He did not easily give in to the restrictions and problems of advancing age, although it was obvious he was indeed slowing down. He was now in his mid-seventies, being born in Preston on 17 September 1863, of wealthy and hard-working parents whom he had looked up to for guidance in his early years, and was soon emulating their aspirations. As he grew, small in stature but large in ambition, he took advantage of all the opportunities that a good education could offer, then following on from attending Oxford, he chose to become articled to a solicitor, rather than follow his father into the flourishing business of running three spinning mills.

It was as well that he chose this path for a while, for he gained an insight into the

The wedding of Col. Stephen Simpson to Nathalie Hesketh, 1903.

legal aspects of these factories. When his elder brother died, he then felt able to take over the business with a certain mastery, flair and authority, a position that he rather enjoyed. He was definitely well qualified and suited to the job, having previously assisted his father for much of his time. At the age of 40, in 1903 he married an heiress, a 30 year old Bolton mill owner's daughter, producing a son and three daughters in quick succession. Sadly his wife died in 1921, leaving him the task of managing four lively young offspring. He always had tremendous energy himself, doing most activities at a trot, whilst expecting others to keep up with him. With a fairly high register to his voice, he was not easily ignored when demanding attention.

During the First World War, 1914-18, although by then 50 years of age, he enthusiastically took over the recruitment drive in his district, becoming a Brevet-Colonel, a title that he clung to for the rest of his life. The position of Lord Lieutenant of Lancashire gave him another pinnacle of influence, allowing him to be presented at Court, to further his ambitions. He was a great social climber, acquiring from the College of Heraldry a suitable coat of arms, which was displayed on all occasions, and all fitting places.

Although having great ambition, he was a kindly man in many ways, with soft brown eyes and fair wavy hair, and took responsibility for all the members (mainly female after both the wars), of his large dependant family.

Grandfather – Colonel Stephen Simpson

At the time of his marriage, having previously moved from Preston, to live in a Southport town house, Stephen Simpson felt that he had reached the stage of buying a country estate to house his growing family and upon which to lavish his wealth. Thus at the turn of the century, he bought Bowerswood, a beautiful Victorian house near Garstang, encompassed by two farms, parklands, outbuildings and stabling for his horses.

He loved the place, putting much time and effort into developing well laid out gardens, lawns and walkways. His carefully planned rose garden of chosen blooms, were much admired, and he took a delight in discussing every variety with his gardener, another rose addict! Up to a goodly age, he toured the lawns every morning with a dandelion digger, to pull out 50 of the troublesome plants before breakfast. He travelled at least three times a week into Preston to the spinning factories, or the 'works' as they were called, to oversee the smooth running of production. When I arrived at Bowerswood, this was still the norm, for wire drawing, and the spinning of copper cables as one of its products, became an essential part of the war effort.

The Colonel, as he was always called, wrote letters in a fine nineteenth century script with language to match. He loved delving into historical matters which he recorded, could complete crosswords with great speed and accuracy, had strong religious beliefs, and sang his Christmas carols in Latin. The library at Bowerswood had an eclectic mix of books, some centuries old, others the latest publications. These were housed on long bookshelves that had frilly curtains of soft leather hanging down for some three inches from the upper shelves, thus excluding much of the dust from settling on the book tops.

The Colonel spent time sitting in his large leather chair in his library, writing letters, and was an avid reader of classical novels, to which he sometimes enjoyed listening, on the Home Service on Sunday evenings. He took a little whisky and water while listening to the nine o'clock news. This was always brought to him by the parlour maid, Nellie, who filled the spill jar on the mantle-shelf, then banked up the fire with a log or two and a shovel of fir cones kept in a big brass scuttle in the hearth, previously collected from the lawns under the fir trees. Being a pipe smoker from long habit, his moustache became tinted slightly with yellow and the aroma of his preferred tobacco clung to the library curtains and himself, for many hours until the morning, when windows were thrown open to dispel the lingering traces of tobacco smoke.

Having been brought up in the Victorian era, he changed very little to accommodate the ways of the twentieth century. He liked his own way and could be irascible when challenged. But his nineteenth century ideals, mannerisms, speech and habits added to his charm. He still ran his household in a Victorian manner, with an orderly timetable, and all who lived there had to conform to this way of life, including ourselves when we arrived in 1939. It was rarely an irksome task, for the house was well run during the thirties and thereafter, with a decreasing and more elderly staff, some of whom had been there for many years. He assumed the mantle also of caring for his staff, indoors and out, by paying for all medical treatment as required, taking his responsibilities very seriously.

Aunt Flo-Jane, 1937.

This care extended also to his five aging sisters, the survivors out of seven girls, and also his two daughters and two grandchildren, I being one of them. During this troubled time, we were all welcomed into the shelter of this family home. Great grandfather had died towards the latter part of the nineteenth century, and therefore my grandfather took on the mantle as head of family after his elder brother Isaac died.

My grandfather had many recollections of his family from the past. This example was about his eldest sister from about the late 1890s. In the strict order of Victorian England, younger sisters were not encouraged to marry before the eldest had done so. Before the First World War, Florence Jane (known as Flo-Jane), being the eldest of Grandfather's sisters, and running his household for him, needed to be 'found a good husband' before the other girls had a chance of marital bliss. She had a mean, waspish and bossy nature, but nevertheless Grandfather had 'lured' a wealthy and eminently suitable suitor, Lord Grey, to meet this good-looking eldest sister, who owned a considerable dowry, left by her maternal Grandmother. Lord Grey duly presented himself at three o'clock and was shown into the drawing room, where he waited patiently for his host to appear.

The loud angry voice of Florence (Flo-Jane) could be heard clearly through the door to the dining room: 'I will not tolerate such insolence from you, your work is slapdash, and I cannot put up with another day of this behaviour!'

Flo-Jane was holding forth and scolding the poor parlourmaid with such venom, that the girl burst into tears, and ran hastily from the room. Lord Grey could hear this unpleasant scolding and much more besides, a tirade to shatter the peaceful afternoon. Grandfather hastened down and into the drawing room with the sound of the scolding of the parlourmaid, who had dropped a pail, still reverberating in his ears. As he entered, he was met by the sight of a hastily departing Lord Grey, who had unexpectedly remembered another appointment that could not wait!

By the time I arrived at Bowerswood, aunt Florence who never married, and the only one that I do not remember at all, died when I was about three, although I have seen photographs of her with me! But there were many stories about her in the family, and Grandfather had a ready store of them with which to entertain us as we grew older. She became a byword for shrewish behaviour or bossiness, so when anyone behaved in an overbearing manner they were accused of 'being a Flo-Jane'.

William and Mary Hargreaves in later life (approximately 1936).

Another example from the 1890s followed on from the previous event when his third sister, my Aunt Mary, who was the only one to eventually marry, escaped this Victorian 'order of marriage!' After his university studies, Grandfather often invited graduates he knew to visit him. One of them, William Hargreaves, just down from Dublin University, was invited to stay by Grandfather, at about the time of the upheaval with Flo Jane. Whilst on his visit, he fell in love with a younger sister, the very shy Mary. This was in 1894, just before he had booked a passage to the Malay Straits. He explained his intention of starting a public school for boys there and needed a wife to accompany him. He had witnessed the flight of Lord Grey from the house, and was hesitant to mention the matter of choosing a wife from Grandfather's sisters, in case he was fobbed off with Flo-Jane, still unspoken for, and secretly caring only to have Mary, who happened to be his third cousin.

Grandfather told us that his aged mother, realising that word would get around of

Aunt Caroline.

Flo-Jane's temper, and worried about the problem of finding so many suitable husbands for all the girls, was pleased to accept an offer for his sister Mary and to take her abroad. So, after the banns had been read in the local church, she followed William to Malaya on her own the next month, boarding a ship at Tilbury, with her ladies maid, and was married in Penang Cathedral when she eventually arrived. The school which they started so long ago is today a thriving first class public school in Malaysia, with the new Sports Hall in 2010 being named the 'Hargreaves Building'.

My great-grandfather worked long hours in his factories in Preston and London, and expected his seven daughters to make good marriages, whilst his sons would expand his empire of spinning mills. But his three youngest daughters, being as well educated as their brothers, had other ideas of using their knowledge, and had no plans for getting married. My aunt Nona told me that at an early age Beatrice, herself and Gertrude had decided they had no intention of handing over their 'marriage portion' or dowry to some man to misuse, as was the custom, whilst they would be kept housebound – they wished to travel, and this was their incentive to learn at least two languages as well as the usual accomplishments for young ladies. The two world wars only slightly altered their plans, whilst aiding them to branch out on their own.

All this set a freer trend for the younger sisters, Helen having died of a fever, a few years previously. They were all adventurous and spirited ladies. Caroline (Coco) who was born in 1870 helped with the welfare of the girls who toiled at the Works in Preston. Before the outbreak of the First World War, she was very happy to become engaged to a very jolly and kindly Captain Thompson. Like so many others, he was killed in 1917. She served as a Voluntary Aid Detachment nurse in a hospital in France, which took an almost direct hit, where they were both working and she herself was sent home wounded, and almost completely deaf. Courageously, she started working again in the hospital in Preston for a while to forget her lost love, and, deaf though she was, in 1921 when Grandmother died, she went to help run Grandfather's household very efficiently with Flo-Jane.

Caroline as a VAD nurse in World War I.

Caroline taught me elementary sign language, which proved to be very useful in my later life.

Of the three spirited sisters, Gertrude became a war correspondent for *The Times* newspaper, having first spread her wings as a successful author. Beatrice ran an equally successful lending library, and Nona, the musical one, organised a music school for singing, dancing and piano playing. They ran these enterprises in Cairo, and were well known, well-loved, and wizened like brown walnuts from the constant and extreme sunshine.

Every year in the middle of the summer heat, all three travelled back to England, usually staying at The Sesame Club (for English overseas visitors) in Park Lane. Beatrice died early in the 1940s, as did aunt Flo-Jane, creating a kind of calm in the family. But during this time, due to the London bombing, Bowerswood became a more popular port of call for the other two, where they could meet up with Mary from Malaya, and the resident Caroline.

I am sure that Grandfather made the best of our arrival from Ireland in 1939, and as the months passed we busied ourselves with our governess Janet, having our meals with her in the nursery, but never in the big formal room. We also soon found out about several wartime restrictions that were in operation. Petrol was rationed from 1939 onwards, which did not visibly affect us children, but the rationing of bacon, butter and sugar certainly did, and when asking for certain favourite foods, we were offered some other substitute, with the repeated phrase, 'Don't you realise there's a war on?' Christmas that year did not really bite into our consciousness, for all the adults made huge efforts to

Three of my aunts –
Caroline, Nona and Gertrude.

create a normal seasonal atmosphere for us, and for our cousins who joined us. Our farming neighbours ensured that the occupants of Grandfather's household did not go short of essential foods.

My great-aunts Gertrude (Gee) and Nona had arrived, to make lovely creative paper decorations, and with Aunt Coco, they filled the house with fairy lights and fantastic creations to completely captivate us, the two wide eyed little girls. My Papa's fairies flew out of their envelope, for knowing how important they were to me, Mother and Janet pinned them in various places around the upper parts of the house, for I still felt very lonely, missed Miss Robinson, and in this huge house I felt somewhat misplaced.

Aunt Gee joined in this creative bonanza, for she was an extremely good artist, and painted a large picture of Father Christmas with a full sack, standing in a little bedroom with two sleeping children. This was hung up on Christmas Eve along the banisters, lining the halfway landing, and next to it on either side, were placed several large socks for Christmas gifts. It could be seen from both the hallway below, and the upper landing where the Ottoman stood with its cushioned seat in front of the landing window. All these preparations heightened the excitement and anticipation that were new to us, and by bedtime we soon obediently went to bed and fell asleep.

On Christmas morning my young life was changed by a Christmas present!

Hearing the cockerels crowing their pre-sunrise alarms from the farm next door, we awakened very early next morning, opened the bedroom quietly, and were intent on exploring, but soon spied the Christmas stockings on the staircase. They now had names on them with things in them, so Jane lifted down both of our stockings. In hers were a few sweets, a jigsaw puzzle, other games and a Pooh bear, together with a book all about this little animal. But I did not envy my sister's toys as I usually did, because I had a Piglet! And a little shoulder bag to carry him in! Piglet held a small bag of jelly-babies between his paws and arrived with what looked like a small trunk of handmade clothes for every occasion, including his pyjamas! I now had a tangible friend to share my experiences with and to whom I could whisper my secrets, and he almost never left my side for the next ten years.

Piglet dressed in a navy blue bands-
man's outfit made in 1948
by my mother.

The Simpson Family in 1881, from left to right, back row:
Helen (1865-1910), Isaac (1860-1910), Mary (1867-1948), Jane (1833-1914), Stephen, sen. (1832-91),
Caroline (1870-1945), Florence (1862-1941), Stephen (1863-1950).
Front row: Beatrice (1873-1943), Gertrude (1869-1957), Nona (1877-1957)

THE FARAWAY TREE

In the summer sunshine the flowers waved their heads continually in the breeze. By this time of the year we were riding our small bicycles to and fro between home and Garstang, or were travelling with Janet in the trap, pulled by Poppy, the cob, with little fear from motor traffic, for the simple reason there was hardly any! We saw many other horse drawn vehicles instead, and a few horse riders. It was not long before I started exploring the interior of grandfather's house, having circumvented the outside and grounds very thoroughly, with and without my sister. The drawing room was a large and elegant formal area, with long French windows, a large open fireplace, a display cabinet, and a variety of comfortable chairs, with a pink and grey colour theme. There was a grand piano, that was often played beautifully by my great aunts. The hallway also had French windows, and a large, open and much used hearth. Leading from the hall, one came to the well-stocked library which was Grandfather's preferred lair. It always smelled faintly of pipe tobacco and I hesitated many times before disturbing him there.

The big dining room, which had been a billiards room in 1908, boasted a lantern window above it in the ceiling. It could be reached through the library, or along the long staff passage from the kitchens, by going through the 'green baize door' from the hallway, but we were told firmly never to go through this door, for it was 'Strictly out of Bounds'. But in a short while, the cook, Mrs Pearson, encouraged us to visit her for milk and the biscuits she made, so we did not advertise this fact to Grandfather or the aunts, and went round to the yard door to avoid being caught and chastised. As an excuse for being there I delivered cream from the farm, and climbed the loft ladder in the stables, to bring a few apples from the large store. She would then cook apple turnovers for us.The gun room, where the guns were secured in locked cupboards, was at the end of the long staff corridor leading from the kitchens. Down here were two outside-staff bedrooms, occasionally used for guests when a shooting party was afoot. The butler's pantry and store rooms could be accessed along there, and led down to the cellar steps to a well-stocked and cool wine cellar.

There were other areas that were out of bounds to us, namely Grandfather's bedroom, bathroom and dressing room, all situated above a large boiler house below. The boiler was fed with coke, creating an evil smell, I thought, and not a place we cared to investigate! My three aunts had their individual rooms, and there were another three for visitors. Above these were the staff bedrooms, accessed by a steep staircase to the upper floor. Also up there, I found an access door to the roof, storing this information away for further secret exploration. Down the corridor to the big bathroom, the floorboards were covered with deep green linoleum, and were always well polished with beeswax, the aroma of which pervaded the whole of that floor and when

Great-aunt Caroline (Coco)

Bowerswood's green room windows.

walking on it, always squeaked. It spoke of 'clean!'

My deaf old Aunt Coco, with her long face and even longer drop earrings, was a constant figure in the shifting, changing population of Bowerswood. Her room was at the foot of the steep, narrow staircase to the upper floor. When she retired to bed, she locked her door, sleeping soundly until the morning. Being locked in was usually of no relevance to others, and was never remarked upon. However, on one particular morning, this habitual practise had more serious consequences! She had locked herself in for the night as usual, but could not be aroused the next day.

'Caroline, Caroline, where are you? It's past breakfast time!' Grandfather called out at his shrillest, when he missed her at breakfast. He sent up Nellie to rouse her, but she was unsuccessful with her mission. No amount of knocking or banging produced any response. General panic ensued, and fearing that she had died, everyone offered various solutions. Then Stirsaker, our practical minded old gardener, went for the ladder to enter by the window which was open, but the house was a tall Victorian building, and proved to be too high for his garden ladder to reach the bedroom window. Eventually he ran to Mr Jackson's Farm, returning with the long hay-stack ladder. Then the gardener persuaded his trembling son, being the lightest person, to climb this very tall and flimsy wooden affair.

'Jus' unlock t' door fer us, and cum aht o' theer throo t' door!' his father said, whilst placing the other shorter and stronger ladder against the wall. For safety he first attached a rope onto his son, then to the upper rungs of the stout ladder, fearing he might fall. The lad climbed to her window sill, then put his leg first over the threshold, and followed this by the rest of his body and through the window opening , tumbling in onto the floor.

Aunt Coco, startled by the sight of a grubby urchin entering her room through the window, and believing him to be a robber, attacked him quite unmercifully with her umbrella that was leaning by her bed while screaming at the top of her voice, then unlocked the door to summon help! When her excitement calmed down, she explained later that she had gone to bed with a bad cold, had taken a sleeping tablet to help her rest, but had fallen into a deep slumber until the next day.

We had a big bedroom at the back of the house, with three beds, and three windows through which to view different parts of the grounds. It was known as the green room, and I could gaze longingly over the back fence to watch tantalising new activities from Mr Jackson's farm. The second window at the side, revealed the long lawns and the woods beyond. The tall trees

Part of the cobbled yard.

there were occupied each year by rooks, whose strident and insistent cries, heralded the onset of building new nests. From my bed I watched the changing weather patterns, first of all as blue skies, then pink and grey streaks of hurrying cloud formations, which passed continually overhead to make up a backdrop for the tall trees in the woods swaying in the wind all the while, as the birds wheeled around creating flight patterns, before settling onto their nests. In the garden, the flower beds were planted with sweet smelling perennial flowers, such as polyanthus, carnations or wallflowers, which were used regularly for cut flower arrangements in the house.

The third window offered views of the busy cobbled back yard, which led to the various stables, garages and sheds, where fine green moss grew between the stones. These outhouses contained four cars, three horses named Duke, Duchess and Poppy, two bicycles, the trap, and the Governess cart, pulled by the cob, Poppy, and an Atco motor mower. The mower could be ridden around the lawns, then down to the tip in the trees beyond the vegetable garden, to be emptied on the ever growing piles of rotting grass, with its distinctive, pungent smell.

The old carriage, requiring the services of both our horses, Duke and Duchess, and the coachman Fletcher, now evoked memories of grander days, not so long past, but was quietly disintegrating into oblivion in another garage, like the embers of a dying bonfire that eventually settles into ash.

Duke, Duchess and coachman Fletcher, with Grandfather in front and Melene, Valerie and Mary seated in the carriage.

We counted the array of cars in the yard, with my mother's Austin 7, Uncle Barney's MG magnet, Uncle Stephen's Morris 12 and of course grandfather's grey Lanchester. He had never mastered the art of driving cars, nor did he intend to do so. Without the

Above Uncle Barney in his car and below, Aunt Melene, Uncle Barney, and Grand-father's car

aid of four legs between the shafts to pull his trap, he was stuck in a 'nineteenth century time-warp', so he employed an old chauffeur, who acted as handyman as well. As petrol rationing bit into reality, the three other family cars were 'Laid up for the Duration' in the spare garages and shed, where they were polished, oiled and wrapped up in horse blankets. Eventually even the Lanchester had to be laid up as well, while my mother's small car was re-instated, because the petrol allowance that was given to Grandfather as a mill owner producing vital war materials, permitted greater mileage from her more economical car.

As time passed, with no petrol for the Atco, the lawns became less manicured and were drastically reduced again as more vegetables were grown. The remaining grass areas were now scythed regularly by a couple of older farm hands who were experts in the finer arts of wielding sharp scythes. Duke and Duchess, together with Poppy, enjoyed food from the hay store for their winter feed. Now the Governess cart came out again, and the trap, newly renovated to be pulled by Duchess, was our mainstay for travelling back and forth to do essential shopping. It did not take us long to help harness Poppy, a gentle creature who was clearly used to children, and it was on this cob I had my first experience of riding, on a leading rein, until I became skilful enough to control her myself. At other times, she happily ran free with the other two horses in the paddock in front of the house. Above the garages and stables there were cool, dry rooms for storing large quantities of apples, collected every harvest time, from the extensive orchards. The horses also had a useful change to their diet on bruised and damaged fruit.

The staff in Grandfather's household was ruled by the cook, Mrs Pearson, a red-headed, hardworking Lancashire lady, in her fifties. Annie worked for her in the kitchen, with her sister helping with simple tasks. In addition there was Nellie, who was about 60, trim and thin, who was now the house/parlour maid, having been a ladies' maid when younger. With this experience she helped my old aunts willingly when they came to stay. She was very good friends with Mrs Pearson, and preferred to use her spare time helping her friend in the kitchen. Due to the scarcity of food during the war, they became very inventive with the menus at mealtimes.

The external staff were either past the calling up age or medically unfit to serve in the armed forces. This applied to old

Val's car

Mrs. Pearson and Nellie

Stirsaker, and his two sons. One had asthma and the other flat feet. They all lived in Garstang, and either worked in the garden, or did maintenance work around this large property. As the war progressed, changes to the staff occurred, and the old coachman, Fletcher, retired. Bill Drummond from Lancaster was installed as the chauffeur. Another gardener handyman-cum-forester, Jack Lockwood, also joined us to make the estate more profitable for the war effort, and other itinerants, looking for a job, were sometimes employed for casual work.

Travelling into Preston occasionally, we started to notice many large barrage balloons, the size of a small house, hovering relatively low in the sky with ropes dangling beneath them. We feared these strange objects, whilst not realizing the significance of their protection from low flying enemy aircraft. Then we started to hear the first of the bombs in the distance, the wails of the sirens, which warned the civilian population to take cover. We started to see a proliferation of different air-raid shelters rapidly springing up. At first the children, then adults, were issued with 'Siren Suits', one piece outfits in navy blue, also sported by Winston Churchill, made of brushed up serge, and sold inexpensively to the general public, to wear for extra warmth in the shelters during night raids.

On one occasion Mother took us, with Janet, for a few days summer 'holiday' to Fleetwood, the nearest seaside town to Bowerswood. Having booked in to a small hotel with a large first floor family room, we were surprised to see the beach fenced off with prominent 'No Entry' signs everywhere. That week was quite hot, so instead of the expected beach holiday and sea bathing, we all made do with the large outdoor pool, sit-

My sister and I in siren suits

uated on Fleetwood promenade, and watched fascinated the daily Punch and Judy show, joining in with some organised childrens' games, run by the Women's Guild.

But the most memorable activity during this trip was watching at night, out of our upper bedroom window, the targeting and blowing up, by practising coastal batteries with their shore based naval guns, of various small old

Garstang, Lancashire, 1932,

ships and other assorted items. These had been towed out for some miles onto the vast shallow Morecombe sands. The coastal entry channels to Liverpool and Preston needed to be protected, because these ports were the nearest landing points for the Canadian and American convoys bringing food, munitions and military equipment. Testing the distances and accuracy of range for the gunners afforded the watchers a nightly firework display.

We were all provided with gas masks, to be taken everywhere, as protection against gas attacks, like those of the First World War, plus a ration book. Each week was carefully marked off in this book, by the grocer that you were registered with, when buying the allocated rations allowed to each person. The small share of the essential foods and other commodities, such as clothes, fuel, furniture and soap, according to one's age and needs, were also all marked up in this book. We went to Bartlett's Grocers in Garstang, where the small amounts of butter, lard, and cheese were carefully cut off with a cheese wire to the exact weight, then wrapped up in sugar paper. Exact amounts of tea and sugar, were weighed out into cones of the same paper.

On one occasion, I sat with my piglet on the counter corner during these operations, waiting to go to the paper shop to collect my *Sunny Stories*, a weekly magazine book by Enid Blyton for little girls, full of magical tales of 'The Faraway Tree'. From these stories I started to develop my own mental picture – a fictional world which I associated with the tall trees in the Spinney, that I could see from the landing window, situated in the middle of the paddock around which the horses grazed. For quite a few years I was sure that my fairies, now lodging there, had found a new home in those trees, one of which I named 'The Faraway Tree'.

THE PAINTBOX

I have interesting memories of a Christmas holiday, when all the family congregated at Bowerswood. It was a very cold winter. Mother, my sister and I, arrived from our boarding school and in addition Aunt Melene came to join us for the festivities, having travelled alone. Mother was confronted with Grandfather's immediate concerns about having sufficient food, because like everyone at the time, shortages and rationing made life difficult. With so many people around him, Grandfather became a little irritated and occasionally confused, now having reached his eighties, which led to the occasional flashpoint in the household.

Bowerswood from the paddock in winter.

'My bacon has been burned again!' he complained. 'It's a pity, it's all so strictly rationed, but I'll make no comment to Pearson. She might take offence and leave. Good cooks are like gold dust at present.' Then he added, 'she is very inventive with the menu though. But has a temper and takes it out on Nellie, who is a hard worker. Not surprising – she's a redhead!' Grandfather's logic was often rather suspect.

By the next morning his humour was restored, because after breakfast Drummond drove him to the Works in Preston, now using my mother's little Austin 7 to save petrol. He went personally to hand out his Christmas boxes for the staff at the Works. At the same time he instructed Willie Chadderton, his manager, to make alternative arrangements to stagger the workers' time off. The background to this was a notification sent from the ministry to increase once again copper spinning production. At this stage of the hostilities, this commodity was considered a critical item for the 'war effort' and there was an enormous demand for stranded copper wire. He also wanted to check out the new air-raid shelters, recently constructed deep below the factory, with space for all the workers. Therefore, he and Rose, the office manager, went down underground to

The Syke Street Works.

The oldest employee, Henry Preston.

check the arrangements. I was aware of the events just mentioned because I had accompanied Grandfather on this particular trip to the factory. I watched an old man working there called Henry Preston, with a very long beard! In order to divert my attention from him, I was placed upon a tall stool in the office, so that I could reach the sloping book-keeper's desk, where Rose provided me with lots of scrap paper and a big box of coloured crayons. This arrangement kept me happily occupied, while Grandfather concluded his business for the day. I heard the conversations, but could make no sense of 'staggering the workers time off.'

The buses that we all relied on so much had reduced their timetables once more, so the damaged horse-drawn trap was repaired yet again, fairly successfully. Duchess needed re-shoeing and although the poor horse was now becoming too old for this continuous work, with her slower gait and greying muzzle, she had to be brought back into service. Duke was of similar age, better for riding, and could be swapped around, although he was not so placid between the traces (the straps connecting the harness to the load).

By 23 December, it was time to finish putting up the decorations. What a disaster it all looked! Old Stirsaker, the gardener with his son, brought in a tree from Lower Wood, and wedged it into a supporting container in the library. 'It's not BIG enough this year,' my deaf Aunt Caroline complained, getting out the tree decorations and attempting to sort them out all over the floor. Grandfather was often short tempered with her.

'She thinks that she's helping, but she cannot hear anybody – I think the war-time bomb blast not only shattered her hearing, but her wits as well, and I do struggle with having such a deaf sister to run my household,' he complained. But everybody was used to her odd ways. She dressed in clothes that were in vogue in about 1910, similar to my other two old aunts. Indeed Gee and Nona, equally eccentric, ar-

Caroline in 1940.

33

Aunt Melene, Wendy and Jane.

rived, via the London train during the afternoon, as did the post, with a puzzling letter to Nona from Mrs Riddle. In it was enclosed a dress belt, to match the dress that she had been sent, but not received the previous week. In Mrs Riddle's accompanying letter she enthused about the lovely Shantung silk that she had requested her dressmaker to make up for her friend. 'Maybe it will arrive after the holiday period.' Nona was always an optimist, and thought well of everybody.

By the day before Christmas Eve, it was cook's day for ceremoniously stirring the Christmas puddings, cleverly created from everything but the usual ingredients, for dried fruits were now totally unobtainable, and with dried egg powder now being rationed, baking powder had to suffice. The habit of wrapping silver 'three-penny bits' in grease-proof paper, to put one under each person's plate was observed.

'I don't know whether we have enough silver three-penny bits saved for the occasion,' said Aunt Melene, but her comment was being ignored by everybody, and Grandfather had other matters on his mind. He didn't heed her either.

'I have sent Drummond to pick up the goose from the station in the trap. He can take the grandchildren with him. I hope the girls behave themselves and sit quietly. They are very excitable, so I doubt it. When he arrives back, he can help Stirsaker, to pluck the bird.' He was becoming aware that the gardener now had severe arthritis, therefore would have struggled with this task alone. So we went to the station to fetch the Christmas dinner – a Cumbrian goose sent by our cousins, while Drummond allowed us to hold the reins in turn, pretending to be in control of the trap. Having successfully re-turned from the station, the plucking started in earnest. Stirsaker wanted the feathers from the goose to line the nesting boxes for the hens in the orchard, in their little henhouse. He showed me how it was done, but still being very young, I became covered with feathers and this caused a fair amount of havoc! My aunt Gee decided that I was safer drawing some pictures, therefore I was quickly removed from the interesting and flighty feathers which had been like a snowstorm.

Meanwhile, Mother and Jane decorated the tree indoors, with much quarrelling between Mother and Aunt Melene, who, as the elder sister, felt she should be in charge. Her husband Barney was in the same regiment as my father, and therefore was also away. Grandfather's pronouncement on him was, 'what a fussy little man he is with an insistent manner.' I thought that was a compliment. When at his home in

Uncle Barney and Aunt Melene.

the Lodge, at the end of the drive, he made beautiful models of aircraft, which he hung from the beams in his house, and as a result I liked him for it. I also played with his two ageing dogs, the spaniel, George, and the golden retriever, Jerry. It was probably just as well that children often see the world with different eyes...

It had been an increasingly difficult year with ever more rationing, all the men away, and more women than Grandfather cared to have in the house at one time, so his peaceful existence had been turned into turmoil. 'We will make do as best we might this Christmas,' he said.

Caroline, Grandfather, Jane, Dudley Foster and I.

The whole family attended Church for the Christmas Day morning service in Garstang, filling the family pew. Melene, always full of chat, told Mother their brother Stephen had money difficulties, and said it was no wonder when he gambled so much. We heard these comments but did not understand them.

The two new women, who were employed over the festive season, seemed willing enough, but a little surly. Gee and Nona could be quite demanding of their services regardless of war-time conditions. An example of this occurred two days earlier, when Aunt Nona insisted that the two ladies should stick up more anti-bomb nets on the upper windows, to save shattering glass if we were near enough to be affected by a blast from Preston Docks or the munitions factory.

Cook and Nellie were as usual very inventive for our Christmas luncheon, cooking the goose and stretching out the rations for the festivities by including a variety of bread stuffing, force-meat balls (taken from a recipe by Hannah Glasse, 1747) extra vegetables and other foods which helped preserve our stock of rations. Stirsaker had brought in some goose eggs, three brace of pigeons, and four buck rabbits from Jacksons Farm, and gave them to Drummond, for hanging in the cold store, all welcome additions to augment our stores. We pulled home-made Christmas crackers, listened to the King's speech, ate a tiny piece of cake, washed down with a little Madeira wine, and finally fruit from our apple store, completed our Christmas meal. Everyone tried to create a party atmosphere. We were better off that year than many others, and gave thanks for it.

By Boxing Day, the intermittent snow showers continued, and as it fell it became much thicker. The land took on the appearance of a well-designed Christmas card, which created a reflective glow around the house, making it feel very cold inside, as well as looking like a bright snow palace fit for the 'Snow Queen' of my storybook, shining within this white landscape. But it was a day full of surprises.

First to arrive for lunch was Dudley Foster – Aunt Melene said that he sometimes traded on Grandfather's friendship a bit, for he was a lonely man in his fifties, yet was very good company for Grandfather, who, when sitting talking to him, created exquisite hand-made embroideries, a pastime which he always undertook on his travels. Aunt Nona found him far too prissy with his mincing manners, yet he was invaluable on Boxing Day, making table decorations for the evening celebrations, and entertaining us girls for hours by demonstrating the art of fancy needlework. This is a skill that I continued to use all my life, because I have always enjoyed making things with many kinds of material.

Then we were all shocked by the following unpleasant incident, suddenly exploding into an otherwise peaceful Boxing Day holiday. At 11am, all the staff were invited into the library, where the Christmas tree stood, along with the presents beneath. These were handed out, in rank order to the various staff, depending on whether they worked inside or outside. They were all allowed to wear their own Sunday best for the occasion. The staff all filed in to face the three old aunts, who were sitting reading out the labels, finding the correct recipients for the parcels. Without warning, Nona suddenly leapt up to her feet.

'She is wearing my lost dress!' And with rising anger and a series of further probing questions she demanded, 'where did you get it?' At first the girl, a temporary parlour maid, denied all knowledge of wrongdoing.

'I'll prove you wrong then!' cried Nona over her shoulder, as she rushed up to her room with alacrity, albeit now 73 years of age, to fetch the matching belt as evidence. In her haste she turned and tripped, falling down the stairs and landed at the foot in a heap, with a broken ankle. The doctor was hastily sent for from Garstang. Unfortunately the regular doctor was not contactable, therefore a second apparently 'inferior' choice was settled upon.

'I do not care for him much, or his religion, but he will have to suffice for this occasion,' commented Grandfather. My aunt was splinted and bandaged, and the alleged thief, being now detained and dressed in her own clothes again, was taken by the constabulary for questioning.

'It seems one cannot be too careful with employing trustworthy persons,' was the consensus of opinion, expressed by my flustered aunts from Egypt.

Thereafter, the day became quite merry. Mr and Mrs Price-Stretch arrived in their yellow Rolls, to show it off. He was a noisy man who wore a monocle, plus-fours and a 'pork pie' hat. His wife appeared equally forceful, and liked to take charge of the conversation if she could.

Coming down the drive, I remember hearing the muffled clip-clop of horses' hooves which had been tied in little bags of sacking for safety in the snow. Mother's cousins, the two Miss Heskeths, had just arrived in their ancient trap, along with their nephew, bearing a gift of two bottles of fine claret. Soon I pranced about in my new heavy footwear, which were boys walking shoes. The reason for the choice of boys' shoes was because my

The Price-Stretches visiting for Christmas.

mother had discovered that all girls' shoes required seven coupons, but the boys' footwear only three, so girls often wore boys' shoes to save on clothing coupons. Feet were measured, and if found to be larger than the stipulated norm for that age, extra coupons were issued to accommodate the growing child.

Looking towards the front paddock.

After a light Boxing Day lunch, Dudley Foster and Grandfather strolled through the orchard to Bowers House farm, to see the Jacksons and give them their Christmas box, and thank them for the goose eggs. Mrs Jackson gave him a present for 'the girls' to bring back to the house. As farming activities had to continue every day, Grandfather went briefly with Mr Jackson to admire the milking herd, then refreshed by the stroll, they shed their snow laden overcoats and returned to the library in front of the fire to listen to the afternoon play on the wireless, *The Moonstone* by Willkie Collins, and ate warm muffins and strawberry jam for tea. Aunt Gee sat with them, comparing embroidery notes with Dudley, while both worked diligently with their special crewel needles and coloured threads.

We opened Mrs Jackson's gift, and found it contained a picture of a donkey, made of cork, together with a tail attached to a pin. This game was called Blind Man's Tail, and needed accurate positioning of the tail onto the donkey when the player was blindfolded. We played Snakes and Ladders, and learned how to play Snap and Bezique with old Aunt Nona, who was now laid upon the sofa with her leg propped up. This was followed eventually by Solitaire which we played for hours.

Aunt Gee embroidered as well as her sisters, and made beautiful handbags. She carried around a large bag containing many skeins of coloured silks, and would pull out a thread of some vibrant colour for her work. She would ask me frequently whether it would be 'right for this or that leaf', but as she was somewhat colour-blind, I diplomatically tended to agree with her, and her choices lent an air of mystery and vibrancy to her work. She brought me two presents for Christmas, the first being a pair of red leather slippers from Egypt with curved-up toes, like those of the genie in the story of Aladdin. But I must admit that the greatest present for me was Gee's present of a paint box containing high quality paints and three sable brushes.

'I'll teach you how to use all these pretty colours and make your own fairy pictures, to match your father's lovely paintings,' she promised, and she was as good as her word.

Suddenly I was as quiet as a mouse, sitting in a corner somewhere – I was now in my element. In my mind's eye, I created the illusion of how my fairies were flying out once again from my own paintbox, with a little help from Aunt Gee, who enthusiastically encouraged my blossoming imagination.

BOWERS HOUSE HARVEST

From the vantage point of the boundary fence, which skirted the grounds of Bower-swood, one could see a magnificent seventeenth century building, Bowers House Farm. Lining the path to the ancient front door was a row of even more ancient yew trees which showed up starkly against the white façade of the farmhouse. Inside the entrance hallway was a very wide and sloping staircase with shallow treads. It was probably built at the same time as the house itself. Within the staircase's supporting structure, there was a cleverly designed secret priest's hole, a small hidden room created during the religious wars. In addition, beyond the room, was an entrance to a subterranean passageway which led to another building, a hall, approximately two miles away. I roamed about in this lovely house, not realising its historical significance at that age. The farmer's wife was happy enough to let me play, or help her in the ancient kitchen, covered with faded rag rugs and which housed an enormous kitchen range, fuelled by wood or coal, and probably as old as the house!

When I remarked to Grandfather that it would be a pity if the bombs flattened everything, he walked over to the farm to chat with the farmer. Very soon afterwards, new rolls of pre-glued window-netting ordered by Grandfather, arrived for use on their priceless leaded-lights, which ensured that none of them were shattered from bomb blasts. At this time, we had heard a few explosions, and had felt the

Bowers House Farm.

shock waves sometimes, but experienced nothing which created any serious damage.

Along our boundary was the little lane which led from the farm to the fields; an old gate in the back fence, an exit into the lane, became irresistible to my wandering spirit. Often, I was awake, up with the birds, and went out quietly to go and watch the cows ambling in for early milking, as well as to watch Martha, the farmer's daughter, who was helping drive the cows in, and who wore wooden clogs. She was a careworn and cheerful woman of about 35, with untidy hair and a missing front tooth, wearing a floral overall, and of course, those clogs that clattered on the yard cobbles.

Being an inquisitive girl in my grandfather's house, I needed plenty of activity, because otherwise there was not enough to keep me occupied. In terms of support for me from other members of the household, there were limitations. First the great aunts, whilst being very kind, were two generations, and an era away from me. Second, my mother often occupied herself variously with the WVS (Women's Voluntary Service), war work in the village, or with helping run the household, during which time Janet was supposed to be looking after us. Finally, as for my sister, being a little older, she loved reading, and fared better than I. She had other things to do, and was often annoyed by having a younger sister trailing after her.

On one occasion, while peering out of my bedroom window, I spotted Martha who was busy on most mornings in the farm dairy. I was drawn like a pin to a magnet, watching her bustling activities. As the men milked the cows, she was occupied cooling the newly-collected milk. The milk was poured through a metal-ribbed hollow cooler with cold water coursing through, then down past a sieve which removed any unwanted solids before it was poured into a waiting churn. They filled at least three or four churns each day. The churns were loaded onto the back of the tractor, and taken to the end of the mile-long drive, ready for collection by the milk lorry. Her father and brother George, always did the milking, before turning the beasts out again into the pasture. I followed Martha about, wanting to help, and shooed the cows out into the fields with her. Often, I was given a cup of still warm milk from Martha, and a little jug of cream to take back to the kitchen in Bowerswood for breakfast.

Martha remonstrated at seeing my sandals. 'Tha mus' put watter-proof clogs on thy feet in't dairy! It's better fer thy feet in't shippon weer its gey slaipe!' ('You must put waterproof clogs on your feet in the dairy. It's better for your feet in the cow byre where it's very slippery.')

I skipped back to our kitchen with the cream, and told Mother later what Martha had said. What luck! A few weeks later, we visited the cobblers, because it was discovered that clogs only required two coupons instead of seven, of one's allowance, these being defined as essential 'work clothes'. Therefore, very soon I appeared in a pair of lovely red clogs fastened with buttons. They were indeed as warm as Martha had predicted, because of the thick wooden soles, and during holiday times were my preferred footwear when outside. Furthermore, they were delightfully noisy!

During the summer holiday months, my sister and I spent a lot of time at the Jackson's farm, probably getting in the way, but sometimes helping with harvesting. The harvest was always assisted by neighbouring farmers and friends, to supplement the farm's own labour force. I became a little runner for Martha with the 'Baggins' or refreshments for the men working in the fields, which Mrs Jackson had prepared. I was too small to do the 'stooking' (stacking) of the corn sheaves but rode on the old Fordson tractor beside Mr Jackson while he pulled the binder, creating bundles of corn which were then tied in sheaves. It was a two-man operation, before the advent of the combine harvesters.

The sheaves of corn were stood up, and leaned against each other in double rows of six, to dry in the wind. At intervals, they were turned to expose the wet sides for drying. Three or four men walked behind the tractor doing this job, and it was all quite a labour intensive activity. A few days later, provided that there had been little rain, and all seemed dry, the sheaves would be collected on a trailer from around the field, stacked high against the 'gates'

Mr Jackson on the binder,
Jane and George on the tractor.

placed at each end of the trailer. Once loaded, they were taken to the farmyard, where they were off-loaded, and turned into corn stacks, in readiness for threshing day. Some farm hands were much more adept at building the corn stacks in a safe, stable manner, therefore were preferred to the other farmhands who were more skilled at throwing heavy sheaves of corn

The Dutch barn.

high up onto the stack tops. At the top, the stack 'builders' would then construct the stack, layer by layer. More stacks were then created, and covered with tarpaulins to protect against rain, weighed down at their corners with bricks. These corn stacks were set up in each field as they were cut, this being the most convenient place for storage. Eventually even the Dutch barn was used for the final sheaves, which also served as convenient protection against rain and damage to the crop.

During this time, some of the men involved in the harvest brought their small bore shotguns, for the opportunity of bagging their 'rabbit suppers' in the fields. In addition, this activity had the benefit of keeping down the vermin which ran from under the stooks. I learned early to handle a small ladies' shotgun, and to skin my rabbit too, once shot. When a little older, I was taught to shoot pigeons by Bill Drummond and Jack Lockwood – this all added generously to our food supplies because we had a lot of pigeons!

All awaited threshing day, and a date was set for the arrival of the threshers. Several large machines appeared down the driveway, headed by a traction engine, accompanied by a large body of men. This was a threshing contractor who visited each farm in turn in the district. By combining work forces, it greatly speeded up the threshing process. We found it exciting to watch and other farm children joined us, while their parents worked elsewhere. The areas adjacent to the stooks became very crowded with people and machines, and was very noisy too, and lasted two or three days. All those involved in threshing ate their 'Baggins' in relays, to ensure that threshing was maintained continuously throughout the working day. We became involved in fetching food and billy cans of cold tea from the kitchen for the thirsty workers.

Enormous drive belts were attached between the steam engine drive wheel and the thresher. The engine was fired up with coke, contained in a hopper at the rear. Once its power was built up, it was set to work, to drive the thresher, which separated the corn from its stalks, and subsequently the chaff from the corn. The corn was finally blown into container trucks, which had arrived, to transport it to the flour mills. It was a very dusty, complicated business. We were soon covered with a fine white dust. In one part of the thresher, the straw was baled and expelled from the end of the machine. Normally, the straw bales were stacked in the barn for cattle bedding. Typically, numerous mice scurried around in the barns, but nobody took much notice of them that day. Several wandering hens, thinking that they had found a heavenly nest in the barn, were soon disillusioned when they were hastily moved, as more bales were placed there. Finally, all was gathered in safely. Soon we were waving the contractors goodbye, as the steam engine, machines, lorries and men moved to another farm for similar repeat perform-ances.

Farm labourers were in short supply, because the Armed Forces claimed all available young people. Therefore, attention was turned towards other sources of manpower for work on the farm. Mr Jackson was of-fered two young men from the Young Offenders Centre. They arrived one day, but

Jack, Albert, Mrs Jackson, Martha, Mr Jackson, George, old Robin, and the sheepdog Jep in front of Mr Jackson.

one of them hated working outside on the farm from the start, and was really frightened of the cows.

'I ain't going nowhere near those bleeding beasts!' he declared. He became so awk-ward and surly, that poor Mr Jackson realised he couldn't be trusted with livestock. He asked the Young Offenders Centre if he could give him back, suggesting that he was more suited to a farm with no animals. The other young man, Albert, was much more of an asset. He was about sixteen years old, a bit of a dreamer, and couldn't write. On one occasion, when I went in to watch Mrs Jackson making bread in her large kitchen range, I offered to teach Albert to write his name. Interestingly, I found out subsequently that *nobody* at the farm could read or write, except Martha, who had a very elementary ability and Mr Jackson, who only knew his numbers. This was my first lesson in real-ising that literacy was not a priority for many people in farming communities.

At Bowerswood, one day my sister and I went up through the little door onto the roof to explore the 'valleys' between the tall sloping roofs. A couple of men had come up to clean out a chimney stack, because a rook had fallen down one of the tall chimneys, and had created a fall of soot in the library below. Very gingerly, and undetected, we peered around the roof stacks and into the gulleys, with 'hide and seek' in mind. Sud-denly, we spotted a bag in an unobtrusive corner of the roof. Both of us took hold to pull it out. 'Look! It has patterns on it like Aunt Coco's work bag,' Jane said, 'and it is very heavy! I don't think we can carry it.' We knew it was not one of the workmen's toolkits, so Jane sent me to fetch Nellie, who carried it down with our help.

'It's silver from around the house that's been missing for ages! And things from your Aunts room, and the kitchen!' Nellie could easily identify where the items had come from, so Aunt Melene and Mother set about unravelling the mystery of how, when and by whom the missing articles had been stored on the roof. Nothing came to mind, there-fore they decided to empty the bag, refill it with wrapped up pieces of wood and stones, and replaced it partly hidden in the corner. There it lay for some time. Thus the matter was held in abeyance until a few weeks later, when we broke a pane of glass in the bath-room.

'Get that handyman Peter to mend it, before the rain comes in. He's quite a good glazier,' and Grandfather pressed my aunt to organise it. In my usual way, I wandered around, following the handyman, to watch him working. He smiled sweetly at me for a little while, but then shooed me away, saying: 'Be off with you now, stop following me around, and go and play with your dollies! I've got work to do.' I melted away around the corner, for fear of another telling off, but continued to watch the man's progress.

Later, he left the bathroom in his soft-soled shoes, but his progress could be traced because the shoes squeaked along the green linoleum floor as he climbed the upper floor stairs, and then onto the roof. I shot off to tell Mother what I had seen, and she quickly summoned help from the staff, telling us to stay well out of the way. Of course, they were ready to catch the man red-handed, as he very quietly descended the stairs with the offending colourful bag, thinking he had recovered his 'loot' without being spotted. Perhaps this was my first lesson in the ways of the world, when one could not trust everybody, even when they had a ready smile.

PIGLET'S ADVENTURE

During the Second World War many young people were evacuated from areas that were considered to be in danger of the bombing, to places that were not thought of to be in imminent danger. This included the surrounding countryside of Preston, with its active dockyards and several ordnance factories, where mill workers were mobilised for the increasing war work of manufacturing munitions and aircraft. Numbers of barrage balloons were used as anti-aircraft obstacles to protect such industry, but stray bombs, having missed their primary targets, often landed and exploded in unexpected sites, and were frightening, dangerous and deadly.

At the beginning of the war, having travelled from Northern Ireland, we lived with Grandfather, in his Victorian house near Garstang, a mere twelve miles from Preston docks. So it was decided that for safety we girls should attend a school in remote Kirkby Lonsdale as boarders, during the term time, and we eventually settled in, with about 45 other

The Biggins.

youngsters of assorted ages, whose parents were on active service for the war effort in some form, or other, and therefore had no settled homes at that time.

The school, built in 1869, was leased from its previous owner occupant. It was a large ornate nineteenth century building, stone built, with mullion windows and four castellated turrets and was surrounded by extensive grounds. Each of the turrets towered above a corner of the main building and was well covered by Virginia creeper. Windows peeped out through this mass of greenery, and birds darted out from their well-hidden nests. The carved oak door lay within a stone porch, which also housed a long metal bell-pull that was surrounded at ceiling height by house martins' nests, from whence in the springtime the birds could be seen swooping out to feed on flying insects.

Stepping into the shady interior, there was a large square hallway, wood panelled from floor to ceiling, with an impressive wide staircase with carved balustrades, which rose to the next floor in a graceful curve to join the gallery that surrounded it. The bedrooms, were of generous proportions, and each having a wash basin, provided eight dormitories for six children in each. At the top of the stairs, there was a room used as a Sick Bay. The advantage of this room in such a cold house was the presence of a fireplace, often used, and it also boasted a balcony, reached by French windows, out of which a measles, or chicken-pox covered child could sit with Matron, to benefit from the sunshine.

Downstairs the main rooms, all oak-panelled, were used as class rooms, then a smaller sitting room and staff room that faced two dining rooms, on either side of a long corridor to the kitchen facilities with more doors. These gave the feeling of hidden secrets behind so many closed rooms. The ancient lighting system was barely adequate to light up these vast panelled rooms, which appeared to the children now living there, to be a somewhat daunting new home. All the children had brought their favourite toys for comfort, and I was no exception, for having left my fairies in Ireland, I'd transferred my affections firmly to my little eight-inch Piglet, who could fit in my pocket, while my sister had her Pooh Bear. My paper fairies and precious paintbox were left safely in their bag at grandfather's house during term time.

On the lawn at Biggins the week before the fire.

As far as possible, the effects of war touched the youngsters only rarely, but all lived in a fairly austere vegetarian regime; were dressed alike in shorts and Aertex shirts; taken walking regularly in the countryside; learned about fossils, plant life and how to climb trees and were encouraged to learn piano and take riding lessons as extras after ordinary lessons.

The China birds

My dear Papa appeared one weekend, to take us out riding, and spend a short time with us. He had taken a room with Mother in the Green Dragon in nearby Kirkby Lonsdale, where we were delighted to be taken for a meal. We met with an elderly lady who stayed there permanently at the time, having been completely bombed out of her home near Liverpool. She told us wistfully of her home, now destroyed, whist opening her large, capacious carpet bag of many colours.

'My things in this bag are all my possessions that I am left with. Perhaps we should not set so much store by our belongings, for at least I have my life,' Mrs Sitchell said philosophically. Then she pulled out of her bag, two well wrapped china figurines of exotic birds, about three inches tall, saying, 'These two have survived a century in my family, so you two young girls shall now have them. Give my survivors a lot of care to last another century!'

We came away with two colourful china birds, both of which I still have to this day, one being broken, for my sister did not care for the one she was given, and threw it on the floor in temper, which was subsequently repaired very carefully by my mother. So they stand on my mantle shelf as a reminder of that brave old lady of so long ago.

Trips were organised for very special occasions, but because these tended to need a train ride to get anywhere, they became almost impossible, for trains were increasingly needed for troop movements as the war advanced. Travelling by train was a hazardous activity, and the blackout restrictions were so strictly enforced, that stations had few or no lights to recognise the approaching destinations, and no heating was used on the trains due to lack of fuel.

The Biggins as it looked when we arrived.

By 1942 a pattern of living had emerged in this large household in the backwater of Westmorland, (now a part of Cumbria) as the war continued to enmesh thousands elsewhere with grim reality. In Europe and further south in England, they were much closer to the war. We rode our bicycles, played in the grounds, learned our various lessons the Montessori way, had cold baths every morning and ran round the lawns barefoot as a daily exercise regardless of the weather. They said it would produce strong and healthy feet, but also caused a proliferation of chilblains! Nevertheless, we seemed to thrive on this spartan and well-ordered life.

Suddenly all this changed!

During the Christmas holidays of that year, with re-stricted travelling, no parents available, and many de-stroyed homes, there were twelve children including my sister and myself, who had to stay in the school for their holidays. All were encouraged to make paper-chain hangings, and decorate a large tree, to make the occasion as festive as possible, whilst staff wrapped up parcels to fit in with known wishes sent to Father Christmas, by the children.

Three of the staff decided to take nine of the children to Morecambe, to see a pantomime, and had saved enough petrol coupons to take three cars for the journey. I, together with two other youngsters, had succumbed to chicken pox and missed out on the trip. We were thus tucked up instead in the sick room, tended by Miss

Jane and I in kilts on the lawn.

Goodall. The two Heads, tall Miss King and elderly, rotund Miss Crane were downstairs in the building – all the other staff had gone home for Christmas, except the cook.

Nobody envisaged any danger in this situation.

The three cars set off with the chattering children for their New Year's treat in More-cambe, to watch the matinee show, leaving a well-lit and gaily decorated house, with table laid and all prepared for a Christmas party to be enjoyed on their return. I remember feeling so sad to have missed this outing, so I curled myself up on a cushion by the sickroom fire, which was a large Victorian grate, banked up with wood logs for fuel to give us all some warmth, and talked privately to Piglet, my toy and my confidant, to whom I would whisper my thoughts when lonely.

Miss Crane struggled to balance her books of the school finances in the library, totally oblivious of anything around her, and was startled when Miss King rushed in and said urgently, 'I can smell burning wood! I think we are on fire!'

She had crossed the vast hallway, and neither of them knew immediately from which direction it came. Soon it became apparent though, that the house was indeed on fire, for the smoke quickly filled the hallway, emanating from a ground floor room, and soon visibility was reduced to nothing.

Miss Crane shouted, 'I'll ring the fire brigade and police, and you go up to warn Goody and the children!' With that, she darted out to find the phone in the smoke filled hallway. Miss King, with her long, thin legs, bounded up to the sickroom in the swirling smoke, shouting a warning to us in the sick bay, and urging us to retreat out onto the balcony. She assumed that Miss Crane was going to follow her up the stairs, for it was impossible to find a way out on the ground floor, but when she turned round to look, she was horrified to see Miss Crane, having dialled 999, laying unconscious on the lower steps, with the phone from the hall table still in her hand.

The house was rapidly filling with blinding smoke, with the acrid smell of the burning wood filling our noses and making us all cough and splutter, while trying to see through running eyes. She dashed back into the sick room for a towel, which she soaked in the basin, whilst urging us, the watchers, now terrified, to sit out on the balcony. She grabbed Miss Goodall, wetting another towel to protect her also from the smoke, and together they carefully descended the smouldering stairs, grabbing an arm apiece of the unconscious figure lying on the bottom step. Between them they dragged and slid the prostrate woman up the broad oak staircase, step by step.

They eventually pulled her up to the landing and into the sick room, closing the door to give them some respite from the smoke. Unconscious, but still breathing, they manoeuvred Miss Crane out onto the balcony, and shut that window too. It was cooler there, but the air was rapidly filling with unpleasant fumes. Miss Goodall had taken eight sheets out to effect an escape by trying to make a temporary ladder, knotting them together, but then she realized that they were a few feet short and did not entirely reach the safety of the ground. Then the glass in the balcony door shattered with a startling burst of noise, showering our precarious perch with shards of glass. There was no going back for any of us...

By now, the flames were attacking the solid oak door, and eventually it crashed in, and with a surge of energy, being fanned by the now open balcony door, it devoured the contents of the room in about ten seconds. And in a few more minutes, the floor in the room caved in and was completely destroyed!

Eyeing the too short makeshift rope, Miss King cried, 'We'll have to jump the

The great fire at a Kirkby Lonsdale mansion used as Moorland School.

last part! The children, being lighter, might be alright. Goody, you take them. But I cannot leave Florence unconscious here.'

Fear makes heroes of the most timid of us, and this moment was no exception. With fumbling fingers the sheet rope ladder was attached to the balustrade, and thrown over towards the ground. Miss Goodall, being a PE teacher of about 35, descended part way to take us children down, one at a time and reached up for the first one. She had urged the strongest child, a lanky thirteen year old, to follow her, and having reached as far as she dared go, coaxed the boy to jump the last few feet. He survived this jump by rolling over and over as he went. However, Miss Goodall, hanging on to the knots, could not now regain her upper position, and they could not persuade me or the other frightened girl to descend without holding on to a teacher, for at that time I had not yet learned how to climb a rope. I peered over the balustrade in absolute horror.

But help at last was at hand, and none too soon, for the heat was now overwhelming us and we would soon disappear into the onslaught of the advancing fire.

Fire at the school seen from the rear where the fire brigade fought the flames.

Among the acrid smoke fumes, and over the terrifying noise of the persistent conflagration, noises could be heard of shouting people, and a clanking bell of the fire engine. Firemen quickly arrived at our side of the building, and soon spotted the imminent danger of the marooned group. With great speed, a ladder was brought to Miss Goodall's assistance, while another party of strong firemen with ladders, brought down all of us frightened survivors from the balcony one of whom grabbed both of us girls hastily as the remnants of our ledge disappeared from view. I clung like a limpet to this fireman, and needed much persuading to release him. We were carefully loaded into an ambulance, for dispatching to the Westmorland General Hospital. But my memory does not recall any further than that point, for I think my brain by then could take no more.

The unconscious Miss Crane eventually recovered in the hospital, and the firemen finally quelled the terrible fire after 24 hours hard work, leaving the shell of a beautiful building completely gutted. It was only fit thereafter to house the barn owls, who silently glided in the evenings to take over this ghostly reminder of a once proud house.

The Biggins five years after the fire.

A telephone call to the theatre at Morecambe that night ensured that the pantomime party were taken to temporary holiday accommodation by friends; and a local mill owner in Rawtenstall, father of a child at the school, came with his lorry and workers to salvage as many of the belongings as he could, much of it found in the cloakrooms and cupboards, beyond the untouched kitchens.

The cause of the fire eventually proved to have been started by old and faulty wiring severely overloaded during that period. My sister and I mourned the loss of our few toys, which had been cherished with much love and attention, because of the very fact that they were indeed so few. But the greatest loss for me was my Piglet, my companion and 'almost alive' toy to whom I was inseparable and had been clutching desperately on the ledge.

With great determination, the school re-opened again at the end of January in another leased vacant country house near Clitheroe, and we all tried to put the experience behind us, but certainly never forgot. The clothes, shoes and belongings at the mill were sifted out, cleaned, and eventually returned to their owners, if known and if worth it, but sadly a large pile was not.

A few months later in the spring, when I had returned for my Easter holidays to Grandfather, a little parcel arrived for me at his house. I thought it was an Easter present, but when I opened it, a small shoebox was revealed, now lined with cotton wool. Inside was my beloved Piglet, found at the site of the fire, who had been washed, and re-dressed in a simple sailor suit. Accompanying him was a little letter. It said, 'I have been on a winter holiday to the seaside but wish to come home now to you, because I am lonely.' I also had been lonely for my toy... but not any more!

NUNK KNOWLES

By the end of January 1943, the staff of our boarding school had rented another large empty country house, which was in the small market town of Clitheroe, Lancashire. It had the curious name of Nunk Knowles. The school staff set about acquiring new or second hand equipment and furniture, and with great enthusiasm opened its doors to its pupils, aged 3 to 16. As the war progressed, the school slowly increased its complement of boarders as a result of more bombing and as more absentee parents became involved in war work.

The new Moorhead School.

The building, perhaps Edwardian, was not as old as the previous one in Kirby Lonsdale, but had similarities which worked well for a school. On both floors of the building, there were large and spacious rooms. In the hallway, there was an impressive inglenook fireplace which dominated the entrance. Unlike the previous school, whose oak panelling darkened much of its interior, in this school, the whole place appeared much larger and lighter. Similar to Kirby Lonsdale, there was a stone porch at the main front entrance door, into which the swifts or house martins flew freely in the spring, creating their mud 'houses' within its roof. In front of the entrance, there was a large circle of gravel around which visiting cars could negotiate, when arriving at, or leaving the school. Since we were all encouraged to have bicycles, this area soon became a miniature racetrack for the younger children on their tricycles. Since the long driveway up to the school was a private road, the older children were able to ride up and down in complete safety.

The gardens were extensive, with well stocked borders of perennial plants; peonies, oriental poppies, and lupins sat happily amongst the hollyhocks, geums, and delphiniums, whilst the knapfolias, known as red-hot-pokers, and carnations flashed colour to delight the eye with perfumes from them to tease the senses. The gardens were divided up with rows of old yews, creating a heavenly playground of wide lawns for the spirited children, whose imagination and creativity were completely unbridled. We had to run round these lawns, each day before breakfast in bare feet, the school's head teacher believing that the exercise would make them stronger. There were also two old gardeners who tended the grounds, which included the large and well stocked kitchen garden. This was a bonus, because the school was strictly vegetarian. As a result of this, we were fed extremely well, despite wartime food restrictions, and we truly benefitted from it.

Whenever it was fine weather, we regularly had our afternoon rest spread out on the lawn whilst one of the teachers read a story out loud – but I rarely heard the endings through falling asleep so promptly.

Known today as Moorland School, the building overlooked the fields bordering the River Ribble, and was high enough to command a good view of the surrounding countryside. One neighbour in the vicinity, just along the river, was the cement works. Below the school, we could enter a park which had footpaths along the river valley. This enabled us to view the activities of the Works, and ride about the No-Mans-Land scrub areas on our bikes, creating make believe games of the cops-and-robbers variety. Between the school and the river, there were several acres of green fields, sloping toward the river. These fields were bounded by the main Waddington road to Yorkshire, across which spanned an ancient stone bridge, connecting with a steep escarpment on the other side of the river.

Sleeping on the lawn at Nunk Knowles.

These fields became out of bounds for a while, when several 'butterfly bombs' were discovered. These were German anti-personnel bombs (in German called *Sprengbombe Dickwandig* 2 kg, abbreviated to SD2) which were pretty things for innocent children to pick up, but unfortunately deadly! In order to make the fields safe once again, they were carefully swept by military experts while we received pictures and talks about their dangers. In the middle of this field was an electricity sub-station like a small green metal hut. I only remember it because of the large printed swear word I saw across its door, 'Fuck'. With this new discovery, I went back into school, shouting the word out loud, whilst saying 'What does this mean?' I got thoroughly smacked and told never to use such a wicked word again. Not understanding my wrongdoing, I was really fearful of saying anything, so it was not until my late teens that I understood its meaning and would have totally forgotten this trivial incident but for the severe beating I received. Adults never learn!

The river flowed through more of the same country, the other side of the river being bordered by the steep woods of Waddow Hall, whose grounds were used for Girl Guiding activities. We were invited to join in the camp groups occasionally from our school. Inspired by the Girl Guiding 'merit of achievement' badges, Miss Goodall started a new Wild Wooder's Group, encompassing all ages for boys and girls. Every child made a 'Merit Belt', fashioned in the handicraft class, of hessian and coloured wool, onto which was sewn coloured wooden beads. Each bead had a value – gold, red, pink, orange, yellow, blue and green according to the skill needed to complete a task. I remember my first two gold beads, for painting, and garden making! I was a very energetic and competitive child for things that I liked doing and creative too, therefore my belt and its patterns made from coloured beads grew almost faster than for anybody else.

This beautiful and tranquil countryside around the school was disturbed by the sudden appearance of a great many soldiers, seemingly hundreds of them, all with different missions. It transpired that the East Lancashire Regiment was on manoeuvres to train the infantry up and down Pendle Hill, with full battle dress packs on their backs, night and day. We could see from our school the outline of this steep and rounded hill. It was said to be the home of the Pendle Witches, a group of poor misunderstood women living there in the seventeenth century, who peddled herbal medicines. They were hanged in 1612 at Lancaster Assizes for cursing their tormentors.

Pendle Hill and the surrounding area was a fairly hostile, steep and boggy environment. Here the Army used a great many fields, whose gateposts had been painted red to indicate the areas requisitioned by the Ministry of Defence for army training use. The military activity did restrict some of our trips. For example, small groups of children were accompanied by one of our staff to walk to Clitheroe Stables for their regular riding lessons. Normally, we would be allocated our horse then ride towards the paths up Pendle Hill, but since the arrival of the soldiers, we were requested by army personnel or by notices placed in prominent places, to use alternative routes for our rides, then return again different ways in order to reach the stables which were in the centre of Clitheroe.

Another group of soldiers appeared to spend much of their time occupying the river banks. Subsequently, we discovered that these were the Royal Engineers, working for many weeks to train soldiers in the art of building bailey bridges (temporary lattice steel bridges, manufactured in modular form). The purpose of their training was to help the army with their cross-country movements in continental Europe, by devising and practising methods of river crossings. They used various equipment, including bailey bridges, floating pontoons, aerial slings for equipment and zip wires for personnel. The flat meadows bordering the river below our school were ideal places for these activities, especially the use of the raised escarpment and the Waddow Hall woods on the other side of the river. Waddow Hall was being used temporarily as an isolation hospital for children during wartime, to avoid the risks of enemy bombing further south.

With the arrival of the military, tents sprung up in rows, like mushrooms in the surrounding fields, and troops took over lodgings all around the town. One Easter holiday when we were requested not to return to Bowerswood because everyone there had flu, Mother searched diligently for some accommodation for Jane, me and herself, for just a couple of weeks, while the school was closed. She had been required by the War directives to find a job, now that her two children were of school age, therefore took one as assistant matron in our school, which luckily became available. Being a Land Army girl was not really her style – she had sampled this for a couple of weeks before joining the school, nor did she fancy factory work.

She tried to find rooms nearby, just for Easter, and eventually had to settle for a place in a small cul-de-sac on the outskirts of the town, because everywhere else was full. This short road with about 24 houses had a recreation ground for children at the far end in a small field, where a row of swings, a slide and a large climbing frame was positioned. Our accommodation was a small terraced house in Park Road opposite this playground, sharing two rooms upstairs and two down, with no bathroom, and a row of six toilets in the yard. This was the smallest living space that I had ever seen!

Mother with a cow.

The toilets had square toilet paper with writing all over it, threaded on a long string. Our toilet, The Privy, was to be avoided if at all possible, because it was so smelly, and because it had a somewhat rough wooden seat.

'This will be like camping. It will be fun!' my desperate and determined Mother was not to be discouraged. The owner had the upstairs front room, and we three shared the back bedroom, where I was now on a camp bed. The kindly Mrs Tompkins cooked our evening meal on the small gas stove, and then heated water on it for a bedtime wash.

'Where is the bathroom and basin?' I soon found out, as she lifted me onto the draining board, saying 'sit.' There was no bathroom or basin! And the 'privy' was No. 3 across the yard. So I put my feet in the Belfast sink (a box-like ceramic sink), hot water was poured in from the kettle, and I was washed all over with the minimum of fuss. Jane was given the same treatment, even though she was a year and a half older, protesting loudly. I remember it all so well.

The next few days were filled by making friends with the children in the street, who devised games on the playground. We watched three bigger boys creating a 'tent' with two sheets against the far corner walls. Soon they had filled it with creatures, three rabbits, two caged mice, a guinea pig, some caterpillars, and a talkative caged bird. I was hopping from foot to foot, wanting to see inside. Chalked on a piece of cardboard was a notice: 'THE ZOO – 1d. TO ENTER' (Note: 1d. referred to a British penny in circulation until 1971. The letter 'd' derives from the Roman word *denarius*).

Entrepreneurial skills were developing fast in these young boys! So I skipped home to Mother for a penny, and waited in the growing queue to have my penny's worth in 'The zoo'. I was allowed to hold the rabbit in my lap, thinking wishfully that I had one of my own. Then I spent ages trying to get the parrot to say something meaningful, before relinquishing at last my place in the 'zoo' to the next child in the queue.

But my luck ran out with the playground equipment.

I did what all adventurous children do, and climbed with the others over everything, finishing up on a swing, but could not force it high enough for my liking. One of the bigger girls came over to push it for me, as I cried out with great glee, 'Higher! Higher!' At the highest point of the swing I slipped, and with a great shriek, I fell to the concrete below, and lay motionless with my eyes closed.

Apparently I had blacked out for a few moments before waking, and then was extremely sick. A neighbour carried me into the house, and laid me on the sofa, where I was wrapped in a blanket to stop my shivering. I complained loudly of a headache, so was kept in the dark, sleeping for the rest of the day. At suppertime, when I did at last feel a little better, a knock at the door revealed the two 'zoo' keepers. As an act of kindness, they had brought the rabbit for me to play with on my knee, loaned me the parrot for me to converse in bird-talk gobbledegook , and then gave me two pennies from their takings, as recompense for having hurt myself. Such are the kind ways of some children, to help cheer each other up. After a few days I was soon running around again.

The following week we attended a town fete in the Market Hall in Clitheroe, where the Royal Engineers) Regiment entertained the townspeople with music, sandwiches and cakes, army style. They set up a Housey-Housey game with the sergeant being the caller, and then organised a country dance to which every age group joined in. Their military band had formed a Dance Quintet for social occasions, much appreciated by the locals. This activity was considered by the army to be a way of 'keeping up the

Clitheroe Castle Place, 1940.

morale' of the civilian population, and a recompense, in lieu of the many disruptions they had caused to life in the town. These socials events were soon a regular feature in the town calendar, and both regiments joined in for these off-duty activities, whenever they could.

A local girl, Kathleen Barton, was well known as a classical contralto and attended several choirs, as well as being an all-round singer of great talent. She was often engaged to perform at the events organised by the army. On the first of these occasions which we attended from our accommodation in Park Road my mother helped repair Kathleen's torn dress. Before long we all became good friends. Mother loved sewing and designing dresses, and produced one from some unwanted curtain material for Kathleen to wear at the next social event. It was the turning point for our lodgings too!

Kathleen lived in her now deceased parents shop 'Barton's Drapers' in King Street, a three storey building of ample proportions, fronted by the shop. She was as lonely as my mother was, because her fiancée was a captain in the Navy. She also needed to have paying lodgers 'to make ends meet'. So a deal was quickly struck, and we moved into this big house, with one other lodger, a Mr Jack Smithson. He had one room on the first floor, and worked for a bakery delivery service, travelling all over Lancashire, returning four days a week to meet his girlfriend Muriel at the house. She wore a calliper on her leg, an old fashioned solution to assist mobility for the dreaded and then incurable, disease of polio from which she suffered when young. Jane and I slept on the top floor, where I carefully arranged our dollies along the window sill. The first evening came, and with it a thunderous knocking on the ground floor door, to be heard from three floors above.

'There's a light in the window on the top floor with dolls along it! Where are your blackout curtains? Haven't you read your regulations?' I could hear the angry conversation from over the bannisters, and hastily rushed to rectify our mistake, because we were all used to this on-going problem. Mother made great apologies to the Air-Raid warden, explaining about our recent arrival, and doing her best to 'pour oil on this particular troubled water'.

The following morning came another knock, equally thunderous, but this was a friendly milkman, with a horse, and two churns on the back of his float. He asked for our jugs, and then dipped a metal canister into the churn which was hanging by its handle on its lip. He scooped up enough milk for our needs and a little extra besides! There were three sizes of these measuring canisters to choose from, a quart, a pint and a gill (former British Imperial quantities, equivalent to 1136 ml, 568 ml, and 142 ml respectively), so we carefully retreated to the kitchen with our full jug, while the horse kept on chewing its breakfast inside its nosebag, which was hanging from its neck. I went outside again to watch another very large horse, a big dray, walking up the hill, whilst pulling his daily load. In this case, it was a station wagon, carrying packages for the shops in the town, and likewise, this horse also carried a nosebag of oats round his neck.

At the end of the holiday, I did not want to return to school as a boarder. In the first instance I refused to explain why, but very slowly after patient coaxing from Mother and Miss Goodall, I admitted for the first time that I had been suffering from persistent bullying. The children responsible for this behaviour had been at the school also in Kirkby Lonsdale, and now I found they were still with me. We all shared bedrooms, of six children of mixed ages per room, and I, being a very small person, was easy to 'tease' or take advantage of. On one occasion, I had been stabbed in the back with a lead pencil by an older child, the embedded and dissolved lead still being there to this day. This angry child was allocated the bed next to mine!

One very cruel game was to place a pillowslip over my head and arms, and tie me up with a dressing-gown cord, demanding a non-existent password to release me. There were many nights that I was left in this state, and I

Jane and I with our new knitted cardigans for school.

was very frightened too. For comfort, I would revert to talking in secret to my imaginary fairies. The bullies swore to devise other 'games' if I told anybody, but they did so anyway, and regularly. Many games were much worse, such as standing still for ages in one of the urine pots that were lined up in the middle of the bedrooms! So I kept my own council, becoming a loner, for fear of exacerbating the situation. For example, I worked alone on my little garden, which I had been given outside. With some useful advice from adults on choosing seeds, I created a real show of flowers in it! It became as colourful as the cardigan that one of my aunts had knitted for us so cleverly.

Having found lodgings with Kathleen near enough to walk to school, my mother now decided for my sake to change me to another dormitory of younger children on the other side of the house, and to have Jane and I stay with her as day girls at the weekends. With this, the pattern of life altered yet again for both of us. We re-adjusted to another way of life, part boarder, part day girl, but still participated in all the activities offered to the boarders. Nothing seemed to stay the same for very long, I thought.

Fortunately, we did not miss out on our education, which was taught in the style of the Montessori Method, a very enlightened way of teaching in those days, which used individual rewarded programmes for each child to follow in core subjects. A blue bead was offered for a completed assignment, green ones for distances of walks finished, with a square pink one for a good illustration, so maybe I was really working for the little rewards.

We also had the services of an older retired Oxford Don, who visited once a week to take some of us on fossil hunting outings. Since he was a very keen geologist, we were able to explore many interesting areas that we would otherwise never have visited, and we were given the benefit of his enthusiasm. This resulted in much more understanding of the geographical and geological principals of our world, a fact that stood me in good stead when I was older.

Learning at this school encouraged me to be very independent, more of a thinker, and I thrived well with these teaching methods. One of the main benefits was to encourage individual development, which was otherwise not possible when participating only in group classroom activities. I had a natural preference for a few subjects, but because of the school's enlightened curriculum, I took to other subjects with great enthusiasm through this individual approach. Young as I was, it enabled me to work out strategies of learning, the benefits and rewards for doing so, and to be a survivor as well.

Clitheroe crossroads.

THUNDERBOLT

The school was ideally placed for the children to go on country rambles. Two of the teachers often took advantage of good weather to take groups of us Treasure Hunting. Such outdoor excursions coincided with a message from the Ministry of Agriculture, which put out an illustrated leaflet, requesting the collection from hedgerows of a variety of essential herbs that grew amongst the herbage. These herbs were in great demand for the 'war effort'. Once we had learnt to identify the various plants, we then drew them in our books. As requested by the Ministry, we collected all types of herbs which were sorted into large piles. The teachers made moveable wooden racks in our geography room, tied the herbs onto them, and when full they were hauled up to the ceiling to dry. The goosegrass or alternatively, the sticky bud plant or cleaver, was the most prolific, but when dried and treated, was a wonderful treatment for infections – I admit that I don't know the biochemistry behind all of this. Sage and borage were in plentiful supply, and in late summer, we collected armfuls of foxgloves, and buckets full of rose hips from which syrup was made. After drying, all the herbs were passed on to the Women's Voluntary Service centre in the town. For our efforts, we received a handsome pay-out of five pence per pound in weight for most of them, but a huge seven shillings and sixpence per pound for foxgloves. A shilling a day for a good day's work, but I think our enthusiasm waned a little, because most of us got only sixpence each, and a small share of the barter. This was one of our remunerative war efforts, because pharmaceutical companies were desperately short of raw materials required for production of medicines. Paper, string, cardboard and milk bottle tops were also important collectable items for re-cycling. Adults encouraged all children to add to their ever growing stockpiles, which were then regularly collected for further processing.

The River Ribble winds through a large flood plain, past Clitheroe which lies slightly higher up the shallow river valley side, and flows on towards Preston and the Ribble Estuary in the Irish Sea. During the wetter periods in the year, the flood plain becomes somewhat waterlogged. The melting snows from many nearby hills swell the river, coursing down in torrents, spectacular and very fast. The level rises, and overflows over the plains. This used to happen repeatedly and, when very cold, caused layer after layer of ice to form, thus creating an extremely thick layer of ice.

During one winter, when the temperature dropped quickly and severely the field of ice was a sight to behold, being at least two feet thick. As a result, local people and troops alike, took advantage of this new 'ice-rink'. While the children took

The River Ribble near the school.

their toboggans out to play on it, the adults dusted down their ancient skates and pressed them into service again. For two or three weeks it remained intact until the weather changed, and rising temperatures inevitably caused the ice to thaw.

I slept in a dormitory overlooking the river, which was partly obscured by the trees below us. One night, we had all gone to bed and were sleeping peacefully, when suddenly the house shook like an earthquake. A tremendous explosion rent the air, which went on for some minutes. It was followed by several more crashes, until gradually silence reigned once again. We were all persuaded back into our beds, having to withdraw from the windows, through which we could see nothing in the night because of the thick hoar frost patterns on the panes. But it was a different story the following day. The sight outside was indescribable.

Large slabs of ice had been thrown up in the air by the extreme pressure of advancing water beneath, flowing off the hills. This had coincided with resistance from the inflowing spring tide, which flowed up the river as far as Ribchester. The ice now covered the meadows on both sides of the river. There were even slabs of ice which had landed in the park trees. Indeed, ice was scattered over a wide area in a haphazard fashion, large and small pieces, often piled up high in large heaps. Even the trees didn't escape the onslaught, because smaller shards of ice were balanced amongst the highest branches. Some pieces blocked the roads and the area was quite impassable for some time, until the bigger blocks melted sufficiently to make them light enough to be moved, however it took weeks before it was all gone. I don't think I have ever seen such an awe inspiring sight, demonstrating the extreme power of nature.

On another occasion, we witnessed a different type of explosion, however not as dramatic as the exploding ice. Around Clitheroe there were a great many mills, which had been built to harness energy from the fast flowing rivers. One of these mills unfortunately had been bombed, and was now a ruin. Nevertheless, one of the two chimneys belonging to the mill remained standing in the corner of the yard. It was safe and needed no further attention until a barrage balloon collided with it, which then made it too unsafe to leave. The town council decided it must be demolished; notices were displayed in prominent positions, advising everyone of the demolition date, but especially warning the public to keep away, and watch at a safe distance. This inevitably drew a large crowd, like bees around a honey pot. The army demolition squad was involved in the process, but had difficulty in moving the ever growing crowd back to a safe position. Being an event of great interest, of course we children were there, as a group from school. We all waited with mounting excitement and anticipation, expecting a great explosion, as we could see men in the distance moving around the base of the structure.

All of a sudden – a small gunshot noise was heard, followed by an enormous billowing of smoke. Slowly and gracefully the chimney sank down to the ground, creating a kind of ballerina skirt around its base with dust and smoke, pirouetting around its demise as if it were a stunning ballet. It created no

The demolition

noise, no fuss, no mess, and certainly not the spectacle expected to entertain the crowds, who were somewhat disappointed with the event. They all wandered home again silently, leaving the site within minutes.

Clitheroe is situated high above the banks of the River Ribble, crowned by a square Norman Keep, which had a hole blasted out of one side in 1645, rendering it uninhabitable for future occupiers. Otherwise it was still a fairly strong fortress. Its outline can be seen for many miles around, with adjoining land made into a public park with a beautiful Victorian wrought iron bandstand built upon it. As children, we roamed in the park and through the Keep, often sitting on the castle slopes to listen to the band. There were rings of individual slatted seats around the bandstand. At weekends in fine weather every available place was taken, including much of the grassed slopes around, in anticipation and enjoyment of the band concerts held there. We all attended them and very soon got to know favourite pieces of music, which the band enjoyed playing.

Mother had bought me a present from a shop specialising in miniature items. It was a small bugle, 'Piglet size' and thus accompanied Piglet now the proud owner of his own instrument. Since I had been learning to play the piano, I deemed myself clever enough to rule manuscript lines on my paper and draw musical staves on it, during one open-air concert. Then I wrote out the notes of *God Save the King* so that, still in my make-believe world, Piglet could play the National Anthem at the end of the concert. Mother and Kathleen were quite surprised at my efforts, and Kathleen decided at the end of the concert to show it to the bandmaster, Jim Grant, for his comments and possible corrections. He was amazed to

The Bandstand near Clitheroe Castle.

see that every value and position of each note was correct.

"Would you like me to teach you some music theory after school sometime?" he offered, while looking at my efforts. He obviously thought that it was worth it. When he called round to discuss musical scores with Kathleen, who often sang with the band, he always spent time with Jane and I, giving us the theory for brass playing. It was essentially the playing of one line of music at a time, and without using all ten fingers, as I had been taught on my piano. Instead, we learnt that playing those notes was through the valves of an entirely different type of instrument, which required dexterity, timing and different skills.

Interestingly, from this time onward, Jim Grant influenced my appreciation and interest in music greatly, so I'm devoting a few paragraphs to him here. He became a great friend of ours and in particular inspired me in future years to play in a brass band. This was an interest which I subsequently enthused about, and passed on to my four sons. As this generation has matured, it has influenced the musical choices in their lives.

Jim Grant was born in 1899, and was one of the older bandsmen in the Royal Engineers by the outbreak of World War II. He was a tall, thin man with grey hair, who had the complexion of an habitual smoker. During wartime the Recruiting Officers sought young able-bodied men for active service but also selected older reservists for non-combatant roles. Being too old for an active fighting role the band was an appropriate place for Jim, because he had served in the First World War as a boy trumpeter, joining at the age of fifteen. He was a Londoner originally, and gained great skills eventually, playing every instrument in the band. He became the Regimental Band Master, teaching aspiring young bandsmen to play. He also held regular teaching sessions in his own time for potential players from the civilian population.

Jim Grant

By 1943, during which time the regiment was actively practising temporary bridge construction over the Ribble, he organised a wide variety of entertainments – including concerts and dances – which greatly helped maintain the morale and lift flagging spirits. People were only too willing to consider any new distractions, which would take them away from the harsh realities of war. The band travelled extensively around Lancashire to towns and villages that had suitable halls for entertainment. Since a military band, along with all of its instruments, took up a lot of room, they were usually transported in a furniture van, including space for the players too. As required, there were a few volunteers, who usually went with them, to look after the music and the trappings of this mobile concert.

On some of these occasions, my mother, the singer Kathleen, my sister and I would volunteer to help out. Frequently, we travelled to the concert venues at weekends in the van, along with the bandsmen and their instruments. The venues included many of the mill towns in the valleys of East Lancashire, such as Rochdale, Burnley and Blackburn. As we travelled, we often joined in creating ad-hoc music sessions inside the van. Often, this mystified shoppers as we travelled along streets, especially when stopping at traffic lights. Almost invariably, we saw amazed faces with open mouths while the impromptu concert took place inside the vehicle.

I gained a lifelong love of brass band music, on those long trips to the concerts. This was especially the case because of the kindness of the bandsmen, who taught me the rudiments of playing. I even had the opportunity to try to play all the different instruments, gaining a feel for their place in a band. We made ourselves useful too, for example, by keeping the music cards tidy for each player (these were put into the 'lyres' or music holders, on which the score was written for each piece to be played, and attached to each instrument). We learned about the joys of harmony, and to appreciate why four players could sound like a complete band.

The band regularly played in the King Lane Theatre, Clitheroe, to packed audiences, and, as usual, we were keen to help. I remember well one concert, which was planned to end with the *1812 Overture* by Tchaikovsky. As usual, this required a brass fanfare with the trumpeters, the ringing of chimes, and cannon fire, timed with the kettle drums, as its finale. The first two instruments were not a cause for concern on this occasion,

King Lane Theatre, Clitheroe.

however the band chose to replicate the sound of cannon fire using thunderbolts, which is a type of noisy firearm used to create big explosions, but one which allegedly doesn't cause damage.

So much for the theory – the practice turned out to be rather different. I was at the back of the stage, sorting out the music cards with the sheet music, and glanced down one of the long passageways, which bordered the two sides of the theatre. Some soldiers were preparing their instruments to create this dramatic climax to the overture, and were watching their score carefully to anticipate the cannon fire moment. From several past concerts, I knew this moment well, and was ready to watch the action which would fit the music. Bang. Crash. Another – Bang. Crash.

With a thunderous commotion, the ceiling in the passageway came tumbling down the full length, piece by piece, with chunks of plaster and buckets of dust that sprayed over every nook and cranny of the place. The musical finale was a great success for the audience, with noises from the fireworks exploding, and realistic 'smoke' which were plaster trails, and wound about the stage everywhere.

Signalling the normal end of the concert, the fire-doors were opened, and the audience happily left the theatre, enthusing about such a terrific finale to the evening, completely oblivious to the events backstage. What a disaster there.

Immediately afterwards we were ushered out of the back doors of the building, all of us white as snow from the plaster, including the players, who hastily picked up their instruments and cases. As we later gathered, nobody had been allowed back into the building again until the safety of the structure had been assured. This process took a couple weeks, during which time the damage was speedily repaired by an army squad of repairers and decorators. I never saw such fireworks used again until I heard the same piece of music performed some years later, in a safer environment, at Kneller Hall Royal Military School of Music in Middlesex.

Later, the newspapers reported upon the concert but the damage backstage was popularly ascribed by them to bomb damage and remarked 'What a mercy it was, that no one was injured'. Fortunately, they never revealed the true cause of the incident.

BAILEY BRIDGES

Washing day in Kathleen's house in King Street was a complicated affair because she didn't have a washing machine. That might be strange today but was not unusual during the war. First the copper boiler was lit in the corner of the wash-house, using a bed of coal, then supplemented with kindling. Items of clothing were boiled and washed in rotation, by placing them in the boiling water, with the least dirty placed in the tub first. Some of the hot water was taken from the boiler and poured into a dolly tub along with particularly dirty clothes. These were agitated with a five-legged dolly-stool, which had a long-handled cross bar to perform the required agitation as it was rotated back and forth. Then the 'posser' was applied to the tub, forcing water in and out through the clothes with a copper headed type of colander. All this activity was repeated again with clean water. Finally the clothes were fed through wooden rollers of the mangle to wring out as much water as possible, before hanging up to dry. Thank goodness for modern automatic machines; in those days, there wasn't even a twin tub in sight.

My recollections of the chores of washing remain quite vivid because, while I was ill and confined to the house for several weeks, I watched this activity frequently. The reason for my illness was a verruca, an infectious complaint more common in the early part of the century than today. At school I had found that my foot

had become more and more painful, so I was taken to the doctor. He diagnosed the ailment on the sole of my foot. It was decided to take me to Blackburn Infirmary to have the growth cut out, because its roots had spread to a large proportion of my sole and instep.

This was an occasion that I shall never forget. When we arrived, I was put in the WS ward, a place with my own initials I thought, until I found out it meant the Women's Surgical ward. Preparing for the operation was a dreadful experience and a fight, because the staff tried to put a chloroform mask on me. As a result, I kicked, I scratched and bit the poor nurse holding me, finishing up by rolling onto the floor. They were not to be defeated. Treating me slightly more firmly, I was sedated eventually, and the operation was finally carried out.

In the King Street garden after my operation.

Once I returned to the ward from the operating theatre, it was now full of older women. As a treat, I was offered an orange and a banana, which I had never seen or eaten before. Not knowing what to do with them, I tried eating the outer skins. Of course, I quickly received advice on this. With great pride, I showed off the see-through hole in my foot to the other ladies, where the surgeon had removed an enormous growth. Gradually my foot healed and I made a full recovery. Thereafter, to prevent contracting another verruca, I insisted on protecting my feet by wearing slippers or shoes, a habit which continued for many years.

Just after my stay in the infirmary, my sister Jane suffered from a severe bout of pneumonia. Thanks to the advances in medical knowledge at the time, she was given a course of M & B tablets, the first of the known sulphonamide antibiotics, which saved her from a long, protracted illness that could easily have been fatal. I believe that this antibiotic was discovered in 1937 by May & Baker, and was offered to army personnel by 1942.

It was not always convenient for Grandfather to have us return to Bowerswood for our summer holidays, therefore other activities were changed. Mother took us to Waddington, a village three miles away from Clitheroe, for a little 'camping' holiday, with eight other people – a few adults along with their children – making eleven altogether. Collectively, the adults asked a local farmer to lend a small space in a field near to the village for a week. This was exciting stuff for us all. As ever, Kathleen was involved and had acquired five small tents from the army store via Jim Grant who, together with a friend, helped to put them up. I had become a bit of a loner, and did not want to share, therefore asked to have the smallest one to myself. During this time, we all went to the local inn for meals, and were taken on walks along local roads and paths, a very beautiful area of countryside. On one occasion, when some of them were going to the pub in the evening, I asked my mother to bring back to my tent some of the coloured bottle tops, that I had seen in the pub. These provided two friends of mine and myself with hours of play, pretending that the different colours were opposing armies.

But I didn't have my tent to myself.

On the first night I was startled by the snuffling of a creature poking his nose under the side of my canvas. In no time at all, I was joined by a black and white collie dog, wriggling continually and wagging his tail in communication. Very soon he had found a warm spot and climbed into my sleeping bag with me, damp fur, muddy paws and all. It was like having a live teddy bear to cuddle, and one which washed my face too. Next day, my horrified mother tried to shoo him away back to the farm, but

The collie dog.

62

had to resign herself to my new smelly dog companion for that week, only realising too late that he had come with his own 'friends', the fleas, and lots to share with me.

The films shown during wartime invariably followed the same pattern: first, a major feature film, then an extended newsreel, followed finally by a secondary film. Sometimes, there were special showings for children, which missed out the distressing newsreels, and advertised as suitable for the very young. On these occasions, longer Walt Disney films were shown, such as *Bambi* and *Snow White*, at which I cried heartily when I saw the frightening witch.

We occasionally went by train to Preston, which seemed quite an adventure. During this time, all the station signs were taken down to confuse potential enemy infiltrators, and the station lighting was considerably reduced to become completely ineffective. One had to rely on the stationmaster to call out the name of the station very loudly – it was very bad luck if you missed this announcement. Whenever possible, we attempted to travel in the daytime only, but the length of our journey was often dependent upon whether we had to give way to troop movement trains, because they had priority over all other rail traffic.

I remember one instance of this when I had to have some reconstructive surgery done on my inward turning teeth, at a specialist dental practice in Liverpool. Unfortunately, we arrived three hours late for the appointment. Very apologetically, Mother explained the circumstances behind our lateness but the specialist was somewhat dismissive about it. 'What do you expect during these troubled times. It happens all the time.' Nevertheless, a little more constructively, asked, 'Can you get home later? If so, I'll deal with your daughter now.' He gave me a piece of dental modelling wax to play with to keep me quiet. He now dipped it in hot water to soften, saying, 'Be quick, as it soon hardens,' so I hastily turned it into a cat, and had it finished by the time it was my turn.

We went to Preston one holiday to see the comedian George Formby, who sang and played a ukulele at the Guild Hall in a Christmas Pantomime. We sat in the front row of the theatre with a group of other children to watch *Peter Pan*. I was not so pleased, though, when a few of us were ushered up on to the stage in a row to sing 'Yes, we have no bananas.' as a canvas 'prompt', containing the words, rolled down in front of us. At that stage I could neither read fluently nor write easily, and still barely knew what a banana was anyway, so I hung on to Jane's hand and would not be parted from her, while I tried not to cry.

On another occasion we went to the cinema to see *Snow White*. It was pitch black at the station and cold – so very cold! A thin veil of cloud hid the millions of twinkling stars that usually made the darkness bearable, thus giving the sky above shape and depth, but without these points of reference the world was a terrifying nothingness. I walked on, clutching Mother's hand, my other hand plunged deep into my pocket where I could feel two big pennies and a silver three penny piece jingling about. Mother carried a hooded torch whose beam danced along the pavement edge to guide us to the station where we intended to catch the next train, though its time of arrival was variable.

I then sat with my mother on the platform bench in the total dark, remembering the poor, apparently dead, Snow White whose downfall was engineered by a terrible black witch. Her cackles of glee and harmful abilities seemed to reappear again, as a passenger brushed past me in the dark, and my fear returned and I stifled my sobs.

At that moment we heard a train, with its chugging engine belching plumes of smoke and steam, the fire box glowing faintly in the darkness. As it drew closer the brakes squealed and the monster train arrived out of the dark to stop by the platform. Suddenly there were lots of people including many soldiers, who had been hidden by the shadows, crowding onto the platform. The porter shouted the name of the next station, 'Preston Station, northbound. All aboard, leaving in three mintues.' He repeated this as he strode along with his downward shuttered railwayman's lamp, the platform was quickly emptying but still devoid of any light and was as dark as the inside of the carriages.

Over the 13,000 miles of railway lines, all station signs has been taken down due to fears of invasion, and everybody had to rely on the annoucements of the porters or station masters. We had been drilled into showing no tell tale lights to any stray enemy aircraft. In haste we aimed for a carriage door, being jostled by the crowds, and I was lifted into the train by an airman standing by the door, as another man pulled Mother unceremoniously into the train.

Doors were slammed as the train started to move again, all within the three minutes allowed and, as the train moved, people began to rearrange themselves goodnaturedly to maximise the space. Cases were stacked up to create makeshift seats while kit bags were softer options. We had boarded a troop train which picked up some civilians at night but travelled on very tight timetables. The priority of our hard pressed railways was to carry servicemen who were now augmented by overseas personnel.

These were mainly Americans who had recently joined our forces seemed to be everywhere, with their easy going and kindly ways. They were creative too, for the man who had hauled me on board soon checked that the blackout blinds were closed on all windows before rigging up a light. It was still very cold and people's breath rose in little clouds. Trains were not heated at that time so save on fuel, but the warmth of a really packed carriage soon began to raise the temperature. Cigarettes were passed around, increasing the fog-like atmosphere, like a sea mist creeping up the estuary, obscuring the view from one end of our carriage to the other. People were now talking and asking questions of the Americans.

'Where have you come from?' 'Have you family back home?' were the two questions most often asked, usually resulting in long discussions about the differences between the two countries, languages and customs. The American who had lifted me onto the train, now sat me on his knee so that I wasn't squashed on the floor and several other children perched on servicemen's knees.

'Where have you been to be out so late, little lady?' he asked. His simple question brought forth a lengthy reply, 'We've been to see Snow White but she got killed by the wicked witch, and now she might be on the train to kill someone else!' I wailed and started to cry again.

'No, no, she is saved by the Prince in the end, I promise you and he kills the witch. I've seen the movie. Now have a piece of candy and dry your eyes.' Smiling he broke up a big bar of chocolate and handed little pieces to all the children as the other airmen searched in their pockets to give out sweets to other passengers.

My American friend searched around for a distraction to keep me from thinking about the film. He noticed my hands were still in my pockets and asked, 'What have you got in your pocket?' I was wearing my sister's outgrown blue coat with a navy velvet collar and flaps that concealed pockets, and within them I was jingling the two pennies and silver three penny piece.

'These are for playing Tiddlywinks,' I said, 'they work just as well as real winks.' Now that I had someone to show the game to I was keen to demonstrate and soon forgot all fears of the wicked witch.

It was the longest and most unexpected train journey I had experienced and my memories of it far exceed any about Snow White and the witch. I asked my American friend what he did in the forces because these men from afar wore strange uniforms, unlike my father's green-brown Army uniform.

'I fly little airplanes to France and back. In fact I can show you what I mean as I've made these for my kids back at home. These are made from an English penny in our aircraft servicing department. We are making them to take back Stateside for our kids.'

He then fished out of his pocket a little copper Spitfird that was highly polished, with a safety pin soldered onto its reverse side. He pinned it onto the lapel of my coat where it shone brightly against the navy blue material.

'A Yankee present for you to keep little lady. I shall be thinking of you when I'm flying high tomorrow night.'

I do hope that he returned safely with his little flight of aircraft after the war. I've often thought about it when I wear my small Spitfire, now plated with gold to keep it shining.

During this period of my life I was either in the Clitheroe area or at Bowerswood. I remember the sad day when an aircraft came gliding through the low clouds on a

The aircraft which crashed on Pendle Hill.

cold murky February day and crashed into Pendle Hill. The weather was appalling, and we found out later that this was one of five American Republic Thunderbolt planes, P-47Ds, which had flown from Norfolk to Wharton in Lancashire. This particular plane had been circling round to find a break in the low clouds, but unfortunately ran out of fuel and crashed into the side of the hill, killing the pilot. Pieces of the plane, bullets and weapons were found for weeks afterwards spread over Pendle Hill, and of course the area was made out of bounds to all of us young scavengers, for fear of one of us picking up some live ammunition.

About this time, we became aware of an influx of farm workers around the district, cheerful men who whistled and sang strange songs while they worked. They were given the job of 'luking', a northern word meaning gathering rocks and stones out of fields, to make the land easier for growing crops. It also could mean clearing thistles and nettles for the same purpose, and this meant that more land was made available for producing larger amounts of food. I discovered that these men were Italian Prisoners of War, dressed in brown overalls with yellow circles on their backs. They lived in a camp nearby, but as they seemed to have no intention of escaping anywhere, they were allowed to wander about freely when not working.

Rides for children across the River Ribble.

Our teachers told us that they had spoken with some of these POWs, who had reportedly said they were very happy to be working in England, and were very frightened of war, the Germans, and guns, treating all the children with great kindness. We thought they seemed to be very homesick.

The Royal Engineers worked hard on their various constructions down by the river, and rumour had it that they had perfected some of their contraptions. The Bailey Bridges had been designed originally by Donald Bailey, a British Civil Engineer, who worked for the British War Office. He tinkered with model bridge designs at home, especially using toy construction components from his box of Meccano pieces. He offered his designs to the War Office as possible temporary bridging solutions for use during the liberation of continental Europe. The River Ribble at Clitheroe proved to be a suitable testing ground for the trials of the various bridges.

In readiness for taking part in the Normandy landings, the Royal Engineers had started to prepare to ship out their belongings, to dismantle their camps and remove equipment from around the town and surrounding fields. However, before leaving, and as a means of celebrating their time in Clitheroe, they decided to hold a Jamboree Day, just like a big agricultural show, but army style. This was held on the flat fields by the river, open for all the townspeople, making it a holiday occasion during which all the bridges and equipment for crossing the river were made available to inspect and try out. Some of them had been made into 'fun rides' for smaller children. Jane and I quickly climbed into various 'rides', especially the ones that took us over the river and back.

We were excited by the occasion. Jack Smithson had his hands full with us because he had offered to take us both for the afternoon, accompanied by his friend, Muriel Bywater. She took photographs with her very efficient Brownie camera to mark the occasion, especially when the soldiers arranged themselves for a group photograph for the crowds of onlookers to record the occasion.

Jack Smithson and Muriel Bywater.

'Can I take one of you both?' I was keen to try out her new toy.

Everybody could walk on the Bailey bridges, trying out several different models, and the pontoon bridges too, soon competed for attention, with rides being offered to the daring and eager youths on the zip wires across the river. There were canoe races, as well as other competitions, for any of the young people who vied for speed and excitement while competing against the young soldiers. Refreshment tents and other entertainments, like Hoopla stalls, were set out to delight everyone, while the band played for the afternoon.

Later on, a large wooden floor was spread out on the field under an enormous marquee for dancing, lit by coloured lights. This activity competed strongly for customers, from the over-spill of people in the beer and food tents around the field. We

The Sappers before leaving.

all danced the hokey-kokey, and ate ice-creams. The music changed tempo as the lights dimmed to provide a more romantic atmosphere for the late night dancers. Finally we youngsters were packed off home to bed, but could still hear much laughter and the band music playing well into the night's warm breeze.

Acouple of days later when we all ran back down to see how things were progressing for the soldiers, we were amazed to find the mists rolling over a peaceful and clean field, green and tranquil in the morning light, with not a soldier, a tent or a bridge to be seen.

As my father would have said:

> *The night shall be filled with music,*
> *As the cares that infest the day,*
> *Shall fold their tents like the Arabs,*
> *And silently steal away.*

HENS AND COAL MINES

Percy and Helen Ridley who lived in Shildon, County Durham, were friends of my parents. Percy was manager of the Midland Bank, located on the Main Street, in the town. They lived in a beautiful old bank building, which had mullioned stone windows, and had all the charm of an early 'Arts & Crafts' style. It was built in 1899 for the York and County Bank and is now a listed building, and has been converted to a family house. During the war, when I first stayed there it was a busy commercial bank serving numerous businesses in Shildon. The town was located at the heart of a coal mining area, and was also at the crossroads of a thriving railway repair industry, along with associated shunting yards, and a busy main railway station.

During one particular Easter holiday, when my sister was staying for a month with her Godmother, I was invited by these friends, Pop (as he was always known) and Helen, to spend some time with them, and was duly dispatched for my unexpected trip to Shildon on the train. Children often travelled alone in those days, in the care of the guard, who offloaded their charges at the chosen destination handing them over to an appropriate waiting adult. I was full of excitement, and happy to see this new place.

Midland Bank House, Shildon.

Helen was a delightful person, with great charm, quietly spoken with a slight Durham accent and a ready smile. She organised a little bedroom for me overlooking the Main Street in the town. This was the first time I realised how noisy the centre of a town could be, in particular, in the evenings men would be ejected routinely from the various local hostelries. They were always in varying stages of inebriation and would sing and shout boisterously together on their way home. Unluckily for me, they often passed below my window, at which point I would cover my head with the plumpest eiderdown I had ever seen, to lessen the noise, while learning a few new choice words to be looked up later. Pop was a keen, political person, but also quite a comic with a broad smile. Often, I wanted to ask him the meaning of an odd word which I might have heard from the night's revellers, but I was reluctant to do so, based on the negative experience I'd had at school. Invariably, I chose the quiet option, as being the safest policy and never asked.

Early the following day I went exploring the house, which tended to be my habit. Very quickly, I found Nora, Helen's stalwart helper, who was dusting and cleaning the bank before opening time. I offered to help, and duly chose to walk along the

Helen Ridley.

tops of the counters, using my little duster, to remove dust from the uppermost ledges that I claimed were very dusty. Balancing myself at this height was bound to court trouble. Nora was a bit cross, no doubt taking my comments as criticism. Therefore, she banished me from the room completely, saying she was worried about me falling off. Thereafter, Helen told me not to bother Nora again while she was cleaning.

Later on I watched Helen making bread, which she baked three times a week, in the big kitchen. The dough was made with fresh yeast and left on the table by the hot range to rise, before being divided up, shaped, and put into tins for baking. Here Helen invited me to get involved, and I was now in my element. I was so pleased to make my first loaf of bread under Helen's eye, although it ended up becoming a hard, grey, solid lump as a result of being over-handled, over-kneaded and over baked. But with practise and a little encouragement, I improved until my efforts were finally edible. Nevertheless, the comment for my first efforts received a 'Not bad' from Pop. As far as I was concerned, that meant success.

The house was a peaceful and beautifully furnished home with leaded-light windows and broad window seats. The place was always full of flowers, tastefully arranged. Helen was an extremely good painter in her spare time, and was happy to set me up with paints and good quality paper, which kept me happily occupied for hours on the dining room table. She also had a piano that I enjoyed playing, practicing the same pieces over and over again. Unfortunately, this annoyed Pop so much that this activity was soon stopped.

In the garden I spied an entrance to an underground air-raid shelter, which had been well stocked with bedding, food and other necessities. The door was shut, but never locked, in case of emergencies. It was three quarters buried in the earth, but around it, hiding the entrance, were many mixed flowers, tall hollyhocks, delphiniums and dahlias, and a lawn, edging a well-used vegetable plot. The larger part of the garden at the rear had been fenced off, and used to allow a variety of hens to roam around outside a small henhouse. When I asked if I could feed the hens, I learned of the wartime restrictions relating to hen keeping.

'First we save every scrap of waste food, and put all the peelings, bones, and waste vegetables

Nora in Pop's garden

in that big pan to boil up very well. Raw potato peelings are poisonous to hens.' Helen continued, 'We are registered as hen keepers, so we're not allowed to have egg rations. But instead, we can use our coupons for an agreed amount of hen mash called 'Balancer Meal'. It's never enough, so we mix it with our daily boil-up of scraps, and feed them this mixture.'

Helen's goose

The mixture smelt awful, especially the process of mixing the mash with the boiled-up pan full of waste. Surprisingly, when I scattered this disgusting mixture on the ground for the waiting hens, it was soon gobbled up with glee. Then I collected eggs from the warm nesting boxes where some of the hens were sitting clucking, and who objected profusely to getting out of the way when pushed to relinquish their clutch of eggs. They were a mixed collection of hens and included one goose. This lone bird happily intermingled with the hens, and Helen said it always behaved noisily and was also a wonderful alarm against intruders.

I enjoyed looking after the friendly and nosey hens, which soon became accustomed to me picking them up. I could set one on my knee and sit in the sunshine to stroke its soft and springy feathered coat, while it crooned its hen-talk for hours. There were deep brown hens, black hens, grey-speckled ones and a variety of white hens with black collars and tails. There were also small bantams with long tails. Helen could identify which hen laid which egg by the colours of the shells.

We went shopping to Darlington one day on the bus, and saw notices all over the town, stuck on the walls and fences, depicting slogans such as 'Is your journey really necessary?' or 'Walls have ears.' and 'Careless talk costs lives.' 'Waste not, want not.' was more understandable to me, but the other sayings were a bit too abstract to understand then.

We went to a large department store called Binns. It was my first experience of a big store of this kind. Almost immediately I became rooted to the spot while I watched a sort of railway travelling across the ceiling. As part of this process, I watched the girl at the counter serving a customer, who received the customer's money for an item being purchased, and put it into a round box with the bill. Next, she closed the lid of the round box, and then pulled a lever on a string. Instantly the little 'boat', as I called it, travelled along wires, across the ceiling and up to the next floor where it disappeared through a hole into the cash office. It returned a few minutes later via the same route carrying the receipted bill and the change.

For me this was fascinating – I couldn't believe the ingenuity of this contraption, and promptly asked if I could send something in it to travel through the hole as well. The kindly salesgirl indulged me, and we put two sweets in with a note to say 'Please return again.' I was delighted when they returned, now multiplied with four more, and another note saying 'Enjoy.' So Helen and I shared them with the salesgirl, two for each of us. Such fun moments are remembered for years.

Helen bought me a little torch for use at night because, due to wartime restrictions, street lights were switched off to avoid drawing the attention of German bomber aircraft to the positions of houses, villages or towns. Having lived for about four years without any artificial light outside, many people became much more aware of the stars and planets in the night sky, and I learned for example how to find the North Star and Orion's Belt. We could also watch the beams of aircraft searchlights criss-crossing the skies that made intricate patterns in the sky.

Helen took me to meet a girl, a little older than me, with the Irish name of Maeve, who offered to take me around and show me the town. We enjoyed visiting various places, but this did not last long. She was fanatically keen on football, and also on one of the young men who played in the team. On one occasion, when we went to watch a match with her, I was quite unhappy to find that we had to stand for hours, it seemed, in the cold and then the rain, shouting at yellow and black-striped figures playing with a ball. I promptly declined any further visits, and our friendship soon waned to a full stop.

Shildon is renowned as being 'the cradle of the railways', and grew quickly once the Stockton to Darlington Railway Company built their workshops and the very first passenger railway station there in 1825. At this time, passengers travelled to Stockton-on-Tees. The town grew quickly,

The old Shildon Station.

especially through the expansion of opencast coalfields.

One day, Helen suggested that we went for a picnic on some beautiful spot in the surrounding country before it was finally despoiled by the engulfing coal mine. We took our basket of food, set up a good place for our picnic on a rug, which Helen then sat upon in the sunshine, and I wandered off to explore the rim of the fenced off land, picking the wild flowers there. I collected a good handful, reaching out ever closer to the fence, put a hand on it to steady myself, and then clutched at fresh air. No fence.

I tumbled headlong down into a large hole, whose slopes had been hidden by the lush grass, sliding in the mud and stones, and threw out my arms and feet to break the fall, but not so successfully. Work had started on the clearance of the land, and now it was truly a dangerous place for the unwary. When I eventually came to rest from my sliding, rolling, tumbling and being somewhat scratched from the brambles, I called out to Helen in great fear. I was quite a long way down.

'Helen. I don't know where I am, but I think I'm a long way down. My leg hurts. I can't climb out.' I was frightened, having landed in a large depression in the ground, which kept on shifting underneath me and I could not help myself. I cried out, 'The ground keeps moving. I daren't move.'

Helen called back to say she would get help, and told me to keep very, very still. She feared that I would slide even further down into the hole, because while walking around the fenced rim, she could see the area of excavation, where the removal of tons of topsoil had been piled up, while trees had been uprooted and stone walls knocked down. It had the appearance of a lunar landscape, dangerous and forbidding. We had heard that the land would be returned to its former state once the opencast mining activities had finished. But at this very moment I couldn't imagine the remotest possibility of this ever happening, for how could they ever remember later how it looked like now?

It soon became very cold, and I started to shiver in my thin summer frock, because I was out of the sunshine. In my terrified state, I imagined that this cold crevice would somehow lead down into a dark, dangerous and mysterious world underground. I swore fervently that I would never go exploring alone again, but this was a forlorn hope for the future, knowing my nature.

In a little while and with much relief, I heard voices from a distance, far below me. Soon two men from the shunting yard came up with a stretcher, and made short work of traversing the moving earth and getting me down to level ground. Eventually, they delivered me back to Bank House, shivering and in increasing pain.

The doctor was sent for, and it was established that I had broken my ankle. So now I was bound up and forcibly made to rest. The remainder of my holiday was

Wendy Stuart.

spent either painting pictures, with my now much-used paintbox, or practising on the piano, but only when we thought it was a suitable time not to disturb Pop.

Helen came in from shopping one day with a small bag of paints in little china dishes. She showed me how to renew all my used-up colours with the new paints. In addition, she had bought me a notebook, with a slim pencil attached, for writing down little painting tips, which she was in the habit of telling me. Even to this day, in my treasured folder of paintings, I still have a couple of pictures that we did on that holiday.

Pop wrote in my autograph book a little poem, but Helen was not too pleased about it. Being a religious lady, she thought it mocked the psalm that it parodied. I realised that it was something to do with politics but it was the first time I had heard any disagreement between them. Unfortunately, I never managed to understand either of their arguments.

On the whole they were very much in accord with one another, and exuded such peacefulness, that I loved being there with them. Helen sat with me several times to paint, and showed her undoubted aptitude for painting while helping me to absorb increasingly the painting skills which she had learned in her lifetime.

Pop's Poem

The government is my shepherd, I need not work; it allows me to lie down on good jobs; it leadeth me beside the still factories, it destroyeth my initiative. It leads me in the paths of the parasite for politics sake.

Yea, though I walk through the valley of laziness-deficit spending, I shall fear no evil, for the government is with me, its doles and vote getters, they comfort me. It prepareth an economic utopia for me by appropriating the earnings of my grandchildren.

It filleth my head with baloney, my inefficiency runneth over. Surely the government shall care for me all the days of my life and I shall dwell in a fool's paradise for ever.

We had made plans to visit Middleton-in-Teasdale, and stay in the Ridley's caravan on a sheep farm at Ettersgill, up in the fells. I was very keen to visit the waterfall at High Force, advertised as the highest waterfall in England. But when my ankle had finally healed, our plans had to be adjusted, because there was now no time to stay there. So for the time being, I had to be content with the promise of another visit in the future; a visit that I did make with surprising consequences.

THE RED FEZ

My Aunts Gee, Nona and Mary were often at Bowerswood during the summer months, and met up with the resident Coco which coincided with my long holidays. In addition, my mother's cousin, Norah, stayed there regularly. She lived in Low Abbey, a beautiful, grey stuccoed house in the village of Ellel, near Lancaster. From time to time, she stayed with her four older, unmarried sisters who lived in Lancaster and all suffered ill health. Otherwise, her home in Low Abbey was her retreat, away from the stress of caring for others. She was a little older than my mother. Sadly, she was widowed just before the war, soon after her marriage in 1914, to grandfather's nephew, another Stephen Simpson. Nevertheless, after this tragedy she started a cottage industry spinning and weaving fine woollen

Grandfather's sisters – Mary, Gee and Nona with the author's mother.

cloth in her village, employing widows of the First World War which provided them with a means of earning their living, and this association called The Guild of St. Margaret of Scotland blossomed into a thriving small hand spinning industry at Ellel.

During one summer holiday, she offered to keep the 'ancient' aunts company, they being now in their seventies, but chiefly she came to look after Jane and I because our governess started a new job elsewhere as a wartime civil servant. This was very helpful because we had just started school, and Mother was fully occupied with her part-time WVS activities when not with us at the school. Therefore, our home developed into a household full of aunts. My Aunt Coco managed to run the expanded household admirably, throwing off her deafness like an unasked for gift to be discarded. Coco, Mary, Nona and Gee had an instinctive and close understanding, not often to be seen in sisters.

Norah had no children, had a very sweet nature, and usually wore thick lisle stockings, sensible walking shoes, and tweed skirts. She exuded kindness every moment of the day, and would join in our imaginary games with a will, allowing her light

Norah Simpson

brown hair to unpin itself from the usual bun held in place at her neck. She put on her galoshes (waterproof overshoes) when I insisted on taking her fishing to Mr Jackson's field pond with my homemade rod, a net and a jar. We were much more successful with the net than the rod, and excitedly I put our catch of a few tiddlers into the big cattle trough in the farm yard. There, they grew in safety, becoming quite large fish, unmolested by me, who would otherwise feed them.

As we began to read, for the very first time, about the Faraway Tree in *Sunny Stories*, we wanted to have our own tree house, which would be a secret den to play in. Obligingly, Norah persuaded Stirsaker, the gardener, to shape up two rhododendron bushes, by weaving the branches together, and hollowing out the central parts. He cut some logs for small seats, including a table-sized taller one, and placed them all in the 'Tree Houses'. He gave us both little boards to write the following names: 'Jane's House', and 'Effadika's House'. I didn't want to use my own name, and instead I insisted on using my fairy name. Norah had to crawl in and out through the narrow space each time we held tree parties, but did so willingly, and brought little cups, biscuits, and bottles of pop for these magic occasions.

Sometimes Aunt Melene called in with two of her own protégés from her local Brownie Pack, a group that she organised for the hamlet of Nateby. Occasionally, her two dogs, George and Jerry, a golden retriever and a black and white springer spaniel, with their swishing tails, became tree house visitors. On each occasion, they were quickly evacuated from the play house, being too boisterous, and had to sit outside, panting in the sunshine. One day my aunt showed me an almost perfect ring of small toadstools in the grass, which showed up clearly in the short cut dew covered lawn. She explained that it had been made by dancing fairies from the night before, a story, which I believed in my fanciful mind, only discovering years later the habits of the fungal mycelium that travelled below the surface of the ground to produce the fungi.

The main log pile for the house fire was becoming quite large and had been growing for some time. It was an inspirational place for finding wood for furnishing our make-believe houses. Through our familiarity with the woodpile, Jane and I were able to uncover a crime – theft from our woodpile. This discovery was made on one occasion when I had put to one side a particular shaped piece of wood which I had intended to carry later to the tree house for future use. When I returned next day for my wood, it had gone... and so had most of the wood pile. I checked with Norah, who was aware that quite a lot of chain-saw work was being carried out, but nevertheless was suspicious that something was not quite right. Together, we followed the trail of tree bark debris from the original woodpile until eventually we found a cache of felled trees a little further into the woods.

'Say nothing of this yet, until I find out what is going on.' she asked us, with her most winning smile. 'I do not think your Grandpa would have intended to have those trees cut, but you never know.'

Norah first went to Aunt Melene in her Lodge house and asked tentatively if she was aware of any new tree felling activity going on. Melene, who prided herself on knowing about most things, marched off in her usual strident manner to find Stir-

The old yard and coach house at Bowerswood.

saker the gardener, who when questioned, pointed out that Jack was in charge of tree felling. As an afterthought, he added, 'Jack Lockwood said that the Colonel had ordered a load of wood to be sold somewhere, don't know where, though.'

Without any further preamble, Melene strode into Grandfather's study to ask him what was going on, and using her Aunt Flo-Jane manner, without sparing her words, she put her point over very firmly as to the possibility of theft having taken place. Grandfather was indeed horrified about the whole situation because he had not ordered such a cull of the trees. Using his shrill voice, now raised several decibels, he ordered Melene 'to get to the bottom of it.'

It was taken out of the family's hands when my aunt telephoned their friend, Detective Inspector Hawkins, who advised that there was a thriving business in the district for stolen wood. It would seem that Grandfather's secluded woods had been a prime locality for the thieves. The police went to work, and within a short period of time, managed to apprehend the culprits. One of these was a young estate worker, who was charged with criminal damage and theft by the police. The other gardeners, being very busy, had never thought to question the activities of others in a different part of the grounds. This incident was somewhat disturbing for Grandfather, whom I thought felt vulnerable having staff not able to look after his interests more carefully, and not to mention having had a thief amongst them. I believe that he greatly benefitted from having a sizeable supporting family staying with him at this time.

Grandfather offered us an old trunk of clothes to play with, on the proviso that we were to remove it from his bedroom and move it into a spare room. Norah carefully pulled it out, along the passageway and into another room, eagerly helped by her young charges. She opened this Pandora's Box of delights, which was full of clothes from a past era. There were shawls, fans, dresses, muffs and capes, all wrapped in fine tissue papers, layered in between the folds of the materials. We found evidence of dates of the items, some going back as far as 1730, having found little handbags with dance cards carefully filled in by long-dead suitors and dancing partners. Some of the names were familiar to my growing store of family names, from the Heskeths, Yates, Simpsons, and Bells who were earlier ancestors. Jane and I dressed up in all this finery for some years to come as we grew older and taller until we were seasoned teenagers. We often had days of fun with our dressing up box. Grandfather suggested we might like to keep one item each for our very own, therefore I chose a white crinoline ball gown, trimmed with pink and red, from circa

Jane dressing up.

1854. At a later date, I used this for my wedding dress minus its red trimmings.

Every summer the Garstang Agricultural Show was held on the big field at the northern end of the town, and always on the first Saturday in August. On this occasion it was a glorious summer's day, and as usual there was a selection of livestock lined up in their pens ready to be viewed by the judges and public alike. Jane and I had new dresses for the occasion, made by my mother, along with round straw hats with wide brims and ribbons. We both thought ourselves very smart. Grandfather was asked to be President of the show this year, and therefore was responsible for handing out all the prizes. We were told especially to be on our best behaviour.

The author in a dress from 1854

I was delighted to wander round the animals, keeping out of the way of the show jumpers in the ring. The cattle were duly lined up for inspection and subsequent adjudication. Among various other breeds were Dairy Shorthorns, Ayrshires and Friesians, standing in line next to the Channel Island breeds including the Guernseys, Alderneys and Jerseys. There was one class for 'milking cow and its calf', which meant two animals in the pen, the mother and her baby. I enjoyed observing the differences between these little animals, and would have liked to have played with them. Then I studied the sad faces of the yellow-eyed sheep with curly horns, and different coloured wool. I stroked the bold ones on their noses, and plunged my hands into the thick wool, smelling and feeling the greasy texture each in their turn, thinking that it was too hot that day for such thick coats. Twice I was admonished for wandering off, and Grandfather sat me down in the cordoned off section, which included chairs for his guests. He introduced us to his friends there, pleased that we looked so presentable. But this state of affairs was not to last.

I wandered off again to see the dog show, and tried to attract the attention of the well-behaved animals striding round the ring, following their owners on leads. Although eyeing me speculatively as a possible playmate, all was to no avail because they were too well schooled to be distracted. Having had an ice cream, and a drink, I was drawn back to the animals. I then lifted out of my pocket a little pad of paper and my pencil, to draw a beautiful smiling Jersey cow, which was coloured like a Siamese cat. She had a full udder, and her small calf was standing close to her. So I climbed in to have a closer look at the little animal. The cow, no doubt defending her offspring, thought that my presence was unnecessary in the pen, so she put her head down and firmly lifted me up and then threw me with some force to the other side of this area, where I fell squarely in the cow pats by the fence.

My new round straw hat now sat on one of the cow's horns, with its ribbons waving in the sunshine. The cow, with her big brown eyes, tossed her head in defiance, I thought, looking like a whirling roundabout with fluttering flags. She stamped her feet and tried to throw the hat over her back, behaving like a preening matador, while the owner of the cow hastily went in to retrieve it. Quickly, the farmer picked me up, and fearing that the cow would repeat the action – 'in defence of the calf', he said – he lifted me out of the pen completely. I was taken round to the ladies tent, where his wife cleaned me up. Unfortunately, I was not fit to be seen in public again that day. Too often, it seemed, I got myself into bother.

A couple of weeks later we were all going to the Gisburne Summer Fete, to be held on the lawns of the vicarage. Grandfather asked Nona if she would open the occasion with a little speech. In front of the family, Nona said that she was happy to oblige. A short while later, when she thought that nobody was listening, she was overheard to be muttering under her breath and talking to herself about the task. We all knew that she wanted to be word perfect. In order to practice her speech, she chose to use Mother's room. On this particular occasion, I walked quietly and unnoticed, as was my usual habit, into the room and sat on a chair in the corner. Having nothing to say, I simply kept quiet, and remained undetected. I always loved being with my eccentric Aunt and listening to her singing, with Egyptian overtones, so I was hoping to ask her to sing something, but now was not the time.

Nona had been a dancing, singing and music teacher, in Gezirah, Cairo. She lived with Aunt Gee and Aunt Beatrice (who had died by this time) in an old colonial house with the same name, Gezirah House, where she taught her pupils. She was as

perky as a little bird, wizened like a walnut, with piercing brown eyes, very thin and never still. She was always pointing her toes in little prancing steps, as she jangled the many bracelets on her arms. Her clothes were of light materials, in colour and weight, as scarves floated from her shoulders or waist, according to her whim. Her liveliness rubbed off on me whenever I was with her, and I skipped by her side happily when we went out for walks. I always tried hard to please her, and to learn well whenever she showed me any new piano piece because she was a very demanding teacher.

Now, I return to Nona's speech rehearsal. Secretively, I watched her, half-dressed for the outing, wearing only her new silk slip, and her pointed shoes, while she gesticulated to an invisible audience. She was practising different

Aunt Nona with Jerry, the Springer Spaniel

phrases and expressions in the long, oval mirror in the room. She tried out several jokes, quickly discarding each one until she found the right one for the occasion. With this success, she waved a silk scarf with a gesture of gaiety over her head, while entreating the audience to give generously for the good cause. Her performance was superb, and I wanted to applaud her.

But at the right moment, when she was otherwise occupied, I slipped out again, to avoid being scolded for being present in her room, without invitation. As the time arrived to leave for the fete, I was ready waiting in the hall. When we finally set off, I sat quietly in the car with the others, alongside Aunt Nona now properly dressed in her best muslin frock, an ornate straw hat, silk gloves and carrying her little bead bag.

Aunt Gee's painting of Egypt.

The garden party in the Vicarage garden was well attended, with all the accoutrements and stalls expected of such an occasion. There was a coconut shy, a sale of work stall and home-made cakes were beckoning eager customers, and a game of croquet was also in progress. I was again clean and tidy with my straw hat on, and newly polished shoes shining in the sunshine. Grandfather, Aunt Gee and Jane sat with me next to Mother on the little platform that had been erected for the occasion.

At the appropriate moment, the vicar rose to start the proceedings. He introduced Aunt Nona, who stood up and delivered a magnificent speech, full of entertaining jokes and stories. She had what one might call great stage appeal. The crowd clapped and cheered at her performance, while I counted off on my fingers all the stories that I had heard beforehand, as well as all the ones that I liked. When she had finished, she bowed to her audience several times, in preparation for sitting down, then I said without thinking, 'You missed out the joke about the Arab in a Red Fez.' Of course, only my Aunt Nona and I knew exactly how I could have heard this piece.

Quickly, with great presence of mind, she replied smilingly, 'Hush. Hush. That joke is too long to entertain the crowds here and now, for they might miss their tea, and I see that everything is now prepared.' With that remark, she stepped away and sat down for her tea. The matter was finally closed, when later in the day my Aunt took me aside, and said quietly, 'If you are going to sit in my room secretly, without my knowing, child, you should not drop yourself in it, by telling me about it afterwards.'

THE REALITY CHECK

By 1944 it was clear from all the wireless reports that the war was drawing to a close. While we did not really understand the significance of the various battles being reported, nor the Allied troop advances which were being cheered about, we knew the general population were showing an upsurge in spirits. Nevertheless, we still had to abide by strict food rationing due to continuing food shortages. Father sent us a very large sealed tin of Australian butter, floating in brine, given to him by the army cook, and definitely a catering pack. Sometimes spare eggs were preserved in jars of 'isinglass' (i.e. sodium silicate). I also took a liking for eating dried egg powder, which I ate raw a teaspoonful at a time. It was mainly sent in tins by the Americans, and was issued for making scrambled eggs. I was discouraged from this habit by being told that because it contained so many preservatives, eating it uncooked would make me sick – and it did. Sweets were still unknown to us, generally speaking, so the hoarding of apples and carrots in our school bags, to nibble later was quite a common snack food. I liked the sweetness of peeled turnips too.

A tin of dried eggs.

One evening I was completely confused by an incident, when briefly two soldiers came to our front door at Barton's shop. My mother welcomed them warmly, then turning to me as I entered the other door she said, 'Here's Wendy, she's grown quite tall now since you last saw her."

'Daddy, Daddy, you've come ho….' I started to shout with glee. But then I stopped in my tracks. Was this man my father? Or was the other one my dear Papa? These two men both looked very much like my father. In that moment of hesitation as I scanned their faces, my brain registering the bald heads, the ginger moustaches, round countenances and smiling blue eyes, and the army uniforms of colonels, I re-alised that neither of them were my father. Of course, the obvious explanation was quickly provided – these were my father's two brothers, Uncle John Stuart of the Kings African Rifles, and Uncle Robin Stuart of the Royal Signals. All three broth-ers, now with the same rank, looked remarkably similar in their army uniforms, and the two of them had called in to say farewell before the 'final push'.

I had yet to make acquaintance with my father's family, and as events unfolded, would do so before long. I was so pleased to see them, because I had known that Uncle John was my Godfather, and now I could thank him for the presents he had sent me. Incidentally, one of my Godmothers who often sent me presents, was called Wendy Strachan, after whom I was named. She was an army nurse and a friend of my parents in the Catterick camp where I was christened on 8 January 1936 so I am told, in a deep snow-laden Yorkshire world. She travelled with the troops abroad, was imprisoned eventually in Singapore, and subsequently killed in a Japanese PoW camp – a fact which I discovered later in life. My other Godmother, Daisy Stuart, had a great influence on me in my teens, and whom I first met when we moved to London.

When I was young, we all suffered a variety of infectious diseases which seemed to have no cures, and therefore we expected to catch them at various times from our school friends. Whooping cough, chicken pox, mumps, scarlet fever, and measles were the main contenders. Knowing the seriousness for adults if they contracted some of these ailments, children were sometimes put together deliberately to catch the disease, in order to 'get it over with' while young, as a kind of 'primitive immunisation'. At that time, comprehensive medical knowledge on such diseases was still in its infancy.

Wendy Strachan.

During the Christmas holidays that year, I contracted measles, and became very red all over. My temperature shot up to an alarming level. There was no cure except to stay in bed in a darkened room (to avoid eye damage) and wait for the virus to run its course and wait until my temperature subsided. For several days, I lay in my little bed on the top floor in Clitheroe, with my dolls occupying the broad window sill. From time to time, I could hear the family all busy decorating the Christmas tree downstairs in the sitting room, while several times people came to see if I was still awake. I dozed fitfully, being very hot, and felt that I was not really there. So my imagination took over those hours.

I knew that I was missing out on the fun, and was unhappy that I could not put my fairy on top of the tree – I had made the fairy carefully out of crepe paper, with a frilly skirt and tissue paper wings, stiffened with pipe-cleaners. Lying in bed, I felt quite weak and lifeless, so I dreamed about what was going on instead, not being

My paper fairy.

able to put my talisman where she was needed. After a while, the voices faded, and in the darkness of night, I decided to see for myself the decorated tree, and find out whether they had put my fairy on top. I remember putting my slippers on, as I had been told, but other ideas and thoughts floated in and out of my consciousness while I negotiated the downward three flights of stairs to the sitting room, to gaze eventually at the well-lit tree. I was greatly relieved to discover that she was indeed there – my fairy at the top of the tree. She was the reincarnation of my Papa's fairy from Ireland.

But where was the family? The house seemed empty. I knew that Jane was asleep upstairs in our top room, and Mr Smithson and Muriel should have been around, because they were staying for Christmas. Where was Mother or Kathleen? I opened the back door, and immediately the air outside felt very cold and chilly – it was just as well that I had been wearing my dressing gown in bed. I walked down the ginnel between the shops, but could see none of the family in front of Barton's Drapers. I stood perplexed for a few minutes on the pavement, with even more bizarre thoughts crowding in. I could hear people singing carols, watched some happy people with party hats on, carrying dimmed and hooded torches, walking along the pavement, and decided that I should go there too. I turned to face the singers because surely that was where they all must be.

Someone took hold of my hand. I looked up into a smiling face, a face that I recognised. 'Where have you come from? You look a bit cold. Where are you going?' I felt pleased to have found my friend, and said, 'I only wanted to see the tree with my fairy on top of it. It's in the sitting room.'

Wisely, the Air Raid Warden carried on talking to me, believing me to be sleep-walking, and said, 'Well, I would like to see your fairy, show it to me now.' I obediently retraced my steps and entered the house, stopping in front of the tree, where I promptly fell into a deep sleep on the floor. I was carried upstairs again, put to bed, where I slept soundly for the next 24 hours. Mother and Kathleen had been in the other room in the house wrapping up parcels, never imagining that an eight year old child with measles would get out of bed, and start sleep-walking. They were horrified by what had happened.

Two days later when I had recovered a little, I was carried down again for Christmas Day, but now wrapped in a large blanket, with my temperature coming down and, covered though I was with red spots, I joined in the celebrations for a short while. All the parcels were wrapped in brown paper, the only kind available during the war. They were tied up neatly with war-time string made from rolled paper, and saved in the string box of various lengths – Sellotape had not yet been invented. Mine was a curious shape and heavy, so it was unwrapped for me, to reveal a lantern slide projector, with sets of slides of eight Walt Disney pictures or cartoons. That evening we sat together, entranced with the novelty of it all – a little later it was put away for me to learn how to use, when I had recovered from measles.

I was told of my midnight adventure at a much later date. Such is the power of an active and delirious mind; I can still recall it, my thoughts perhaps, but not all the actions of sleep-walking.

My mother had gone to school in London, in the 1920s with her school-friend, Celia Johnson, who eventually became a successful actress in the West End and Broadway. Therefore, when Celia appeared in a film with John Mills in the cast, she was very keen to see it and took Jane and I to the cinema in Preston. The film was called *In Which We Serve* and was made as a patriotic war film in 1942 to encourage the serving troops. We did not often go to the cinema, therefore every such occasion was considered a great treat. It was even directed by another of Mother's favourites, Noel Coward, for good measure. So we took the train from Clitheroe to Preston Station one Saturday, with Piglet, and the pictures of my fairies in my handbag slung over my shoulder, crammed also with a packet of sandwiches.

All film performances were divided into four parts, the trailers, the 'B' film, the Newsreel of latest events, and lastly the main 'A' film. The 'B' film was often a cartoon, catering for all tastes, and thus I remembered seeing *Bambi*, the Walt Disney film that had been out for a couple of years, so both Jane and I were

A poster from the 1942 film.

very keen to see it. It proved to be a sad film, about a fawn losing its mother, and I was unhappy about it. But I remembered most of all the appalling Newsreel pictures, which totally overshadowed the enjoyment of the other two films. There was an overall commentary by the news reader, his speech racing on, in a high-pitched voice, with cheerful or patriotic music in the background. The newsreader finished each piece on an optimistic note, that we were winning, whatever the odds.

It was the first time that I became aware of the full horrors of what war meant. We were seeing battle weary troops struggling through alien countryside, seeing the desecration of towns, ours or theirs, watching ships being blown up, and worst of all, hearing of unspeakable rumours of Japanese cruelties. The anxiety of course was of knowing that they still had to be defeated, somehow. Why the Japanese were in the war was beyond my comprehension but from this moment onwards I worried that these people were possibly coming to our country, and for the first time I was terribly, terribly afraid.

This anxiety about invasion by the enemy was not helped by the continual radio broadcasts from notorious Nazi sympathisers such as William Joyce. Through the Nazi's English-language radio programme, 'Germany Calling', he made daily broadcasts, in a fake British upper-class voice. He asserted various German victories, while revelling in Allied losses and, all the while, spoken in a jeering and menacing tone. Although we were told that nothing in the broadcasts was based on truth, it was still very unsettling. The broadcasts started in 1939, and continued until 1946, when Joyce was caught, brought back to Britain and hung as a traitor. As a result of these broadcasts, I now feared for my father, and my uncles, and other people that I knew in Father's regiment, who were actively fighting with their units against the enemy. I found it very hard to shake off these feelings of fear.

Eventually came the moment when the rumours about the ending of the war became fact, and 'Peace' arrived, which was declared eventually on 8 May 1945. It seems that this great historical moment totally passed me by, because I have no

recollection of that day. I was still attending Moreland School within its protected environment and
day to day activities. I believe we probably had a
'Peace Party', because we always did for everybody's birthday, the King's birthday and St George's
Day. Of course, one became aware of parties normally, because the food always looked a bit special;
and we would play Pass the parcel, Musical Chairs
and other similar music-orientated games, using the
one good record, played on a portable record player.
It was Johann Strauss' *Radetzky March*, and we all
knew every note of the piece.

But for me the news of the end of the War was
overshadowed by the death at the end of April 1945
of my dear Aunt Caroline (Coco). This was of more
importance and significance to me than almost any-

Aunt Caroline (Coco) off to a party.

thing else. She was my kind, deaf old aunt, who had been a true companion to my
grandfather, her brother, for so many years since the death of Grandma in the 1920s.
I loved her for her kindness, her eccentricities, for wearing strange feathered hats
and dangling jewellery. One example of this eccentricity, was the time when she installed in her room, just for the fun, two very large and shiny-yellow glass Christmas
spheres, which then hung on permanent display swinging from the corners of her
wardrobe, to eke out the Christmas spirit, into the rest of the year. She was full of
fun, for as long as I knew her.

Aunt Mary, Grandfather's married sister now came to stay at Bowerswood. She
and Uncle Will had moved to England when he retired his work as a headmaster in
Malaya. He had died in November 1939, and now Aunt Mary stepped in to try to
fill Coco's place. She travelled from her daughter-in-law's house in London, to become her brother's helper.

She was there to welcome her two sisters, Gee and Nona from Cairo for their

summer visit, which lessened the sad feelings a little
for my grandfather, who said to me wistfully, 'Your
Aunt Coco was my true rock through these past
times, child. How shall I now continue?' I do not
think he believed that I understood him, or would
remember his words, being far too young in his
eyes. But even now, I remember this quite clearly.

Any really momentous events such as the end of
the War were often masked by other 'more important' things when we were very young. I tended to
retain in my mind only those matters which were
important to me or which impinged on my immediate daily activities such as my new Clarks sandals,
bought for the coming holidays, with their pungent

Aunt Mary Hargreaves, 1950.

InsideBowerswood, painted by Aunt Mary.

new leather smell when I ran about in wet grass. They were much more important to me than war news, as were the plans to move to London at the end of the school year.

Grandfather had been down to London to do stocktaking at his London factory, and suggested that we hasten to find a house or flat while they were plentiful. We needed to pack up our school belongings at Easter, at the school in Clitheroe, and also at our lodgings with Kathleen. Mother's plan was for us to move to London in the September of 1945, and for Jane and I to attend St Paul's Girls' School in Hammersmith.

First, our school belongings were brought to Bowerswood. Here, they were repacked carefully, with the aunts assisting. For the first time the enormity of leaving our home and grandfather swept over me. I cried for some while, sulked a little, then went roaming around the house and garden, and visited the farm to say goodbye to Martha. Eventually, having reinforced my memories of my beloved home, I was assured by the promises from everyone that I could return for my holidays... forever. I needed a constant reassurance of continuity.

I did not know what lay ahead of me, and too fast the reality was taking over at last. But I packed my little pictures of the fairies, now very travel worn and grubby after five years... and Piglet also, into my shoulder bag, as my insurance against the future.

THE ODDITY OF PEACE

The world had just secured peace in Europe, but was still waiting for the Japanese to be defeated, to deliver the same outcome to the nations of the Far East. It was now, in May 1945, and Mother determined that we should move to London permanently, to find a house, and enrol us into St Paul's Girls' School in Hammersmith, the same school which she had attended. This had been a longer term plan because Grandfather had already been paying into a bursary fund for our education there. But for this fact, I would never have been in London at all.

Still on active service for another two years, Father was now being sent to India with his regiment on the SS *Empress of Australia*, a cruise ship that had been commandeered for troop movement. The country was increasingly being troubled with riots, caused by the partitioning of India, and the troops were being used to help keep the peace. He was extremely worried about his own family being settled in a new town so far away. Before leaving for India, Father conveyed his anxieties to Jim Grant, our musical friend in Clitheroe. Father knew that Jim was now demobbed, and was also travelling to London to assist the re-housing of his mother.

SS Empress of Australia..

Once, I overheard the conversation, 'Can you assist Valerie to find a suitable temporary flat, while hunting for a permanent house? I'll be back on leave in six months.' He added, 'She is very determined, and there's no stopping her. So please keep an eye on things for her, if anything happens to me. We shall be thrown into the thick of things there and in these troubled times, one never knows.'

After some discussions between them, a plan was agreed between Father and Jim, and shortly afterwards Jim set off for London, ahead of us. All too soon the time came again for us to say goodbye to my kindly Father, after having had a brief afternoon together in Lancashire, with many tears, and loving farewells. We travelled south to stay temporarily in an old hotel, situated in Holland Park, in the west of London. My Aunt Daisy Stuart had helped find the hotel, which was close to her house in Addison Avenue.

My mother was a very determined lady with strong views on many things, having had a passionate temperament, but she also had artistic and creative talents. Having been influenced in childhood by the outspoken and energetic aunts in the Simpson family, it is not so surprising, that this experience manifested itself in different ways in her. She was very kind, extremely sociable, and an excellent organiser. Some might say she was even 'bossy', or maybe a 'control freak' in modern parlance but she got things done, whatever the circumstances.

THE ODDITY OF PEACE

It must have been difficult for her, being married in 1933 to a career soldier, who was more frequently away from home than being present, and having to cope with the changes and challenges during the war. Especially before the war, her life had been one of relative affluence, being able to please herself financially and socially, through her wealthy family. Her skills as a hostess were to be admired, as she was strongly convinced that the elegance of entertaining should not be lost. Therefore, almost every month an excuse was found to entertain, be it a birthday or simply a party, and where possible celebrated in style. She was attractive and bubbly natured, with a

Val Stuart, the author's mother.

ready smile, but a hidden craftiness which did not really show, unless she was thwarted by anyone.

One of her better-known characteristics was her determination to have her own way – which she usually did. This trait was spoken of in whispers, and at timely situations, the whole family was forewarned to avoid unnecessary conflict. She had been a debutante in her early twenties, and at the time had developed quite an imperious manner, which she used to good effect.

After a little searching around, we settled for a while at No 40 Holland Park, an impressive Georgian house, with a portico and broad steps to the entrance. It was large enough to be divided into several apartments, and ours was a fairly roomy semi-underground flat, which included the garden behind the house. There were steps rising up from the French windows in the sitting room to the small enclosed garden, which was paved, with a circular pond in the middle and surrounded by beautiful trees. The apartment was also very close to our new school, Noreland Place, a prep school for St. Pauls, which was within easy walking distance.

Steps up to the garden in Holland Park.

Fortunately, our flat was also close to Aunt Daisy's house in Addison Avenue. This lent a kind of mental stability for me, and offered a new opportunity to discover another great aunt from my father's family. I remained somewhat confused by this huge change to my life, and was missing my other aunts from Bowerswood, in Lancashire. Aunt Daisy was my second godmother, and I cast her in my mind as the 'Good Fairy Godmother', a role that she proved to fill admirably at a later date. Our house also had a small single flat on the top floor, which Jim rented, following Father's request to keep an eye on us all. This arrangement worked very well, and Jim offered his help whenever required which was a boon for us, while trying to make the bomb-weary flat habitable.

This new world was brighter and very noisy. I had never seen street lights, or ones that I could remember, or colourful shops displaying their wares in lit up windows. I had never realised that there were street lights in every road in the towns, which, having always lived in rural areas was definitely an alien concept. Unfortunately, I was now unable to see the familiar stars or the changing moon, but conversely, it was easier to walk about

Jane and I in the garden at Holland Park.

in the evening without colliding with objects in the dark. Up to now, for those of us who had been brought up in the countryside, we had undoubtedly been living in a world probably more reminiscent of the early 1800s than the twentieth century. With the absence of almost any cars on the roads, household deliveries came via horse and cart. We noticed that milk now arrived in bottles via either the Express Dairy, which sported a horse-drawn blue van, or the United Dairies, whose livery was red. Both vehicles were pulled by smart little horses, always with their nosebags, and provided a daily delivery of all the essential dairy products. Nevertheless, it was still necessary to register with the appropriate shop, and give them our dairy coupons. Unfortunately, rationing became even more austere in the post war period.

Jim's first priority was to help his mother, who had suffered terribly in London during the Blitz. She had his grandmother staying with her, Alice Cheshire, now deaf and confused, who had stoutly helped where she could throughout the wartime. He was keen to help his mother make a move into her new little house. Jim's original East London home had been flattened by the bombing, but the old lady proudly announced that she had just been allocated a home, in the last few days, in a 'prefab' in Laindon, Basildon, Essex. The 'prefabs' were prefabricated houses, some of which were manufactured from aluminium, but many had roofs made from asbestos, and were designed for one or two people. These houses were erected on site in only four days. This was a very new concept for everyone, and we were very keen to see what they looked like.

We all travelled east on the Underground via the network of lines to Laindon. Her new home was clearly some distance (23 miles) away from her old haunts in East London. In Laindon, we discovered many acres of small shed-like structures which were being erected hastily in rows, on a field without the benefit of any roads.

Instead, as a temporary measure, large and small duckboards were being laid between the houses to provide residents with a reasonably dry and clean access to their homes. Every fourth row of houses were set-out with a wider access to allow wheeled vehicles to pass. As a temporary arrangement, water mains were laid only as far as standpipes, which were installed at the ends of each row of houses. At this stage, there were still no electricity or gas services installed, therefore paraffin lamps, heaters and stoves soon became standard equipment for every house. Paraffin was delivered to the estates by lorries which could just negotiate the narrow tracks created. All-in-all, the new estates were somewhat basic in the early days, especially the requirement to have to fill water containers at the standpipes, and to carry them back to the house. Slowly this situation was improved and water and gas connections were rectified eventually while the new occupants turned their houses into proudly kept homes with well-tended, fenced gardens.

Prefabricated homes, 1940s

Initially, I was truly shocked by the primitive nature of these houses, until I realised that they were palaces by comparison to the bombed out houses and rubble, which Londoners had had to abandon. During my trip to Laindon, I added to my vocabulary new words such as 'Privy', 'Carsy' and 'Jon', all referring to the little square sheds, used as outdoor toilets, located near to the new houses.

Jim needed to find a job now that he was no longer in the Army, so he met up with a young friend who had spent the last five years in the same regiment with him. His name was Sam Dewhurst, from London, who was also demobbed around the same time. Promptly, Sam had returned to his old job in Fleet Street which he had had since he was fourteen (i.e. in 1934). During the war he had gained the rank of sergeant, and had developed a level of self-confidence and maturity, reflected in the way he spoke, though he had kept his Scots dialect. laced with original Scottish pronunciations. He had worked at the Keystone Press Agency as an errand boy, and fortunately for him had found his pre-war job still open. Sam urged Jim to apply for a porter's job, which was currently vacant – he didn't think that the agency would have to wait long to find a suitable candidate.

With his Scots accent, Sam said, 'A mon o' yer age, daesna usually git a look in wi' all the young'ns gannin hame, but I tauld the Boss ye war OK, that ye haed a verra commanding an trustworthy wark, and he shouldna let ye slip through his wee fingers.' [A man of your age doesn't usually get a look in with all the youngsters going home, but I told the boss you were OK, that you had had very commanding and trustworthy work, and that he shouldn't let you slip through his little fingers.]

So with Sam's help, Jim acquired a fairly well paid job with the same firm, as general porter. Reaching work was only a convenient train ride down the Underground's Central Line from Holland Park to Bank station. He liked his job, was always busy, and thrived among his new companions. I was pleased for him. I think that he missed the companionship and work ethic of being in the army and the band.

We persuaded Mother to allow us to go exploring at the weekends, and provided I gave her a sensible plan, all was well. Jim offered to take us one day, to see the big printing houses of one of the national newspapers in Fleet Street and there were several nearby. The *Daily*

St. Pauls Cathedral from Ludgate Hill

Herald, Daily Express, The Mirror, The Times and *The Picture Post* were the names I remembered most. All these famous press strongholds were intermingled with boarded-up bombed-out buildings, a grim reminder of the very recent past, during which time the printing presses had kept on rolling.

It nearly always seemed to be foggy with hundreds of chimneys belonging to

Newspaper printing houses, 1940s.

London's grimy buildings spewing out continuously their wraiths of unending smoke. Whenever any shafts of sunlight shone during the daytime, past the tall spires, and especially on to St Paul's Cathedral at the end of our road, it took on a truly ethereal quality. At once, one could imagine hosts of angels flying high above the gloom and catching touches of sunlight on the tips of their wings. Or was it the edges of a fleeting cloud momentarily lit up by sunshine beyond these clouds, before evaporating into oblivion again? The only other clear colours were brought by the flower sellers, who sat on the steps of St. Pauls, beside their barrows, full of bright and fragrant wares.

When entering one of the printing halls, the sheer noise of the machinery was so intense and loud, I told Jim that I didn't want to go into any other noisy production area – and I kept away from the printing houses for some time after that. Because of the constantly rotating and moving machinery, I was completely awestruck, imagining that there was a harnessed and powerful beast chained down in the building, struggling to be free. With endless strings of moving newsprint resembling a fiery dragon writhing in anger, the moving belts behaved like its many arms and tentacles. There was no stopping the continuous movement of this machinery, nor was there any respite for employees from the noise, as they went about their business in this voiceless world. Eventually I was able to exit the mind-numbing din, my head reverberating with the noise and was somewhat deaf for an hour or so after my visit.

In contrast, the Keystone Press agency where Jim and Sam now worked was different. Instead, they supplied the major newspapers with the latest news pictures received from Reuters, and other sources. These were taken quickly to the newspaper editors, down the road, delivered by errand boys, such as Sam (at the agency, they were referred to as Gofers). Quite a thankless task, I thought, when everybody was shouting 'Go fer this' or 'Go fer that' – hence the name. Sam loved this job, because it gave him the opportunity, as a general runner, to be legitimately inquisitive. As pictures came in of famous film stars, he carefully amassed a pile of my favourites to take home with me, such as Veronica Lake, Gloria Swanson, Paulette Goddard and Jean Kent, all very glamorous, including also Joan Greenwood and Glynis Johns with their gravelly voices. There were so many more. These I stuck into a scrap book, adding to my collection on a weekly basis.

I liked Sam, because he was knowledgeable, cheery, and found time to show us many aspects of work and life in the city. His job was not his ultimate goal, but he needed to earn a living, and evidently put a lot of effort into doing it well, delivering newly-printed photographs with alacrity to the various intended recipients. Thus he

St. Pauls Cathedral surrounded by bombsites, 1940s.

93

gained access to many places, and met a wide variety of people. Now 26 years of age he was a thin, wiry, likable young man, with a quick, decisive attitude to life. He had piercingly bright blue eyes, a wide smile in a freckled face framed by red hair. He sharpened his wits on his many friends with whom he spent his lunchtimes in The Old Bell Pub, or coffee houses in Fleet Street.

There was a café not far from the Keystone building, where we had our lunch with Jim, or Sam. It could be seen across the bombsites from one road to the other, and when walking there, I often looked over the walls and behind the protective boarding down into the rubble of the bombed-out buildings. Often these areas were covered with flowering rose bay willowherb, a tall pink-mauve sweet smelling plant, which readily covered many neglected and undisturbed areas. On one particular site near the café, I saw a great number of cats, with varieties of breeds and colours, and often with their kittens. Quite often they would come purring to me for petting and craving for human company, having lost their owners, but interestingly their off-spring were very wild, and wary of people. I asked Lil, the café owner, where they had all come from.

'Those houses were all bombed, but the surviving cats have lived by their wits for five years now – we do our best to help them with scraps when we can. But many people come here to feed them too. At least they eat the rats and mice… there's a lot of them round here.'

I saw that they were all very thin and scavenging for survival. Cats are natural hunters in the wild with sharp claws, and night vision eyesight, but bombsites will only support the feeding of a limited number of animals. After five years of surviving in their own neighbourhood, the cats had multiplied into quite a large colony, and I could see the necessity of helping them, as Lil told me.

One day while Mother was busy house-hunting, Jane and I went exploring over one of the walls and into this wild area with bags full of scraps from the café, trying to encourage the shy and thin cats to feed. Our endeavours had very surprising and unexpected results.

LONDON AWAKES

Armed with some food provided by Lil from the nearby café, including a jam jar of watered-down milk plus an old plate, we went looking for hungry cats and kittens amongst the ruins of bombed-out buildings in the city centre. Lil had told us that the smaller kittens suffered the most from hunger, due to their size, and inability to fight for their fair share. Picking our way through the rubble was quite precarious. Occasionally, we would follow a cat, which we thought might have some mewling kittens. We were soon in a new fantasy world. With my fertile mind now adding imaginary goblins, inspired by many strange and unusual noises, I followed the sound of what I thought to be of crying kittens, however was amazed by what I eventually found. I had just walked carefully through an archway, and had entered a small partially enclosed room which was well sheltered within the ruined building. A little dark perhaps, but there was enough light to see a cardboard box, about two feet square, and full of blanket material, clothes, and other belongings. I assumed that a little cat had found a safe place for her kittens, and so I approached this den very warily, taking care not to frighten its occupants.

A feral cat in one of the bombsites.

There were no longer any noises coming from the box, so I put down my goodies, and leaned in to have a peep. Moving the blankets aside carefully, I was astonished to find a very young baby, carefully wrapped up and apparently sleeping peacefully, because the child looked well fed and content. In the box I could see a bottle of milk, a pile of clothes and other necessities for the baby, tucked around him, keeping him very snug, but there were no signs of the mother. I hastily went outside to tell Jane of my discovery. We decided that we should carry the box back to the Keystone building, but it was too heavy for our combined efforts. Unsure about what to do, we went for help.

Sam was standing at the Keystone building entrance, so we quickly took him across the bombsite to show him the box. He was also astounded by our find but advised that the Keystone printers building was not the best place for a baby. While thinking of a better location, he picked up the baby carefully, threaded his way through the bombsite, and suggested that we take it to the older lady, Lil, whom he obviously thought would know better how to deal with this situation. By the time we reached the café the wee mite was wide awake again, and I was relieved that an older adult was able to take charge of this precious box.

Sam was now worried about the absent mother, and suggested that he keep a look out for her. In the meantime, Lil warmed some weak milk, wrapped the baby tightly in the blanket, and fed him until he was satisfied. She then found a nappy in her store cupboard, and placed him in an old pram of hers with plenty of bedding. We realised then that Lil had a family of her own, and was not in the least troubled by this newcomer.

By now it was time for us to return to Holland Park with Jim, leaving the problems with Sam and Lil, who had said that they would soon find

Jane and I in London.

the mother. They had suggested that she was probably working. This proved to be correct, because Sam found her back at the bomb site, crying while frantically searching for her child. She was a young woman called Jeannie. With great relief, she went with Sam to the café to be reunited with her baby. Lil suggested that she could stay in one of her upstairs rooms with her child, as a temporary measure, and as recompense for these lodgings, it was agreed that Jeannie would help in the café, whenever Lil was short-handed.

Eventually, Jeannie did this full-time, when her other temporary job came to an end. We heard of these developments from Jim, through Sam who was always kept up to date about Jeannie's circumstances. He said her story was very sad, but not unusual. Her husband, a soldier, had been reported missing, and her place of work had been destroyed by bombing. This meant that she had ended up having no husband, no home, no job, and no money. Knowing that somebody was looking after her, we did not return to Lil's café for a little while, especially because the following week was filled with new developments for us.

We went with Mother to Norland Place School, our new junior school, which was an introduction to yet another chapter in our lives. It was so different and more regimented than our previous schooling experience that I felt very lost. It was an old building, probably Edwardian, with narrow corridors, numerous stairs, small rooms, heated with ancient iron stoves. The stoves were surrounded by tall guard rails onto which, on rainy days, the children draped their coats, creating plumes of steam. On these occasions, there was always the hope of the miracle that they would be dry by home time. The stove smoked continually, and mingled with the steam, created a misty layer of fog in the centre of the room. On better, dry days, each child used its own named peg in the corridor.

All the woodwork was painted with deep green paint, and in the classrooms there were fixed desks with seats attached. Short legged children had problems. The desks had lifting lids, creating a box into which we stored our books, our pencils and crayons. Ink wells were slotted into a hole in the right hand corner, but dip pens were issued at the discretion of the teacher who judged the abilities and readiness of pupils to use them. Those who did not qualify for such use continued to use pencils. Short armed children also had problems. Since I was short-armed and short-legged, I did not fare well. Neither did I agree with the silence rules, which seemed so alien to me. However, I had a kindly and older teacher, Miss Walmsley, who helped me to channel my excitable energy and fertile mind into drawing and writing storybooks for her, whilst doing my best to keep quiet.

One day, a teacher came into the classroom to show us a new pen, which she had acquired from an American soldier. Fountain pens were already available, but expensive. These were the type, which were filled by dipping into a bottle of ink, while operating the 'suction' lever. Her new pen was already filled with ink, which she said was called a biro. It had a marbled bakelite casing and blue-black ink, although we learned that different coloured inks were available too in other models. The biros were very expensive, no doubt due to scarcity, and it took some years before modern production made them a cheap pocket item. Grandfather had given me a fountain pen for my tenth birthday, but I hankered to own a biro. Eventually my Aunt Mary bought me one for my next birthday, bought at a ridiculously high price in those days.

This new, formal classroom education, with information appearing on the front blackboard, was frustrating, because it was too far away and often unintelligible. In addition, I wanted to do as well as I had always done, but being a left-handed child I was soon handicapped by the current belief that I was not using my right hand through laziness, the result being that I had my left hand tied behind my back during many lessons to force the issue. Not all the teachers subscribed to this belief, but it hampered my desire to learn. Nonetheless, I gained an unexpected ability to be ambidextrous.

At lunchtimes we all walked in 'crocodile' formation for ten minutes to a hall where there were cooking facilities for providing hot meals. Along this route were tall old houses, which at one time had railings around their gardens. During the war these had been removed, and collected as scrap metal for armament manufacture. Many times, I wondered if anybody would eventually replace them.

I enjoyed this walk in the autumn. I often had great fun scuffling my feet in the thick layers of damp leaves, which had fallen from the tall plane trees, and enjoyed watching their movement as they were whipped up and whirled about by the wind along the street. I recalled the musty smell of these wet leaves which transported me back to the Lancashire countryside perfumes, untainted by London smoke. This made my homesickness more acute than ever. These trees were everywhere, with coloured patterns of greys and browns on the trunks, and I soon discovered that they shed their bark annually, thus surviving the smoky and smoggy atmosphere.

As part of school activities, we were taken to an unheated indoor swimming pool located beneath a block of flats. Here, the teachers encouraged us to learn how to swim, however this was definitely not a successful activity, the water being far too cold for me and my new friends. On the other hand, various fortnightly trips out to a sports-field were very popular, giving us the chance to play rounders, and other team games. In addition, we also became involved in local activities, including a Victory Day Pageant in Notting Hill Gate, which brought us into contact with the Notting Hill Theatre group. The pageant was colourful and fun, offering many pretty clothes to dress up in. Through this activity I began to make good friends with a few of my classmates.

As well as being eighteen months older than me, my sister Jane was growing up very fast, becoming very self-assured and above all, she was very pretty. She had acquired some of Mother's mannerisms, and fervently wished to demonstrate her readiness for adulthood, by joining the 'elite society' of being a debutante, as early as possible. But the costs were out of the question. (The practise of being presented at court for wealthy young ladies seeking husbands, originally started in the days of George III and Queen Charlotte in approximately 1762, blossomed into having grand balls for these debutantes and continued until 1958. Queen Elizabeth replaced the event with a much more inclusive Royal Garden Party for a wide variety of people.)

Jane was definitely a leader in the making, who often persuaded me to do her bidding, despite the many times that this got us into 'hot water'. Unfortunately for me, I tended to take the blame for us both whenever my crafty sister could manipulate the situatio. By now, I had learned to keep my mouth shut if trouble was brewing, and thereby avoid any potential punishment which otherwise may have been meted out. On the contrary, and to her disadvantage, Jane would 'dig a bigger hole' for herself by continuing to argue her case, whereas the wiser thing would have been to accept defeat.

Mother was asked if she would allow Jane to take part in a Christmas play on

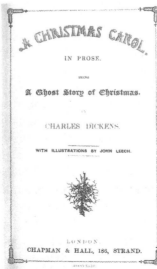

stage, becoming one of Bob Cratchet's children in *A Christmas Carol*. I believe this was being directed by Sybil Thorndyke, whose daughter was also involved in it. It was a non-speaking part, but Jane loved it. For me, I was only a third understudy. At my age, it was sufficient just to be there, but my sister revelled in her part. I was delighted to be involved in the back-stage activities, just as I had been with the band in Lancashire. Therefore, I involved myself in 'helping', whether or not I was actually contributing.

During this time we were taken to see several musicals and plays, especially because now the theatres were just beginning to open their doors again. In any event, this was helped because Mother loved going to the theatre. She took us to see *Peter Pan* as a

Bob Cratchet's family in a Christmas Carol.

straight play, which included the flying sequences, and the pantomimes *Mother Goose*, and *Jack and the Beanstalk* almost immediately afterwards. These caused me many problems, for my logical mind could not work out how the beanstalk could grow so quickly, then someone climb it; and the flying activities in Peter Pan with his flying-fairy companion, Tinkerbell, were so magical to my believing mind, I was totally hooked. Years later, when working on the local theatre backdrop designs for *Midsummer Night's Dream*, *Toad of Toad Hall* and *The Snow Queen* in Lancashire, I recalled my memories of those early, ethereal and magical qualities, experienced at the theatres from my childhood.

Tinkerbell must have been one of my Daddy's fairies. London now had a thriving fairyland for me to believe in. I never wavered for a moment in my beliefs in fairies even when into my teens, or my absent father, who continued to send me little watercolours from India, just as he had done from Europe during the war.

We also went to see *Oklahoma* at the Theatre Royal in Drury Lane, the first musical that I had ever seen. I asked if I could have some of the sheet music so that I could learn to sing the songs. At sixpence a sheet, this was a reasonable request, so I got my music, which I kept until I had an instrument to play it on.

In August 1945, the Japanese capitulated, after the US Air Force dropped atomic bombs on Hiroshima and Nagasaki, with devastating effect. By now, World War II was truly over, having already experienced the German surrender earlier in May. The bombing was widely reported, although the significance of this action was never fully understood by us children. From our perspective, since everyone was relieved that the agony of war was over, none of these events properly registered with us.

The final end of war became a time to celebrate. On 2 September, local parties were held throughout the country. London streets were filled with dancing, and the cheering throngs of a war weary population, mingling with the returning troops, to enjoy several days of jubilation.

The main celebratory event was organised for the following year, as it required substantial planning. Finally, on 8 June 1946, a great victory parade took place through the heart of London, attended by people from all over the world. The route was published in advance, as was a possible rainy forecast for the following day. We hoped to stand in the middle of the Mall, not too far from the temporary public conveniences installed in the park nearby. A large group of us planned to attend and it transpired that everyone in our group wished to travel there the day before, and camp out to secure a place for the following morning.

So armed with a small tent, groundsheets, inflatable pillows, umbrellas, packed food, drink and warm clothes, we headed for the Mall, with much of our equipment carried by the long suffering Jim. We headed for our chosen spot to occupy it in good time. Soon we were joined by several like-minded friends. It rained during the night, but we had come prepared and fared better than other 'fair-weather' people. By 5am we had cleared up our camping equipment and soon got near to the edge of the road, waiting for the action.

We watched the preliminaries of the big parade, the generous use of sand on the route to help prevent horses' hooves from slipping, the dust carts picking up the pre-parade litter scattered by the swelling crowds, then finally the lining of the edges of the route with policemen and soldiers. Intermittently, it remained drizzly, but we didn't care. Hawkers of food, drinks and flags were doing a roaring trade, while a band played on the grass behind us to entertain the crowds, as everybody sang the songs they knew and loved. Finally, the great procession started. First to come was a band, with a regiment of the household cavalry on shiny black steeds, then beautiful well-groomed white horses (known as greys) pulling open carriages and landaus, which transported the Royal family, King George VI, Queen Elizabeth and the two princesses, Elizabeth and Margaret Rose, now in their teens, for everyone to see and cheer. Another carriage followed with the Dowager Queen Mary (George VI's mother), Winston Churchill and other prominent persons in their carriages, while important dignitaries followed in large black Rolls Royce cars, all waving to the crowds.

Churchill in the landeau.

Many bands took part in the parade, including massed bands of the Scottish Pipers, then groups of motor cycles, tanks, mechanised vehicles with a large bomb case, leading gun carriages, followed by the latest farm machinery. Regiments from all the services followed. The Civil Defence Corps, the Land Army and the nurses were all especially cheered so loudly, that it drowned out the accompanying band. It took several hours for all the regiments with their own costumes, bands and banners to pass us by. It was exciting and colourful to watch, but since I was so small I became squashed out of sight and unable to see the parade properly. Jim lifted me up onto his shoulders, where I had an excellent and very exciting vantage point. I leaned forwards in my excitement to see the horses, and grabbed what was in front of me to stabilise my position.

The Victory Parade

This was a bad move.

There was a tall policeman just in front of me, and his helmet was just the right height to grab hold of – which I did, with the result that it came off in my hand. I'm not sure who was the most surprised, the policeman or me. But such was the good humour created by the day that when Jim put me down again, the kindly man let me stand beside him in front of the crowds, holding my hand in case I strayed towards the horses. After a while a roar came from the other direction, and all the carriages came sweeping by again, as my new policeman friend pointed out the King and Queen and the princesses. Here I was watching a fairyland for real, with decorated coaches gleaming, pulled by six magnificent horses apiece, and carrying my 'fairyland' characters to their Victory Celebrations. I was so close that I could nearly touch them.

As the parade passed by, on its return through Admiralty Arch, the crowds followed up the Mall, and finally we found ourselves swept along with the people to

join those in front of Buckingham Palace among the cheering crowds.

We were close enough to watch the Royal family come out onto the balcony, with Winston Churchill and other leaders of various armed forces, waving at the people below. They retreated through the tall balcony windows, only to be recalled again by the roar of the cheering throng. Firework displays were set off in the park, while Londoners and returned soldiers danced ecstatically to competing bands now positioned at the end of the parade, thus the partying continued throughout the night. There were thousands of people, making it impossible to move elsewhere so we had a second night on the Mall amid a mass of noisy revellers.

In 1946, there were no television cameras around, as is normal today, to record and broadcast live the events which we had just experienced, though of course wireless provided the live commentary on the day. In any case, only the very privileged had television sets, although their availability increased drammatically within five years. The victory celebrations had nevertheless been recorded by the Pathé Newsreel cameramen, whose recordings were broadcast later in cinemas and theatres throughout Britain. We knew that we were very privileged to be there amongst those thousands in the crowds.

What a Victory Day to be remembered, and indeed I have done so to this day.

LIFE IN ISLEWORTH

As the years rolled by, the freedom which teenagers had enjoyed during the war years, to travel around the capital, started to be curtailed, through fear for their safety. Of course, this was particularly restrictive for any youngsters with an adventurous spirit.

This was especially true for myself. On so many occasions, just after the war, I was able to roam around London on the Underground, often starting at Holland Park station with my sixpenny ticket, to travel the whole network, which was much smaller than it is today. I would return at the end of the day, very pleased with my afternoon's exploration. The Central Line, from Shepherds Bush to Bank only, traditionally marked in red on the Underground maps, had connections to other lines. These other lines threaded across my map like coloured spaghetti, and provided me with an inviting number of travel possibilities, through various junctions and connections to mainline trains to the coast. The distance of all these destinations was only limited by my pocket money, and certainly not from any fears or dangers from travelling.

I was at home studying a map of the south east coast. Recently, we had been in one of the main railway stations, and we had seen the railway posters, which festooned the walls everywhere, and as usual had me captivated by all the potential discoveries, which they represented. The azure blue areas of the coastlines around

My painting of Shoreham by the Sea in 1946..

London were my new inspiration, which beckoned me. I was seeking a brand new destination. One day, I planned a trip with my sister Jane via Victoria Station to the coastal town of Shoreham. Jane was quite happy to fall in with this plan, and calculated our costs which I submitted to my mother for approval. This was a great opportunity because Mother was fully occupied with house-hunting, so with her ready permission, and augmented with packets of sandwiches and adult instructions carefully written out, Jane and I set off for our seaside jaunt.

We duly arrived at this busy little seaside town, where we enjoyed the delights of colourful seashore shops, crowded fairground booths, and large cones of striped ice creams. We ate these while sheltering from the offshore winds, by leaning behind wooden sea breaks, which divided up the stony shore. I sat there for a long while in the sunshine, and painted the scenes around me on little economy cards with rounded corners, while my sister indulged in beachcombing and paddling. The seaside was a world hitherto unexplored by us during the war, so it was a new excitement for us. From an early age, I had acquired the habit of carrying around with me a small paintbox, a brush and a jar of paint water, as well as a pack of wartime economy postcards in my haversack. After a while, I had completed four small pictures at which point Jane, who wore a watch, said firmly that we must return to the station quickly to catch the homeward train. Hastily I pushed all my belongings into the bag, and ran swiftly after her, just in time to board our train as it started moving.

The train had no corridors, but each carriage accommodated ten passengers, five on each side. The windows were opened by holding a leather strap to let the heavy-framed glass down. In a nearly full carriage, we found two seats and sat down with our backs to the engine, where we watched the countryside receding into the distance amongst the train smoke, like an ebb tide easing away along the shore leaving a kaleidoscope of hazy colour. I proceeded to clean up my paints with tissues, dry the two brushes and tidy up my bag, before arriving home. I wished to jettison the contents of the screw top jar of paint water, now extremely dirty, so I stood up and opened the window, tipping it out onto the track. At least that was my intention – I really should not have done this, because immediately a minor disaster ensued.

With the speed of the train, and movement of the wind, the dirty paint water returned with full force to cover the poor woman sitting peacefully opposite me, changing her cream coloured summer outfit to the mottled browns echoing my shoreline.

After the immediate shock and distress to the woman, then with many apologies from us, we offered to pay for the cleaning of her clothes. I wrote down our address on the back of one of my painted postcards. On a positive note, she said she liked the picture on the reverse, so in haste, I gave her another. When we returned home, I had to admit to Mother my foolishness, and why I nervously awaited a letter and the bill from the poor paint-covered lady. As expected, I was lectured about my carelessness, and also given a fitting punishment at home by Mother.

Some weeks later, we heard a knock at the door, and opened it to admit the same lady to our house.

She said, 'I am so glad to have found you. You had moved from your previous address, and I feared that you were lost to me. It was good of you to give me the two little paintings, which were much admired by my husband and his friends. You paint well.'

Her husband joined in, 'We wondered if you would be willing to paint a little picture of our much loved dog, Sandy who has just died, instead of paying for the dry-cleaning? Here's a recent photo of Sandy.' His wife added, 'A painting of him will remind us of our unusual encounter on the train.' I was much relieved that she was so understanding, and delighted to paint a picture of her dog. Thus I made some new friends, and enjoyed a friendship that lasted a lifetime.

Mother announced in early 1946 that she had found a suitable house for us all, which was a little outside London, a 'mere bus ride away', (approximately twelve miles to the west) she said, which boasted a fairly large garden. We eagerly anticipated seeing the house, and Jim offered to accompany us to Isleworth, catching a train from Waterloo Station on the southern line. The walk to the house was not far from the station. We arrived in a leafy avenue and I remember being told it was a corner house by the bend in the road. I kept on hopping from foot to foot, asking, 'Is it this one? Which house? This one?' as the corner clue gave me several choices.

We finally arrived at a house grandly named No. 1 Canterbury Villas in Woodlands Grove which was carved on the stone gatepost, with No 2 carved on the next door post. It was essentially a semi-detached three-storey late nineteenth century house of yellow London brick, with broad stone steps rising up to an impressive door, sheltered by a stone archway. At the side of the house, a coach-house was attached, now used as a garage, and tack room on the other side. An ancient vine curled over both doors, and circled around two small windows above, letting in light to a coachman's quarters, and a hayloft. Crowning the main door of the house was an intriguing balcony. The house was to be my home for the next seven years, with forays into other places at times, as I grew older. The southern railway passed by the end of our garden, one train every half hour, and surprisingly quickly we never noticed or heard the electric trains as they flashed by.

Canterbury Villas.

The entrance door with beautiful stained-glass windows led into a grand hallway, with doors into two large reception rooms of Victorian proportions, with enormous old fireplaces. Next, one's eye was led up a long broad staircase, to a half-landing in front of an impressive curved stained glass window, then continued up to four bedrooms and a bathroom. By-passing the stairs at ground floor level was the passage-

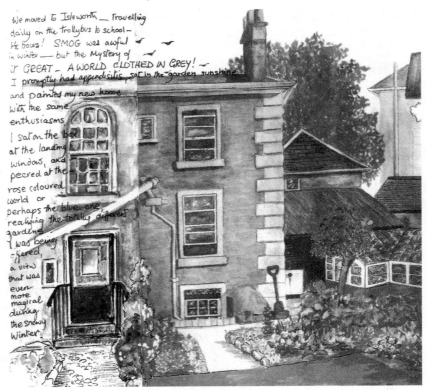

From my notebook a painting of the back of the house.

way to the back garden door, also glazed with colourful glass, which opened onto a flight of wrought iron railed steps, leading down into the garden. Beside this door was the most unusual cloakroom I had seen, with a wide washbasin and china toilet bowl, both covered in beautiful blue flowers, and the toilet covered by a highly polished mahogany seat. I remembered the outside toilets, previously seen in Lancashire and was glad I was here.

As the sun traversed the skies, it filtered through the coloured glass in the garden door, and darted around the hall, piercing the gloomiest corners, while dancing with colourful movements according to the scurrying clouds. These were joined by the same colourful display from the landing window up aloft. They reminded me so strongly of my Irish fairies, that I was totally and instantly at home in this ancient house, to which I was now sure, they had accompanied me. I suspect that the power of my imagination and my unshakable beliefs were helping me into the next stage of my life.

Inside the house, next to the garden door, there was a stairs leading to the basement, which was partly above ground. Here, as expected in a Victorian house, there was a spacious stone-flagged kitchen with a large working iron range, with a wooden maiden for airing clothes above it, which could be raised to the ceiling on pulleys. Two ceramic Belfast sinks were in front of the partly-sunken window through which one could view the garden at eye level. Outside the kitchen door were three pantries with stone shelves for storage of food (or provender, as we called it in those days), one of which boasted a wire-covered window, to keep dairy produce and meat cold.

Fridges and electric washing machines were not yet common in England, but were known of, and we viewed and drooled over them in magazine advertisements. Finally, another door opened into a very large living-room with two cupboards and a coal hole, which was accessed in the front garden by a hatch, for use by the coalman. The front garden could be viewed again at eye level through a similar half-sunken window. Apart from the basement staircase to the ground floor, it was also possible to go out of the basement door and easy enough to run up the outside curved stone staircase to reach the garden. The garden was well laid out but completely overgrown, like a sleeping jungle, and a cat's delight. The pathways led past a greenhouse, round an ancient 'apple/pear' tree (a grafted tree with three different fruited branches) to a submerged air-raid shelter, which was half-filled with water, and full of well-fed snails.

Jane and I rushed around our new territory, inside and out, gleefully finding new corners to exclaim over, and when we found the old wooden staircase to the coachman's room and hayloft we asked if we could have them to make into our dens. They were constructed over two stables at the back of the garage/coach-house, and I think Mother was relieved to find that we both accepted yet another move so readily.

Since we still had school until the summer, we now travelled into Holland Park, firstly on the bus into Kew, where we changed onto the trolleybus into London. As the summer days slipped into autumn, our journeys were often started in near darkness, during which time we started to experience unusually foggy days, which enveloped us for weeks. This was the infamous London smog. This continually repeated autumn weather pattern went on for some years until a significant smog event in London in December 1952, at which time allegedly 12,000 people died, and thereafter smokeless fuels was made compulsory. The fogs were mixed with

A painting of the kitchen.

107

obnoxious fumes, smoke and grime, from hundreds of chimneys and factories, making breathing difficult at times. Our clothes, newly clean at 8am, would become completely black by teatime. The buses crawled along at less than walking speed at times, and we found it quicker to walk in the gloom. As protection from the smog, we tied scarves over our noses and mouths, and were once again carrying personal torches, as we had done in the wartime blackouts, to warn others in the dense fog.

As autumn changed into the winter of 1947, it became so cold that there were days when the fog froze. I remember the winter as a particularly bad one, when two toes on my left foot got frostbite, which took a long time to recover. Snow fell thick and fast until everywhere was completely covered in eighteen inches (about half a metre) or more. This was followed by a very hard and protracted frost, making it impossible to use any wheeled vehicles.

During this time, we ran low on fuel for the kitchen range which heated the whole house, as well as heating the water. The only means to carry fuel back to the house was by foot. However, we soon copied other local children, who were using sledges for their shopping. So we went to the local hardware store and bought as many 28lb. bags (around 13kg) of 'kitchen nuts' (anthracite balls, a smokeless-fuel) as we could load and pull on our sled. Jane and I persuaded another child to help us pull the sled back home. All was well until our combined efforts overturned the sled, spilling our precious cargo at the corner of the road. Picking up every valuable coal nut was a laborious task, especially out of the deep snow. Upon our arrival home, grubby from snow and coal-dust, this helpful venture reminded us of the old adage more haste, less speed.

The grocers was part of the hardware store, and my sister soon offered our services to help other neighbours with their shopping by sledge. Soon, boxes of essential foods were being delivered to several of our neighbours. On each occasion, the boxes were stacked onto the sled, but this time firmly tied on, and delivered safely. During this time, we were given pocket money for the errands, earned our first wage doing something that we enjoyed, made many new friends, and got to know the district where we lived much better.

My confident sister Jane grew extremely quickly once in her teens. She involved herself in everything that she could, taking over whenever she thought she could do better than those around her, and was at least a head taller and one year ahead of me throughout our schooling. She was my role model and I followed her about, believing her to be wonderfully clever, as well as pretty.

Very soon it was time for her to take the Common Entrance Exam required for attending St Paul's School. This she was happy to do, thinking confidently that it was just another step in her schooling. However, there was a small set-back. Mother was horrified to be notified that she had failed the exam, and questions were now being asked about our earlier Montessori education in Clitheroe.

This was deemed to be an inadequate type of formal education, so a plan of how to improve the situation became a major issue. It was discovered that although our Montessori education in Lancashire had been good, we needed a much higher level of mathematics and English, as well as more general knowledge than we possessed.

Without more ado, Mother found a Crammer's School (for intensive core-subject learning), in Hounslow West, for both of us to attend. Jane attended immediately, along with five other pupils, all boys, to improve some of the gaps in her education. Major Drake-Brockman ran this establishment for hopeful participants of entrance exams, while his wife ran a nursery school in the same large, mid-nineteenth house. Jane took and passed the entrance examination again, some weeks later. Due to this success, it was decided to send me on the same crammer's course for the following year before attempting the dreaded exam. By September 1947, my sister was all set for attending St. Paul's School.

Jane and I in Trafalgar Square.

Due to appendicitis, I was suddenly very ill. After being examined by the local doctor, he sent me for an emergency operation in Hounslow Hospital. At this time, operations were not as effective or successful as nowadays, and I finished up with a scar an inch wide and nine inches long, which would not heal easily. I was forced to endure six weeks of bedridden inactivity before being allowed out of bed, by now extremely weak and very listless. I was even more upset when everyone around me planned to see Princess Elizabeth's wedding, arranged for the 20 November, again as a party on the Mall, but was told I would not be allowed to go to this exciting event. I pleaded, even though I realized that I was really not well enough.

'Please may I go to watch the wedding parade too on the Radio Rentals television, it will be in the shop window on their large set in the High Street. Jane could take me? Please?'

But Mother replied with a very firm 'No.' Our local shoemaker, with seven children, who lived at the end of our road, solved the problem by buying or renting a TV set. He suggested to Mother that she could take me to their house to watch the event, whilst she and Jane plus other friends travelled into London to experience the occasion live in the Mall. This was agreed upon.

As it subsequently transpired, it poured down during the wedding procession.

109

Princess Elizabeth's wedding, 1947.

Fortunately, I was the luckier one and avoided the drenching suffered by the rest of the family. The wedding was a splendid occasion, as were the dresses worn by everyone, which still had to be bought by using the allocated clothing coupons, because very strict rationing was now in operation.

As soon as I was well enough from my operation, I was sent to the crammer school. Mother did not want her second daughter to fail Saint Paul's School entrance exam. It was a straight half hour's bus ride to Hounslow West. I found that I was working in a small schoolroom, along with five boys, aiming to take other common-entrance examinations. All six of us settled down to a strict regime of work, rotating with in-depth learning of English grammar with mathematics, algebra and geometry.

For a change we had fewer lessons in Latin, history and geography, but it was plain that we were touching these subjects to acquire more general knowledge. We learned tables and lists by rote, used sharp pencils only, a six-inch ruler for neatness, and never saw an ink pen in the building. Gone were the fun or artistic subjects and games – these were now a thing of the past. Major Drake-Brockman was an old style schoolmaster of about 65, with many creases in his face, framed by thinning hair and he had a grey moustache. He was clear and succinct with his instructions and fair-minded. No idle talking was allowed during his lessons until break time. Everybody knew the rules.

I walked down the road every day for my lunch and crossed a busy main thoroughfare to a café on the opposite side. I paused one day to peer into a junk shop, and spied two sad-looking barn owls, without their protective glass case. In their forlorn and rejected condition, I bought them for two shillings and sixpence (12.5p). The junk shop man wrapped them carefully for me, so I could carry them back to school at the end of my lunch break. Bringing them into the classroom proved to be a very interesting experience.

Once the Major was aware of what I'd bought into the classroom he skipped the planned lesson for that day. He was a keen ornithologist and gave a lengthy and impromptu lecture on the life and habits of owls, including varieties, which I had never heard of or seen. We now saw a different side to this very strict man. To this day, I still have my two owls being a hoarder – proudly mounted on a little wooden stand which I made for them.

The next great surprise from the Major was an invitation from both he and his wife to watch one evening John Barbirolli conducting the Halle Orchestra at the Kew Theatre. It was my first taste of this kind of 'classical' music, and I loved it, especially the works by Vaughan Williams. He said that classical music should be a part of a good education, and discussed this in class next day.

During one rainy day, taking a lunchtime break from my 'cramming' education at the Major's house, I walked up to the parade of shops to a café for lunch, and I was a witness to a fatal accident in the street. I had stopped to watch a youth on a bicycle, coming full tilt out of a side street, on to the main road without stopping. At exactly the same moment, a mother was crossing the road in front of him with her pram. He missed her by inches. But his luck was out, because a fairly fast moving lorry travelling on the main road hit the cyclist squarely on his side, causing the youth to fall in front of the big vehicle. The bicycle spun round to hit the pram, which careered off on its own down the road, without the terrified mother. Tragically the boy was killed. Worse, the head of the luckless boy had been severed from his body, and was now rolling onto the other side of the road.

Pandemonium ensued. In the drizzling rain, the screaming mother ran after her pram to catch it before she lost her child in another accident. I stood with a few other people, my mouth open in horror, to watch as blood from the mangled parts of the body filled the road with bright red trails, spreading onto the wet road surface. I was transfixed, observing the blood as it trailed around in the puddles, coloured with the irridescent patterns of petrol in the water, and mingled with the deepening red life-force seeping away.

Deeply shocked, I went home slowly, missing afternoon schooling, without any explanations to anyone, and sat down in a daze. I started to draw what I had seen, in the privacy of my own room. When questioned later I was unable to provide any answers to my absence from school. It was only when the newspapers reported the accident, that the Major, and then Jim at home, were able to put two and two together, and realised that I had been present at the accident. Two days later I laid out my picture for them, and then nothing more was said about the matter.

GOING SHRIMPING

Once we had moved to our new house, in Woodlands Grove, Isleworth, in 1947, we were pleased to discover there were a great many activities for our age group to take part in. Fortunately, most of these clubs took place at the church hall. Furthermore, the cost to us was simply weekly attendance at church on Sundays. We found that we could learn country dancing, or a variant of it, square dancing, learn ballroom dancing once a week, play badminton, indoor netball or rounders, or even join the brownies and guides. In addition, there were opportunities to play whist, bridge or other card games which were popular at the time. The Girl Guides offered other tantalizing activities.

The vicar, the Reverend Jenkins, was a likeable and energetic young Welshman, who took part in everything possible, and was known as Up-Jenkins behind his back. His odd nickname stemmed, I believe, from a well-known party game. It was obvious to everyone why he gained a very large and young congregation, during which time we competed for places in his choir, with the chance of earning two and six-pence each, for singing at the weddings, which took place at St. Johns Church.

The church soon became a well-known venue for such musical occasions. The choirmaster was Sid Chapman who had very exacting standards to follow. Not wanting to be embarrassed by being associated with a tone-deaf group of choristers, he held lessons each week for any youngster who failed to reach these standards. This task was also undertaken by a few of the older choir members, such as the Middleton brothers, with their deep voices going with their senior status.

In addition, the organist, Don Skipper, who lived two doors away from us, joined in with the Jenkins singing group. I must add that I remain to this day only a modest singer. The church had never before been so full of young enthusiasts.

I made a new friend, Anthea Wendy, who started at the choir on the same day as myself, and also attended Sid Chapman's singing lessons. The photograph of the whole choir, at Don Skipper's wedding, shows Anthea (second from left) and myself

The choir at St. John's Church, Isleworth.

112

(third from left). Anthea had curly auburn hair, a ready smile and a sense of fun. She was two years younger, and lived a few streets away from our house and the local church.

It was not long before I discovered the reason for her keenness to attend everything she could, even though it meant walking quite a distance. This was because her home circumstances were difficult. Her father had been an upholsterer for the underground trains, and subsequently went to Acton during the war to build battle tanks. In doing so, he had entered a so-called 'reserved occupation', where he was not liable to be called up into the armed forces.

It is said that red-haired people had bad tempers, which I only partially disbelieved until I met Anthea's red-headed father. His mean streak not only included stopping

Anthea Wendy Simms.

Anthea's innocent and church-based activities, but also the interests and activities of her Mother, and of her Aunt Aggie. His hostility to people in general was directed at me because he hated 'the bosses' which in my case meant Father, who was an officer in the Army.

He stoked up a malicious rage whenever my father was mentioned as 'the Colonel', or the fact that I came from a more affluent family and lived in a larger house. This was an attitude of mind and state of affairs that I had not hitherto encountered, and found it hard to understand. I had learned to deal with bullying children, but to discover that adults could behave so unpleasantly was a shock. Obviously there were more lessons for me to learn in life.

Anthea's patient mother 'covered' for Anthea whenever she came round to my house to take part in dressmaking. This activity was especially important to us because we needed new circular skirts for the square dancing club, run by the vicar. As expected, Anthea received absolutely no approval from her father.

Nevertheless, we carried out dressmaking on the kitchen table, using colourful curtain material, which had been put away during the war, and therefore didn't require coupons. Coupons were still used for all clothing materials up until 1949, at which time they were abolished. By this time, the 'New Look' came into fashion, whereby skirts became longer and flared.

We spent time cutting our material to the correct patterns, then using Mother's Singer sewing machine we carefully converted our designs into wearable garments. With Mother's advice, being a creative seamstress, we were soon equipped with snazzy skirts, with wide-net underskirts, stiffened well with starch. When we were all set for going to the square dancing club, Anthea came to my house to dress for the occasion. She feared, naturally enough, that her father might ban her from attending, if he saw her new eye-catching outfit, bright as a colourful butterfly.

He would have said, 'Take it back. You cannot have it. We will not accept charity from that Mr Stuart.' At the end of every dancing club session, she changed back

A square dancing group in the 1950s.

again into her previous clothes, just like in the story of Cinderella, before running home again. Nevertheless, she took the skirt to her Aunt Aggie's house to show her Mother, who hid it for her to use on many future occasions.

Once we attended a Square Dancing Rally in the local town, graced by the presence of Princess Margaret Rose, who joined in dancing with us, along with some of her friends. She was approximately seventeen years old then, extremely vivacious, pretty and energetic. My lasting memories of that occasion was of her wearing beautiful clothes. Being closer to our age group it is not so surprising that she was very popular, and her life story, whatever we could find of it in the newspapers, was closely followed by us all.

The house in Isleworth now became the hub of visiting members of our family. Aunt Mary made her home there for four months of that year, and Aunts Gee and Nona came and went to suit their travelling timetable. For a while, we also had visits from my grandfather's cousin, Lena Hinshelwood, who enjoyed her 84th birthday with us in great style, before going into a home for 'gentlewomen.' For a short while Mother had cared for her until this task became too arduous due to Lena's physical and mental demands. Over the years Mother undertook the herculean task of taking in all the aged relatives in turn, as they required looking after, until their eventual demise.

Mother loved organising parties, and celebrations of any kind, and would say 'The more, the merrier.' However, she made sure that everybody was given the right role, including roles for the cook, the housekeeper, the daily cleaner, and a gardener, whilst she orchestrated the proceedings and managed delivery of the alcohol and provisions. She advised the cook in the creation of beautiful food dishes – surprisingly she had an artistic eye as well as being a good cook herself. The unsuspecting guests said of her, 'Val's parties are such fun, hasn't she worked hard.' But she was quite certain that her part was to organise the staff, invite an eclectic mix of people, but not to do any of the actual work herself except manage everyone and to arrange the flowers.

Relatives and friends came and went. There were aunts and cousins such as dear Norah Simpson from Lancaster, and also our northern England friends, Pop and Helen Ridley from Shildon in Durham, and Betty Goodall from the school. One very big surprise was to see my long lost Nanny, my dear Miss Robinson from

Northern Ireland who was having an English holiday. I gleefully took her hand to show her around my new home. All our visitors appreciated being able to stay near London, and we were pleased with the renewal of long-established friendships. I was delighted with the renewed offers of holidays in the north as I still felt a little alien in the London environment. Jane was now busy with her new school, and involved herself even less in my interests and activities – I was definitely the younger sister now.

Jim's very thin-looking sister, Kit Porter, came for a visit to London. She had the same gaunt look, iron-grey hair, but was always full of fun. Her husband owned a jeweller's shop in Bournemouth, Dorset. She was very keen to be taken to see where Jim was now working. I asked if I could go too, because I wanted to visit Lil's cafe and see how the baby in the box from the bomb site had fared. It was now nearly two and a half years since we had found her, however we had always received updates about her via Jim. The very next day, Kit, Jim and I took the Number 657 trolleybus into London, and then changed onto the Underground.

Jim suggested it might be fun to take a ride on the old trams, which we did. We travelled under the ground via the Kingsway Tram Tunnel, then under the Strand, which had two stations only, at the Aldwych and Holborn, and finally emerged at the Embankment in south London.

Although we were not aware of this in 1947, the London Trams were coming to the end of an era, when the last one ran in July 1952, after 91 years of service in the capital.

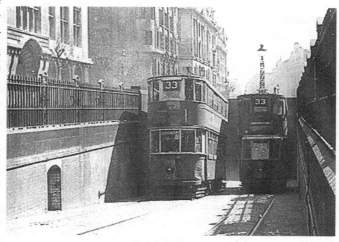

The old tramway.

In 1901, the horse-drawn trams had been withdrawn and replaced with electrified vehicles, drawing their power from overhead lines, which remained unchanged until 1952. Interestingly, the London Trams were designed to be driven in both directions, whereby the driver would make use of the cab at the relevant end, while passengers could rotate the backs of their seats, back or forth, so that they always faced the direction of travel.

Although there were conventional buses, we were always interested in the trolleybuses, introduced in 1931, which due to their large carrying capacity slowly took over from the trams, until also their eventual demise in 1962. The trolleybuses were driven freely similar to normal buses, amongst regular traffic, however because they drew their electrical power also from overhead lines, they were confined to using certain routes only. One drawback with trolleybuses was that, being silent, they could be dangerous for pedestrians, who might unwittingly walk across their path. We experienced that they could 'sneak up' on you unawares, although most of the time the overhead wires gave the game away by twanging and sparking above our heads.

For us children, travelling was always interesting. Travelling underground along the tramway from Aldwych to the Embankment, we experienced excitement in the darkness of the electrical sparks between pantograph and cable, flying aloft like fire-flies flitting in a secret cave, mixed with the strong smells of engine oil. As the tram progressed along the rails, jerking along creating its particular noises, the ticket collector would issue tickets from his chest-high ticket-machine for each passenger.

We were now on our way to Jim's place of work in Fleet Street. I bounded confidently out of the underground station, expecting to experience the familiar street I knew from the past. However, things had changed, and now Fleet Street was a hive of constructional activity. Walking up the road we dodged the builders, the scaffolders, and many men who were determinedly rebuilding many of the bombed sites. We took refuge in the entrance of the Keystone press agency to watch all this activity going on. Gone were the myriads of prowling feline occupants, although we encountered two remaining cats, now sleek and bright eyed with contented smirks on their bewhiskered faces, who were guarding the entrance. Where the rest had gone I knew not.

Jim took his sister in to show her where he worked at the press agency. He had a porter's office, and together with Sam, they were responsible for providing a very slick delivery service of photographs intended for the Fleet Street newspaper offices, with film arriving at Keystone from all over the world. At the agency, photographic prints were developed, then taken quickly to the relevant newspapers for publication the same day. Parcels of special photographic paper, chemicals and printing inks arrived continuously in delivery vans. The use of all these materials in the processes used contributed to the pervading, indefinable chemical smells, found everywhere in the building. London was indeed full of interesting smells. At Keystone, there was also outward-bound stacks of parcels, waiting for transport to the Post Office, for distribution around the world.

Fleet Street.

'You've landed on your feet, lad, make no mistake, at your age.' his younger sister was delighted that after the war he had managed to get a worthwhile job. Nevertheless, I was puzzled by her comments, not really understanding the difficulties of post-war employment, assuming that all adults were capable of achieving whatever they wanted to do in life. Sam and Jim accompanied us for their lunch break down the road to Lil's café, which was now facing a number of new buildings, although there remained a number of boarded up bomb sites, ready for developers to move in and reorganize the rubble.

'Look who I've got with me.' Sam greeted Lil and Jeannie, and walked over to look into a pram, which contained a sleeping child, now at least two years old. The café had been enlarged, redecorated, and buzzed with business people, all needing their lunches. Jeannie was obviously happy with her work, running the café with speed and precision, while Lil kept her eye on the customers, the orders and the bills. From our curiosity over the last two years, we were full of questions for Jeannie. She explained that her husband had been posted as missing and presumed killed. However, investigations by the Red Cross had revealed that he had been wounded, and placed in a prisoner of war camp. The difficulty in tracing him had arisen because he couldn't remember who he was. Nevertheless, he was eventually traced to a British hospital, where he had been sent for convalescence.

'He will be able to come here to join Jeannie soon.' Lil was delighted to offer them a home because her own son had been killed and she had been lonely. It was a godsend to have Jeannie with her, so she was keenly preparing for Jeannie's husband's arrival whenever the hospital released him.

The problems of a lost memory were discussed, but I could not imagine how it would be, not to remember things. I contemplated this matter several times because I was so used to busying myself with my thoughts, imagination and memories, which would so often be added to my drawings or painting books.

Having worked hard for Major Drake-Brockman, under his tutelage I took and passed my Common Entrance exam with confidence, so was now set for moving in the autumn to St Paul's Girls School, in Hammersmith, following in Jane's footsteps.

Kit invited me to stay with her and her husband Bert Porter for the Whitsun holidays in Poole, Dorset. My travelling spirits were raised greatly, and I was excited about this new experience. I was now a very independent young teenager, self-motivated, self-reliant and self-willed. Herein lay my downfall during this holiday.

Kit and I took the train down to Bournemouth Station, where we were met by Bert, who worked in the town at his shop, Bertram Porter's Jewellers, an up-market establishment. We caught the bus to Poole, riding past the harbour and on up the hill to their house. The harbour was empty of water at that time, but during the evening as the tide came in, it filled the enclosed expanse of water silently and secretly. Since this part of the bay was so shallow, the tide moved very slowly. In the evening air, the seaweeds wafted up their pungent summer smell in the warm breeze, reminding me again of the Belfast Lough coastline and the evening sunset in a pink glow over the waterline.

'Tomorrow we will buy some shrimp nets, take a bucket and go shrimping in the bay in our bare feet,' Kit suggested as one of our activities for the holidays. I readily agreed with the plan. The next day we took the bus into Bournemouth to buy our shrimp-nets and to visit Bert. He had offered to take us to lunch and met us at the appointed place. He put a small parcel in front of my plate, which he had brought from his shop. I opened it and discovered a little watch, with a round dial, clear numbers and three hands.

Kit and I with the recorder.

'Congratulations on passing your exam. Now you will need a watch to keep good time for school. Don't overwind it, don't drop it, don't get sand in it and don't get it wet.' Bert was full of instructions, much as a jeweller would to a young girl. Thanking him several times, I put the watch on my wrist.

Before going back to Poole, I found a music shop from which I bought a recorder, made from a new synthetic plastic called Bakelite, along with an instruction manual, for £1.12.6d. I had saved my pocket money and now had the means to play my own music, if I practised hard enough. The church at home encouraged a recorder group and I dearly wished to join it. So now I looked forward to a busy, happy holiday.

Although Kit had suggested that we go shrimping together, she had other things to do, so saw no harm in letting me go down to the beach alone by bus. Kit had packed me sandwiches and a bottle of orange juice in a big paper bag for the day, and reminding me to leave my watch and my recorder on the dressing-table, she gave me my bus fare.

So off I went, happy with my new adventure. Despite Kit's strong advice, and without her checking, I wore my watch, so that I could tell the time and wouldn't miss one of the infrequent buses for my return journey. The water in the bay was at high tide, but just starting to recede, so taking off my shoes and putting them, my cardigan and food bag on the sea wall, I waded in up to my knees. Thankfully, for the shrimps' sake, I was a poor fisherwoman, and netted very little to take back with me. Mostly, I enjoyed the chase of the tiny fish, whilst wading about in the warm sunshine, and listening to the summer buzz of insects and mournful chat of the seabirds, as the sun rose above the masts of the moored sailing boats.

By lunchtime I climbed up onto the wall, ate the sandwiches, and studied my instruction book for learning how to play the recorder, which I had also brought with

Poole Harbour

me in the bag. I then turned my attention to improving my poor fishing skills by renewing my efforts to catch something. Mindful of Bert's earlier remarks, I wrapped up my watch carefully in a hanky, then put it into my sandwich bag and stored it away in the big bag to avoid it getting wet. Then using my hands, I plunged them into the warm water to chase the dozens of escaping fishes into my waiting net,but they all had minds and tail rudders of their own.

Time passed happily, and it was only when the brilliant orange ball of the sinking sun suddenly caught my eye over the water, that I saw the bus starting to travel slowly round the bay. I felt a rising panic, and in haste gathered up my sandals, shrimp net, bucket and cardigan and ran for the bus, arriving at the stop just in time to hop on breathlessly. I was relieved to have caught it, because the long hill home was a steep walk. As I got off, I suddenly realized that I was not carrying the big paper bag with me. I had left my watch and recorder behind.

Regardless of the time, I ran down the hill again, and searched for my bag by the wall where I had been sitting. It was gone. I asked a fisherman who was leaning over the wall if he had seen it.

Kit's photograph of me in Poole with the watch.

'Ask that road sweeper, he's been tidying up.' He said casually, without much enthusiasm. I ran along the road to catch up with the workman, who said that he had indeed put all the rubbish into the bin at the end of the road.

'It was only an empty carrier bag with a screwed up lunch bag in it.' He was baffled by my insistence on finding it. Nevertheless he came over to the bin and reached in to find the discarded paper bag for me, to verify the truth of his words. Inside the bag was the recorder instruction pamphlet, and my screwed up lunch bag. Thankfully, inside the lunch bag was my handkerchief wrapped tightly round my watch. The only loss was the recorder, two hours of my time, and my equilibrium, for because of all this, now there was an explanation to be made.

I caught the next bus up the long hill – that could be explained by saying that I had missed the earlier one, but the loss of my recorder could not be accounted for so easily. In the end, I told the truth of what had happened, and bore the brunt of being chastised for my disobedience in the first instance. It made me think long and hard about the rules set by adults, whether I agreed with them or not. I tried to make up for my behaviour, because basically I liked to please, independent as I was.

Kit took me back at the end of the holidays and stayed at our house for two more days. Before leaving us to return home, she gave me a small long parcel, and said it would remind me of the great holiday that we all had in Poole. I'm so glad that she really thought this, because inside the package was a brand-new recorder. I used it for many years afterwards.

SPORTING CHANCE

At the end of 1948, my dearest father finally returned home, permanently, from India. This moment was hastened by the fact that he was granted 'sick leave', having 'Prickly Heat', a common name for *miliaria rubra*, which was a severe infection of the skin sweat glands. This was suffered by many soldiers who had worked in the tropics, where there was extreme heat.

He had never seen our new house and was greatly impressed by it, especially because it had space for everyone and a large garden with several outbuildings. He decided to occupy the front bedroom, which had a balcony. Since it was the coolest north facing room in the house, this swayed his decision. I wondered why Mother would not share this lovely room, but she preferred her own in the middle part of the house, so I stopped asking what Jane called 'awkward questions', and put it to the back of my mind.

Dad's mantle shelf at Isleworth.

Father used the large front room in the semi-basement next to the kitchen as his study, where the little store rooms off it quickly became his experimental labs for electrical gadgets and a darkroom for photography. He furnished it with a large desk, two big overflowing bookcases, an old, round, pedestal dining table and a couple of comfortable armchairs, along with two carved wooden Chinese Dragon lamps which graced the mantle shelf. These were the principal items in his cosy 'snug'.

Jane and I occupied another large bedroom at the front of the house with a big bay window. From this vantage point, I could watch the milkman with his white horse pulling the red United Dairies milk float; the horse always stopped to graze the large privet hedge. Being the corner house, the milk float stood there every day, for quite some time, for the convenience of the milkman, who radiated from this point, and was able to deliver milk conveniently to several other houses in the street. This cheerful and early worker was also a social focal point whereby various neighbours who popped out to speak with him had the chance to gossip to one another – I was one of these.

Mr Lovely (in his forties and lovely by name, by nature, by temperament and good looks) lived with his aged mother, opposite our house, in a beautiful detached residence. It had a wrap-round garden and wrap-round protecting wall, in which different varieties of fruit trees, surrounded by free-growing parsley, was always in abundance. I envied them the grand piano, which stood in their drawing room and actually said so to him on one occasion. As a result of this comment, I was allowed to practise there, regularly, over the following years, particularly because Mr Lovely realised that we did not have a piano. Since I had learnt to play from the age of five at school, I was very keen to continue practicing, because I was becoming quite proficient. Father remarked to my aunt that I was perfectly safe going there, because he 'batted for the other side'. I never understood what he meant until later, when I was 28, someone enlightened me.

My father soon occupied himself with building a new L-shaped greenhouse on an elevated position in the garden, and built in the ground beneath a large concrete tank of eighteen inches deep, which was then filled with fine stone chippings. Jim had given up the little one-room flat in Holland Park, and was occupying the back bedroom in

Dad's new greenhouse.

our house at that time. He did general jobs for Mother to put the house in order, while helping Father with various more technical or difficult projects. As always, I was keen to join in with any activity instigated, whether I understood the task or not.

In the greenhouse, pipes for moving water in and out to a sump were fitted, and soon waterproof heating wires wound around the interior of the chippings to lightly warm the roots of the plants. Switches to control the twice-daily flow of liquids appeared, and all was ready for working the new soil-free garden – and it worked. Hydroponics.

It seemed to me a miracle to grow wonderfully fat tomatoes and juicy cucumbers on plants rooted in stone chippings, and only fed by water laced with Father's choice of chemicals twice a day. There were one or two exotic indoor plants too for Mother to display in the house. Now, Father's garden was filled with a riot of blooms in every corner, interspersed with exotic vegetables, and probably fed with the same weird concoctions, as in the greenhouse, to produce such results. The garden gave him a peaceful area in which to unwind, but my parents seemed very uneasy with each other, and at that moment I could not put my finger on the reason. Eventually I did find out, to be explained in a later chapter.

During this time, I also learned that Father had hoped to study chemical engineering, but was persuaded by his father to join the army, as was his brother John, and eventually the youngest brother, Robin. So instead of his original wish, he went to R.M.S. Sandhurst, the British Army's Officers training establishment in Surrey.

That first summer home Father took Jane and I on regular long walks. He was obviously a keen sportsman, and very restless. It was a couple of very hot months. He taught us elementary tennis at Redlees Park courts nearby, in which I did not excel, losing

Walking with Father at Kew. sight of the ball, whenever it came too close to me,

although I had very good long sight. He walked us round the local golf course, which he had joined, where he regularly played a first-class game. He took us to the local swimming baths near Twickenham, where he quickly taught me swimming by the simple expedient of showing me how to swim under water before rising to the surface. But finding our way there meant going through Mogden Sewage works, a wonderful 'Moonscape' kind of land, full of large round cinder beds, watered continuously by thin metal arms rotating over the beds. The whole area was scattered liberally on most days with  *Father after the War.* foam, originating from the soap powders which households used, and which gave off a curious smell but not one of sewage. It was always worse on a Monday, and in windy weather the suds could blow for several miles before finally dissipating.

My father, although now officially retired from the army, was insistent that he needed a job, because his restless nature dictated that he was not of retiring age (he informed me that 85 would be about right.) So he acquired a temporary job as Swimming Instructor and Coach for the summer at Twickenham Baths, travelling by bicycle through Mogden Sewage works every day, saying the job would do temporarily, until he found another. And indeed he did.

Jim found a new, better paid job with a courier service, moving from Fleet Street to London Airport. This was only a couple of miles from our house, and involved delivering parcels around the region. The company advertised for more drivers to deliver special packages all over London. My father, thinking this might be fun and more relaxing, applied successfully for a driver's job, as plain Mr George Stuart. He kept his army identity to himself, so that he could blend in with the other drivers. Mistakenly, he thought he was succeeding quite well until his deception was truly rumbled, when one of his colleagues said, 'George, would you write a character reference for me please? I want to apply for my mortgage, and need a referee, so it will lend more weight, you being a Colonel.' Thereafter, he became an unofficial spokesman and correspondent, when necessary, for the men with whom he worked.

Now at home, I was able to learn a great deal more about my father, who until now had been my childhood hero and long-distance mentor. He was always smiling, about five foot ten, with his round bald head, ginger moustache and bright blue eyes, he had a great sense of humour, and could fix anything. He was like this when we lived all those years ago in Northern Ireland before he went away, and in my eyes had not changed a bit. He had a just and fair way of dealing with situations and people wherever he found himself, so he never disappointed my expectations of him, even as we both grew older.

He kept himself fit by swimming and playing golf regularly, but made a lot of time for both of us girls, often joining in with our interests and activities. He attended many social engagements of the regiment as past Colonel, in the Regimental Association, and in the fullness of time ran the southern branch himself. Having an appealing way with the ladies, who were flattered by his charm, he also had a liking for them, perhaps too well at times, because he had had a number of small private dalliances over the years. He was always in demand at dances and parties, being an excellent ballroom dancer. He insisted that I should learn to dance well, so Jane and I were sent weekly to a local dance school to learn ballroom dancing which was in vogue at the time.

Some years later after Father had put on some weight, it was remarked one day, as he took to the dance-floor at a 'Conservative Do' with the stout Mrs Ryde, also an excellent dancer, that, 'They waltzed round the ocean of floor like two stately galleons in perfect harmony and in full sail.'

It seems appropriate at this stage to narrate a little of my father's story because he was the influence and mainstay of my young life. The advice and wisdom he passed on to me over the years was invaluable, even up to his death at the age of 96. He was always recounting little stories and reciting poetry he had learned over the years, which greatly influenced my own interest in writing poetry.

My first evening dress.

Father was christened Godfrey Walter Burleigh Stuart. The name 'George' was completely fictitious. At home he was always known as Goff, but also answered to the regimental nickname, 'Gummy', and was from a large military family of Irish origins. Both he and his middle brother John were born in one of the Hill Stations in India, at the turn of the century. The youngest brother, Robin, was born in England when grandfather retired from India in 1908, and was several years younger. Grandmother Stuart, Alice Mabel, also known as Puss, a fun loving, kind Irishwoman who was known to have a liking for porter, originated from a wealthy shipping family living in Ardmore, south of Londonderry (today known as Derry), and often took her three boys there for holidays. Many stories abounded about their escapades, but one incident is worth telling of their childhood, when the three brothers spent a short holiday nearby with Colonel Barton, their uncle, who owned the Rathmullan Hotel, beside Lough Swilly in Northern Ireland.

In the far north west tip of Ireland, beyond Londonderry and Letterkenny, are the Bluestack Mountains, an eerie and magical place, criss-crossed with many small roads and few hamlets, and where the land drops down steeply into the sea. The shoreline is indented with many creeks, but is bounded by Lough Swilly on its eastern side, which opens out into the sea. It is washed by the flow of high tides twice a day, which flow against the Portsalon River flowing down into the Lough, bringing with it the cries of the seagulls.

The old hotel at Portsalon by Lough Swilly.

The currents around that northern area are strong and quite dangerous, so were to be treated with respect. The three boys loved the untamed area and all the interesting people living there, playing around their uncle's hotel. They used the adjacent farm as their playground, dodging the cows ambling into the dairy, and organised the local boys into little gangs to play cowboys and Indians. A group of them decided to explore along the rocky edges of the Portsalon River, swollen with the continual rain, and the lush grass growing in the field was slippery. Suddenly there was a panic-filled scream, like the cry of a seabird.

This was no seabird. Another scream followed the first.

'Help me. Goff. John.' They both turned round to see Robin, the six year old, slipping down the wet grassy bank, and saw him drop into the water. Immediately the fast flowing river caught hold of him, and propelled the struggling boy along the bank, the current only waiting for the opportunity to whisk him into the faster flow in the middle. All the boys ran along the bank shouting encouragement and instructions, but knowing they were powerless to do anything. None of the village children could swim because they were country boys, with no experience of tides and boats.

With a quick command issued to John, 'Stay by me, I'll need your help.' Goff plunged into the swiftly moving water to find Robin, now sinking yet again, and grabbed him by his trousers. He lost his grip, dropped him and dived yet again to make another snatch at his drowning brother. Fear lent speed to his actions and the memory of the terrified cries of Robin. He was a strong swimmer, and by moving with the flow he now managed to rise to the surface again clutching his burden, his precious young brother, whom he now hauled onto a rock further down the river, whereupon John caught hold of them.

The other children helped and they dragged Robin onto the level field, then turning him over, Goff held his legs up high and emptied him of water, as had been taught by the life-saving class at school. At thirteen, Goff had been a prize swimmer at school in Norfolk, and was forever eternally thankful to have learned to swim. When the dripping and shivering boys eventually arrived home for tea, nothing was said about the incident, because they could not get a word in edgeways or stem their mother's anger at their wet state. They were thoroughly smacked for being drenched, and sent to bed without any supper.

It was only after the village boys had arrived home excitedly, and had told their parents of the harrowing incident of that afternoon, that the story leaked out. This was reported to the local press, the *Londonderry Sentinel*, which published the story. I have no doubt that the newspaper had exaggerated the boys' accounts of events because in Ireland every good Irishman knows that a tale needs to be well embroidered. By all accounts the story was a sensation because it was noticed by the national press, who published further accounts after making contact with the three brothers. Photographs were taken to commemorate the occasion. Young Robin thought it was worth the drenching to have his picture put in the newspaper, not understanding his narrow escape from death. Father was given an award for his bravery.

Years later, when Father was into his nineties, I was holding the citation of the 80 year old award in my hand and I asked him about the circumstances of the incident. He made light of it, saying, 'That was a very long time ago,' but added the details I have recounted.

My father followed an army tradition, because his father, my grandfather, was also a serving soldier. His name was Godfrey Richard Connyngham Stuart and he was born in 1866. He spent much of his Army career in India. He attained the rank of major and survived the great cholera epidemic at Lucknow. He also served in the three great campaigns of Chitral, the North-west Frontier Campaign, and the Tirah Campaign in India, at the end of the nineteenth century. He received military recognition with the CB (Companion of the Bath).

Upon his retirement to Ipswich, he

John, Godfrey, Grandad Stuart and Robin, early 1920s.

became a Deputy Lieutenant for the county of Suffolk, as an honorary position for service in the local community. Father was brought up in Ipswich, and spent his schooldays at St. Felix' School, Felixstowe.

During his service years, Grandfather was noted as an accomplished sportsman, winning many regimental sports trophies, for a variety of sports events – on foot or on horseback. Retiring from the army eventually, he took up Lawn Tennis, playing at a professional level. Both he and his sister, my Aunt Daisy Stuart had been Northern Irish Golf Champions, as shown by the silver cups now in my cupboard.

They came from a family of eight children of a solicitor in Armagh, Major Burleigh Henry Fitzwilliam Stuart; they were all well-educated and keen sportsmen. Five of the children except my grandfather Godfrey, his brother Burleigh, and Daisy were killed in the First World War. I did not really know my grandfather until after the war, but I could instantly recognize the family likeness of bald head, ginger moustache and twinkling blue eyes. By this time, he was getting on in years. He lived in Cheltenham, where I recall he grew beautiful roses. Due to his great interest in tennis, he would always attend Wimbledon, which was a great opportunity for him to stay with us briefly every year and for me to get to know him better.

The Stuart family is shown over the page in the photograph taken in 1903 at

'Dergmoney' in Armagh, Northern Ireland. The picture shows my grandfather Godfrey Stuart who is standing behind my great grandparents with his sister, great-aunt Daisy to his left. His wife Alice Mabel, my grandmother Puss, sits with Uncle John on her knee and my father, young Godfrey is at the front on the grass. My grandfather's elder brother Burleigh is missing from this photograph. Gradually, I discovered the colourful story of my father's life, and of the many countries he visited. The following paragraph provides an outline of his history.

After joining the East Lancashire Regiment he served in Jamaica in the West Indies (in the period 1921-23), in Malta, Egypt and the Sudan (1923-25), and then a spell in India (1925-29). Hardly pausing for breath with a visit home, he was relocated to Shanghai (1931-32), the Western Dessert, then home to be married, all by 1933 and before the outbreak of the Second World War.

A soldier's life in those years was a very busy and much travelled one. I marvelled at his wide knowledge of the world, and badgered him to tell me stories of his life and sometimes I got more than I had bargained for. They were not fairy stories, and my fairies covered their ears in fright.

Father told horrific tales of being in China. They sailed up the Yangzi River to prevent bloodshed between neighbouring groups; and foiled attacks from pirates, who were operating at the behest of Chinese War Lords. On this occasion, the pirates with cutlasses between their teeth, stealthily swam out at night and tried to board the regiment's ships, in the darkness that cloaked the Yangzi River. In retaliation and to foil them, the soldiers quietly floated down explosives on the surface of the water, also in the dark, finally setting them off to do maximum damage to the assailants.

Junks near Nanking, China.

On one occasion, Father was obliged to accompany one of these War Lords who had organised a gathering of chiefs, to broker a peace settlement. Having sat through the niceties of the feast, he was horrified to learn that the entertainment was a public execution, where about 90 men queued up resignedly to be decapitated with a curved sword. Interestingly, my father would talk about these times in detail, but when questioned about the European War, he was more reticent.

At the outbreak of World War Two, he led the 1st battalion of the East Lancashire Regiment as part of the British Expeditionary Force into France in September 1939. His regiment was beaten back slowly by the advancing German forces, and eventually, between May and June 1940, were forced onto the Dunkirk beaches. They were rescued by the famous armada of small boats from across the south coast, not before being shot at during night fall from German planes passing over them. It is recorded that approximately 384,000 soldiers were rescued in this way. One of his men asked, 'Are you not afraid, Sir?'

To which he replied, 'I'm shaking so much inside, I dare not show it, for fear of alerting the enemy, with the sound of my knees knocking, so stand by me and we'll be tall and safe together. We always have a 'Sporting Chance' you know.' I learned this story from a member of his regiment years later.

He was involved in retraining soldiers in 1943 in preparation for taking his battalion on to the Normandy landings of June 1944, however he was not allowed to participate – the official records stated that '…he then had the misfortune to be one of the many extremely able Commanding Officers who were arbitrarily removed by General Montgomery for being too old for active service.' He was by this time in his early forties, and told me that he was very

Father at his desk.

angry at this decision, being still very active. At this point in his life however, maybe his Guardian Fairies were watching over him for he lived to tell the tale.

He joined the staff of Supreme Headquarters Allied Expeditionary Force in France, but when it closed at the end of hostilities in Europe in 1945, he soon found himself in the hot seat of action once again. He was asked to take the 2nd Battalion of his regiment immediately to Dinapore, India, and was appointed Commanding Officer.

Now as Colonel, he moved to Calcutta to stem the serious inter-communal rioting on the eve of Indian Independence, from which I heard some of his most terrifying and gory stories when he finally returned home. He carried an Officer's leather baton, as was the custom, which was given him by an old Irish Colonel who assured him that its hidden depths had fatal teeth within it, to save him from harm. It seemed that even he believed in the protection of the Irish fairies, and indeed it did on several occasions. Within his baton was a fine steel blade, and he explained that when, for instance, he was set upon by a large crowd of cut-throats intent on killing him, he used the hidden

Father in India.

weapon to good effect to extricate himself from the scene and the killer clinging onto his back, while dislocating another from his legs.

With independence, a final leaving parade was held in India, at which Lord Louis

Father and his men, India.

Mountbatten presented the regimental awards. Shortly afterwards, he and his regiment sailed from Bombay on 28 December 1948, being the last regiment to leave India. At home, he appeared to have become a restless man, like a caged tiger. Mother's social life and companions didn't fit the bill for him, and the post-Army environment in which he found himself was no longer a 'Man's world' – at the time, I was too young to be an ideal companion to him.

Father's sporting activities and Army trophies were as spectacular as his father's had been. Young as I was, I thought that sports might now help Father, as a means of absorbing his surplus energy. I did not tell him of my thoughts but recognised his yearnings. For my part, I tried to be a good listener instead, an assistant for his ideas and a small companion when he seemed to need it at times. Unfortunately, Mother, as always, was far too busy socialising or organizing the aged relatives who needed a considerable amount of care – and indeed doing a worthwhile job of it, while Jane packed her life with activities around her new school friends.

On a more positive note, one day we made an excursion in London which subsequently led to a new outlet for some of Father's energies. We had been skating at

Father receiving his presentation from Earl Mountbatten when leaving India in 1947.

Richmond ice rink, and as we returned to catch the bus, walking along the river, I could see many graceful boats skimming the water of the River Thames, travelling in all directions. I really did fancy the activity of rowing, suggesting this to Father. At this idea, he soon shook off some of the despondency and gloominess of spirits, and promised me we would take up rowing; for me this was really exciting.

That was the start of a series of trips to the Thames, when we frequently hired a rowing skiff. Father's job was to sit firmly in the stern of the boat, like a steady rock of ballast, and operate the rudder to steer us. I provided the manpower with the oars. While under his orders, and over time, I gradually increased my stroke speeds, and strength. We rowed regularly around Eel-Pie Island and back, while listening to his exciting tales on almost every occasion. I thought he was such a remarkable man, having lived a charmed life.

He had played his 'Sporting Chance' card so many times.

REAL RED BLOOD.

The journey to school, on my own for the first time, made me feel uneasy emotionally. Travelling without Jane felt such an enormous step to me – and somehow, the journey had transformed itself into an enormous distance to travel and to take such a long time. However, in reality, it was only about an hour by both bus and trolleybus into Hammersmith.

I became more at ease as soon as I recognised other children dressed in the same uniform, so I knew I'd arrive safely at school if I followed them. Since Jane had made friends the year before, she wasn't interested in being lumbered with a younger sister, telling me instead to stand on my own two feet. As you can imagine, the feeling of family rejection at that moment was quite acute. But always to the rescue, Father's advice to me, as I recalled from a previous occasion, was practical and helpful, 'Always smile in adversity and be polite to all. Politeness will often win the day. It gives you time to think silently out your next step. It will be up to you then.'

Spoken when I first started junior school, my father's words now reverberated in my head, as I started that first day at senior school in 1948. This was St. Paul's Girls' School in Brook Green, Hammersmith, an independent, well-known girls' school

St Paul's Girls' School.

in London, which survived the wartime bombing. It catered for approximately 500 pupils at that time, aged from twelve to eighteen.

The school first opened in 1904, having been founded by the Worshipful Company of Mercers. Originally, the Mercers was a trade association for general merchants in textiles, silks and velvets. It was an imposing building of red brick and yellow stone, of a beautiful design by the famous architect Gerald Horsley who was a founder member of the Art Workers' Guild many years before. I thought the building, inside and out, was truly magnificent, and I kept making small drawings when I could, of every corner that took my eye.

The wartime restrictions on purchases of materials and clothing, through the use of ration books (which ended only in 1949), no doubt had a bearing on the design of our uniforms. Unlike the earlier fashion of the times, we had no pleats in our tunics of navy blue, which reached floor level when kneeling. Blue-striped shirts with curved necklines, negating the need for ties, white socks and proper shoes finished off our outfits, with navy-blue trench coats and velour hats sporting the SPGS badge at the front. Off-white tunics and gym shoes were worn for all games. For our summer outfits, we were offered a simple choice of blue or pink dresses, fawn coats and straw hats.

Starting school.

Uniform wearing was strictly adhered to during my time at St. Paul's – however, there is now no longer a requirement for children to do so today. Actually, I was caught out badly on one occasion for not following the dress code when I turned up at school on a very hot day with no socks on. I was promptly instructed to go home to put them on. As you can imagine, this was a long, arduous round trip, but one which I managed eventually, returning to school to present myself to the teacher again, properly dressed.

Sports were a strong feature in the curriculum. Within the school grounds, there were tennis and netball courts, and nearby a sports field for cricket, lacrosse, and a running track, with white lines delineated for the different activities. This vast manicured field, regularly tended, smelled sweet and summery. Being a budding artist, I was always interested in shapes, colours and the form of various natural things, be it flora or fauna. I recall vividly that I laid down sometimes on the grass to see the various insects crawling in the grasses, or experience the joy of feeling the 'green carpet' on my face, smelling the short cut grass and mosses. I'd watch a bird pull out a hidden worm, while gaining a bird's eye view of the world. All these observations were added to my stored knowledge of lives, large or small, to be recalled later when needed as I was drawing or painting. However, the best venue for me was the swimming pool surrounded by changing cubicles, within the school perimeter, and I soon found my preferred sporting activity.

Two other departments also quickly gained my attention. The first was the vast music wing where about twenty practise rooms, with double-doors, lined the upper corridors above the orchestral room and the Singing Hall. The second was the top floor of the main building, a large and well equipped art room. For such a large building and with so many children, it was all remarkably quiet. Perhaps this was not so surprising because a strict rule of silence in all passageways was applied and enforced. This was especially the case along the main corridor which ran past the office occupied by the High Mistress, Miss Osborne, a willowy and a remote Headmistress with a hovering smile, and dark brown hair pulled back into a loose bun.

I found it difficult to acclimatise myself to such a spacious school. My independent spirit was often at variance with the rules

Miss Ainsworth my first form teacher.

set for the pupils, especially if I personally did not see the need for them. However, I liked my first teacher, Miss Ainsworth, who taught science and maths. She was a very tall, thin lady with her hair in a bun, often seen striding purposefully along the corridors in her white coat. She awoke in me a liking for the subject of maths as being so logical, even though I was still struggling with writing many things back to front.

At that age I had a passion for English and history, subjects which seemed to be full of good stories. I also had a passion and an attachment to one of the eighth formers, who looked just like Gordon Jackson, my favourite film star. Since all the senior girls at our midday meal time did table duty, I tried to be on her table when she was presiding over the youngest pupils, so I could secretly drool in her kindly glances.

I was not an ideal pupil. My newly-acquired skills in using my right hand, which was forced on me at junior school, caused me many reversing and spelling errors. The prospect of learning three new languages all but defeated me. However, it was decided in the end that Greek could be dropped, and after struggling a further term with Latin, it also disappeared, but I resolutely persevered with French throughout my time at school.

My English teacher, Miss Higginson, encouraged my imaginative outpourings, whether they were written back to front or not. As a result of this, I was motivated to work long hours for her to perfect the grammar lessons she set. She was probably in her mid-30s, mid-height and of shapely-built proportions, with well-kept wavy, auburn hair and kindly green eyes, which crinkled up provocatively when she smiled, but she never missed a trick.

As I moved up to the next school year, she remained my form teacher, as well as for English. She had come

Miss Higginson

from the North of England, recognised some of my northern difficulties, never criticised my slightly different accent compared to the west London area therefore, I found in her a kind of kindred spirit and humour – although she would have denied such a thing, if she'd ever been challenged. But I sensed in her a sympathetic, warm-hearted adult.

From time to time, I went missing from certain lessons. These were usually the ball games, which I tended to be a bit nervous of, having not quite mastered the skill of seeing or coping with a fast approaching ball in any game. On these occasions, I would usually be found in one of the practice rooms where I would be improving my piano or recorder playing. Practising the recorder had become important because I now played in the wind band, which I thoroughly enjoyed and thought was great fun.

My piano teacher, Miss Parfitt, with loose wisps of grey hair and an encouraging smile, had the patience of a saint, and a soft persuasive voice. She was cultured, with gentle manners and had great patience and understanding for her pupils. Once, she requested that I learn a piece of music; so that I could appreciate its rhythm, I asked if she would play it to me first. This she did, which I listened to carefully before going home to practice it several times over. When I returned to her the next week, I promptly played it from memory, without reading the score in front of me.

'You were supposed to learn to sight read it as you play.' she sighed sadly.

Music also played a large part in our general school life. Gustav Holst had been the music master in my mother's and Aunt Melene's day, who had composed the 'Planet Suite' amongst other well-known orchestral pieces. True to its tradition, we now had Herbert Howells, another famous composer, who led us in choral singing and orchestral pieces, although we were led by Miss Day for our daily singing. She was also a marvellous organist, and as the school boasted a beautiful full-sized organ in the main hall, we were regaled with various recitals from many talented and famous players, who came at regular intervals.

I often spent time in the Art Room, with its high vaulted ceiling and large curved windows, under the auspices of tall, grey-eyed Miss Pasmore, who was a very outspoken lady. She had curved lips, was large-busted, and was always flamboyantly dressed in a flowery smock, with a leather belt around her ample waist to curtail the material of her overall from escaping.

She was an inspired painter, who shared a house with an equally colourful companion, also a painter. Her work was of a soft, sympathetic nature. During my spare time, I was always made welcome in the art department, where I spent hours experimenting with different paints and producing ever larger canvasses. I really flourished in this atmosphere, not least because I felt very comfortable with her.

She was keen for her pupils to meet a painter, Victor Pasmore whose work is now exhibited permanently at the Tate Gallery. I have no idea whether he was perhaps a relative of hers. In any event, he gave us a series of lessons in different forms of abstract art, which he was keen to advocate, and which had the benefit of raising a sense of 'artistic adventure' for this type of art.

About a third of the pupils at the school were of the Jewish faith, and for their daily assembly, they used the Singing Hall, while the remainder of the pupils gathered in the Main Hall for a general Christian assembly.

Victor Pasmore.

Once it had been established which pupils, including myself, had not been confirmed, we were allocated time with an appropriate teacher to prepare for the Confirmation ceremony. White dresses were ordered for everyone. A few weeks later about 45 of us duly attended our Confirmation, on the appointed day at St Paul's Cathedral, all remarkably alike in white dresses and veils. My only recollections from this time was the beautiful music that was played, which filled the interior of this impressive building, and the daylight, which seeped through the many windows in long, slanting shafts. Its beams highlighted the dust particles slowly floating in the sunshine and capturing the movements of a couple of pale moths gyrating in and out of the light.

Of my three godparents, Wendy Strachan had been killed by the Japanese in

Singapore, and Uncle John, the second one, was still abroad in the army. Therefore, my remaining godparent, my Aunt Daisy Stuart attended the ceremony, and presented me with a bible. In it was ascribed a small poem, that I still value:

My godmother, Aunt Daisy.

> *One ship sails East, another sails West,*
> *With the self-same wind that blows,*
> *It's the set of the sails and not the gales,*
> *That determine the way she goes.*

At the conclusion of the ceremony, we came out of the cathedral into bright sunshine. I was keen to skip down Fleet Street and make a surprise visit to Lil and Jeannie, therefore I bought a posy of flowers from the old lady sitting on the steps of the church as a present. My mother and Aunt Daisy came too. At the café, it was a pleasure to see them all again, so happy, after such a long time. Also, I saw there were now four sleek, multi-coloured cats in residence, basking in their happiness and advancing age.

I introduced my mother and godmother then played with the little girl, now about four years old, who was thriving with both her parents. Her father's memory was still not perfect, but it didn't seem to bother him since returning home from the army hospital. He now worked for Lil, helping to expand the business. Jeannie and he were very happy. Since they had become part of my life, I often went to visit them.

My sister Jane, who was strikingly good looking, with her brown hair and bright blue eyes in an oval face, was growing into a lanky teenager. Now she appeared to have an adult worldliness about her, far above her age. She experimented secretively with make-up, while using me to model it for her, and seemed to know everything. Make-up and stockings were definitely only for those who had finally left school – or who attended dancing classes. Academically she was bright and her school work not very taxing to her, so she was always reaching for higher aspirations. She involved herself in the Red Cross detachment, a branch of which was based at St Paul's School. Before long she was a group leader, and suddenly for the first time, I seemed to be needed by my imperious and bossy sister, as a useful member of her detachment.

The question arose about competing for the Limerick Cup, and our St Paul's team of Red Cross First-Aiders was picked out of a large group of girls, to represent our school and we were both selected. Each team was given 'a situation', three 'bodies', suitably made up with fake blisters and fake blood, to represent horrific injuries, a storyline, and suitable props lying around, such as 'in a wood with branches laid about'. This all needed first class play acting and was fun until something happened for real. Suddenly one of the 'bodies' was lying in a pool of real red blood.

Our team had been given a 'kitchen situation', with the usual paraphernalia found in any domestic household. Unfortunately one of the female actors, intending to be one of the 'bodies', had dropped a sharp kitchen knife onto her leg, which had pierced her limb, and as a result a small piece of flesh had been sliced off. In addition, the knife had hit a blood vessel, out of which poured (as I recall thinking at the time) 'real, sticky, red blood.' Without a moment's hesitation, as team leader Jane went into an overdrive of activity, deployed her team correctly, raised the limb, and applied firm pressure while sending for a genuine doctor to attend the competition. We then continued to deal with all the 'fake' injuries as well. Her quick thinking was applauded, the real patient was removed in an ambulance, and we won the Limerick Cup that year.

I admired her greatly and indeed loved her, but was always kept at arm's length by her. I was never able to fully understand such aloof and indifferent behaviour, nor fathom out whether I had annoyed her with some misdemeanour which I had overlooked.

Jane and I as Red Cross nurses.

In London, the Red Cross detachments were called into real service around the city. During one evening, I was sent with a colleague to the London Palladium to man the first-aid post there. We enjoyed this type of posting, because we were able to see some great shows. On this particular occasion, Jo Stafford, a well-known American singer, along with a large American supporting ensemble, sang 'Shrimp Boats are a-coming' and 'Jambalaya'. These were extremely popular shows which enjoyed riotous audience participation and encouragement, who demanded encore after encore.

As often happens, the unexpected occurred. Amid the uproar of the show, a large, round-faced and decidedly pallid man slumped into our First Aid room. He sat on the floor moaning with stomach ache. Using our trained routine, we asked the usual questions about what he had eaten that day and where he had been.

'A've bin eatin' your goddam English food all day, cos there ain't no decent steaks anywhere around here – and A've got a bad head, so A've been chewin' Aspirins.' We then inquired 'How many?'

'A don't know. Dammit. A've been chewin' 'em all day long. Don't seem to help, anyways.' with that statement he was promptly and violently sick. That was a lesson in how not to poison oneself with excessive doses of medicines.

Somewhat novel, another outing for the Red Cross was to the women's prison, at Holloway. This prison was within our area and required Red Cross services from time to time. For example, an inmate might have needed to go to the maternity wing of Hammersmith Hospital, therefore we would be required to accompany her as a precautionary presence.

Since nursing staff were often in short supply at that time, during such cases the ambulance staff first picked up two of us, then a warder, then the prisoner. As always, we waited at the hospital until the prisoner's treatment was complete, and then would accompany them back to the jail. I really hated this part of the Red Cross work, because the prison smelled so dreadful, and the odours of the place clung to all our clothes for days afterwards.

One visit I really enjoyed was to the Chiswick Empire Theatre First Aid post in West London. I remembered the occasion when Joseph Locke, a well-known and popular tenor from Ireland was entertaining for a week and we were very well looked after there. Joseph Locke was a genial host to his friends and all the theatre staff alike, and at the close of each show, he would throw a party for everyone to attend. He would sing all our requests with gusto, and was such a popular tenor amongst my peer group.

At my age we all had autograph books, and I had been instructed to get him to sign a small pile for my friends. The patient man did not seem to mind too much, making jokes about having many absent fans. He entertained us after the show with more Irish stories and songs, which were well known enough for us to join in.

Joseph Locke.

This made me remember nostalgically my time in Ireland, and now, when looking in my autograph book years later, I am reminded of those happy moments in Chiswick. It is also full of the signatures of friends that I made during the years I spent at school, and for me, they were happy times.

My spells spent with the Red Cross served as a bridge between my childhood and a way into adult life. Later on in 1951, during the King's birthday on Horseguard's Parade, I felt that I was moving into adult reality, as Jane and I marched with the Red Cross contingent in the parade.

Jane and I in the Horseguard's Parade, 1951.

Above Bowerswood from the driveway and below as seen from the woods.

Cairo painted in the 1930s by my Aunt Gee.

Above the view from the flat window of Skipton Hall Farm and below my painting of Ettersgill Farm, Teesdale, County Durham.

ETTERSGILL. TEESDALE VALLEY, DURHAM   W.STUAR

We moved to Isleworth — Travelling
daily on the trollybus to school —
½ hours! SMOG was awful
winter — but the Mystery of
GREAT — A WORLD CLOTHED IN GREY!
I promptly had appendisitis, sat in the garden sunshine
and painted my new home
with the same
enthusiasms.
sat on the box
at the landing
window, and
peered at the
rose coloured
world or
perhaps the blue one
realizing the totally different
gardens
was being
offered,
view
that was
even
more
magical
during
the snowy
winter!

ORIGINAL
DRAWING WITH PEN & INK OF OUR BASEMENT KITCHEN.
(REDUCED IN SIZE)

TIGER LILY SMUTS
MY BROWN TABBY

A page from Wendy's notebook when she lived in London.

The field in front of Warlaby Lodge and below, High Force, Teesdale, County Durham.

Above facing the entrance to Bowerswood and below a painting of Letton.

Steps to the garden in Holland Park, London.

Who Am I?

I asked six people this question, for their views!

My cousin Wendy is my last remaining contemporary relative from my Mother's side of the family. Like my Mother she is a very strong and forceful person and not someone to be trifled with. She has always been ultra busy, is very personable and is always helpful of others. She seems to have done everything and been everywhere. A true larger than life character. I like my cousin.

Jeremy Barnes.

For me, Wendy is an inspirational friend- full of life and schemes for the future! She is always willing to give new things a try and usually masters them very quickly. Through her life, she has acquired a range of valuable skills (cooking for large numbers, painting in various medium, sailing and she proved to be an excellent shot when she tried that). These are not necessarily reflected in formal qualifications- but so what! She is also excellent at getting others inspired and to try new things too. She makes classes fun and unexpected.

Mary-Ann Renton

I met Wendy Mary nearly 60 years ago and we have been in touch ever since, but it had been 15 years since we have actually met again, last month.
I was pleased to find her unchanged from the girl who helped me grow up. We sang in the Church Choir together and spent our teens laughing, singing, dancing, acting and generally "hanging out". She was then and still is a very feisty lass of strong opinions that she fiercely defends, but is ready to listen to the others point, and admit to being wrong, if so persuaded by well-argued facts.
She has always been a very hard worker, doing some very physically demanding jobs but still finding the time for her creative talents to find their outlet. She is a wonderful arcivist, unkind persons might say horder, of her family records which she has used in research for a book.
Many of her pictures have hung on my walls and my Autograph Book from 1952 has a very early pencil drawing of hers. I look forward with interest to this new stage for her, and admire her dedication.

Anthea Hammond

Written by a friend who imagined he is speaking from inside Wendy's head.
Wendy

"Who am I? That's a difficult one.

Like most people, I'm never sure. Easier to tell you what I've done and what life has done to me rather than say who I am. In fact I've done lots.
I've raised four boys, in hard times, I've sailed boats, climbed to the topsail of a three-masted schooner - and gained a First Mate's ticket. I've made ceramics and painted pictures, that others have thought lovely enough to buy and - oh yes, - I've written a book about my Gt. Gt. Grandfather's trip with his horse and trap.

At times, I've loved too hard and had my heart broken and - had some nasty illnesses. But parachuting, caving, ballooning etc and other crazy sports are great as pick-me-ups.
I'm frugal. I make do and mend. I like to spend least on essentials and most on desirables - so don't be surprised if you see me in charity shops rifling through the 'ethnic' skirts! Anything colourful !

Some folk think I'm a bit of a tough nut, that I can be self-centred and opinionated. In fact, the 'tough nut' bit is just a front and is my first line of defence against a sometimes harsh world. What they don't see is the thin shell that cracks easily or the heart that hurts quickly.
Inside, like everyone I suppose, I look for recognition, praise, satisfaction if possible, and if I'm really lucky, love.

Inside here, there's an eighteen year old still waiting to find out who she is."

As always,
Your long-standing friend, with love

Mike
September 2008

From Edward.

Wendy – my love.
Highly talented and –extremely stubborn.
Somewhat untidy by my standards, but gets engrossed in things.
Kind and tolerant. A good listener.
Quite fearless and very capable of leading from the front.
Very determined to see things through.
Bright nature, and likes bright clothes.
Highly motivated; resents getting older.

I have known my friend Wendy for many years. A positive & energetic character with a great zest for life. She is interested and notices everything. She has a creative & incisive mind, and possesses that rare combination of persuasive abilities, intellect and organisational skills necessary to carry projects through to completion to a very high standard.
Tom Strickland

In the woods at Bowerswood.

The tennis court at Bowerswood and below inside Bowerswood.
Opposite the old yard and coach house and a painting from my first seaside holiday.

Our first
"Holiday by
the Sea"

W. M. Stuchl 1948

Lookinjg through the orchard. .

THOSE MEN IN BLUE

Our house in Isleworth was quite close to the Royal Military School of Music, at Kneller Hall in Whitton. This meant that, in summer in our garden, we could regularly hear music played by the military bands, which floated eerily on the wind.

There were monthly concerts held in the grounds, with 250 brass bandsmen playing on the great bandstand, surrounded by many flagpoles, their pennants fluttering in the evening breeze.

As the performance progressed and the night became colder and darker, hundreds of coloured lights gradually shone out, highlighting the crescendo of the finale, which was always a dramatic piece of music.

Kneller Hall, Twickenham.

Having spent his life in the army as a Sergeant Tutor Bandsman, Jim knew many people at the School of Music, and was keen to introduce us to his friends. At the first opportunity to do so, the whole family attended. Father was pleased to come with us, and of course, my mother never missed an opportunity to be sociable. We sat on some of the semi-circular arrangement of chairs, covered ourselves with rugs that we had brought, and watched the largest military band, resplendent in their deep navy uniforms decorated with medal ribbons, playing every kind of brass instrument that I had ever seen.

The concert reminded us of the disastrous finale in the King Lane Theatre in Clitheroe some years previously, especially when they started to play the same piece, the '1812 Overture', but fortunately this time it was different. The fireworks and rockets were managed to great artistic effect behind the very large bandstand, and created a magical effect. We came away from the concert in an elated mood.

Afterwards, the adults wished to go to the bar, but because this was run as a military establishment, the choices were clearly between the Officers' Mess, and the

Kneller Hall Bandstand.

Sergeant's Mess. Father had been chatting happily to some of the colourfully-clad officers, two of whom he knew from his regiment, and we started to drift into the Officers' Mess, which was well laid out for supper, when I realised that my mother had got herself into an argument with Jim.

'I can't go in there. I'll just slip into

the Sergeants' Mess for a pint. You go on with Goff.' he said, trying to placate my mother, who said, 'Then I'll go with you.' Mother had not understood that neither man was really welcome or even allowed in each other's bar.

To his credit Jim realised the awkward situation Mother was creating, and hastily said, 'I must just see Peter Dyson about something before he leaves.' And calling out a time of departure to be at the gates, he melted into the crowds. Mother had to follow the rest of us, but did not let the matter rest about the injustice of it all. I was sad for Jim, but at my age, I did not fully understand the intricacies of the social order of the army.

When we arrived home later, a terrible row ensued with Mother demanding the right to choose her friends, while Father was exasperated. 'Don't you ever put me into such a humiliating situation again.' I was beginning to understand certain social distinctions, and as the row continued, I became increasingly aware of the differences between Jim and my father.

At the start of the war, he had originally given Jim a brief, maybe unwisely, to help Mother, Jane and myself by making sure that we found suitable accommodation when we moved to London. Father was anxious to ensure that we were being looked after if he failed to return from the conflict. As a serving soldier Father had no option but to go with his regiment to war, but now he disliked the fact that someone else had seemingly moved in on his home territory.

Jim was kind, reliable, resourceful, musical and hardworking. I liked him greatly for these qualities, having known him since I was a small child when we moved to Clitheroe. But I also loved my father with an instinctive, burning passion, fostered from birth. I knew that he had asked Jim himself to watch over us all during that troubled time. But Jane hated Jim, because he had often sided with Mother when my sister had needed chastising. Jane had a strong will, and resented Mother's guidance as she grew up. This present row was a great opportunity for Jane to vent her feelings. 'Throw him out of our house. He doesn't belong here.' she shouted with venomous glee.

At this point, Mother said 'No, no. Just calm down. We'll all go to bed, and discuss this tomorrow.' The immediate row subsided, everybody disappeared into their rooms, and the matter was shelved for some weeks, no doubt while a lot of private discussions took place. I realised that my mother had great problems with her divided loyalties, and this subject, bubbling beneath the surface of normality, would explode again at a later date, and indeed it did, as will be explained.

Jane was the prime mover in some of our activities in the Girl Guides. Both of us had joined the Isleworth troop when we moved to the area, and Jane soon graduated to a position of responsibility. We were the smartest dressed, and best drilled Girl Guides for Sunday Church Parades, and since she was our patrol leader, we gained the most badges, which we diligently worked hard to acquire.

Summer holidays were eagerly longed for, therefore it was not surprising that the summer camp was much discussed, with plans and preparations made weeks beforehand for this exciting trip to what for us was a completely foreign country too – Wales. Four of the male workers from the church were accompanying us, as well as the Guide leaders and Jane was keen for us both to go.

Since our plan was to travel to Kilgetty, near Tenby in Wales, everything which we needed was eventually loaded onto a small bus (or charabanc, as they were often called then), along with our personal kitbags. In addition, our bus was accompanied by an old lorry loaded with the somewhat heavy, old-fashioned circular, canvas tents and latrine cubicles. It was as well that we took some strong men with us, because all these items were quite unmanageable for us small girls. The cooking facilities were planned to be in a central tent, used also for communal activities, therefore boxes of stores were required to be loaded along with cooking stoves.

When we were Girl Guides.

We arrived on a very hot August day, in the pretty hamlet of Kilgetty. It overlooked the nearby sea with its sandy beach peeping through the trees, although it was quite difficult to see due to the extreme heat which was creating a mirage of wavy images over the tarmac road. We arrived at our destination, a picturesque medium-sized Welsh farm, all whitewashed and gleaming in the sunshine. Driving through the small farm yard, surrounded by the dairy, cow byres and large barns, we saw hens wandering through a steaming midden, and an assortment of other animals peering at us from their pens. We were guided into a field full of meadow flowers and buttercups, humming with the sound of many insects and attracting colourful butterflies. The farmer had removed the cows from our camping field and drive them into another hillier field, before allowing us to enter.

We soon realised the necessity of watching where we walked, and needed to choose carefully the positions for our tents. These were rather old, circular army issue. It was a great relief that we eventually worked out how to erect them with their central pole. All the groundsheets and sleeping bags were arranged like petals on a daisy, with feet to the central pole. Following the same theme, the six circular tents were arranged around the camp fire. We were now set up for our holiday, with instructions to collect milk, bread and eggs daily from the farm in the mornings.

We all went down the cliff path to the shore to play, and swim in the surprisingly warm August sea. By now cleaner, dryer and refreshed, we trooped back for our meal, which had been prepared by the guiders, having erected the cooking tent. They had also built a large camp fire, around which we all sat, happily singing camp fire songs. We learned how to make 'Dampers' made from flour, salt and baking powder, with the resultant dough being wound round sticks and shoved into the hot embers, making a kind of primitive bread, often somewhat burned and tasting of smoke, but delicious. The evening was hot with a rare stillness, the sea shimmering over its glassy surface, and nothing stirred. We all retired to our tents to sleep away the excitements of the day. Along with the others, I fell into a deep sleep – but this summer idyll was not to last.

During the night I was awoken, as the sky rumbled and grumbled amidst the growing thunder clouds which crowded over the heavens, darkening the world. Sudden flashes of lightning lit the scene, to be extinguished again instantly, followed by thunderous crashes which grew ever closer and ever more frequent, until the flashes and crashes seemed to be immediately above us in tandem. This terrifying thunderstorm was now added to by heavy rain lashing down relentlessly on our tent roof, running under the tent sides, and in danger of wetting all our gear.

By now we were all huddled into the middle of the tent, nervous and worried, so we hastily gathered up our sleeping bags and belongings and wrapped them in our groundsheets, piling our bundles in a big heap in the middle beside the central tent-pole. We also put on our boots and extra clothes under our raincoats for warmth, and hoped that the storm would soon end – but worse was to come.

Camp fire cooking as Girl Guides.

Suddenly amidst the fearful noise, there was a whooshing sound as the tent pole broke through the material at the apex of our tent and the whole canvas descended upon us in one graceful movement, like the final deathly moments of the full skirted ballerina in *Swan Lake*, trapping all six of us and the bags into one great heap, while the rain continued to pound us relentlessly from outside. We were very firmly trapped and all so stunned by this turn of events, that we lay quiet, after ascertaining that nobody was hurt, until the rain finally eased off. Then we heard shouts from outside.

Help was now at hand because farmer Jones had been out to inspect the damage around the farm from the storm. After a general consultation with him, we were led with our belongings, into the cow-byre, now swept out, hosed down and liberally scattered with straw, to continue sleeping till daybreak, when the cows returned to be milked. Our personal gear was hastily stored in the provender shed.

We assumed that this was to be our 'tent' for the next week which needed to be swept out, hosed down and re-laid with straw every night. So our tightly arranged campsite was somewhat split. Nevertheless, we settled down for the remainder of the night believing that our camping arrangements would be resolved in the morning without any further mishap, but there was still more excitement to follow.

The bell tent at the camp.

The next day did not quite go as planned. A large tree had been struck by the lightning so the farmer enlisted everybody's help to clear branches and create piles of wood, which benefitted our camp fire greatly. Some of the activities had been so disrupted that we had greater freedom to occupy our free time. The damaged cooking tent needed to be repaired, and I offered to help Jane with

140

it. She declined the offer and suggested that I go and play with my friend Mollie, a girl who was a couple of years older than me. She wanted to explore the animals, the farm machinery, the poultry house and the barns which offered new experiences.

Together, we climbed about in the new cut bales of hay, built a den for ourselves in the warm barn, drank the pop that we had brought in our pockets, and finally, after such a busy and disturbed previous night, in a relaxed state, fell into a deep sleep. Suddenly,

The hay barn at Kilgetty.

we awoke simultaneously, cold and disorientated, and saw circular beams of light, darting around the barn roof, and flashing along the walls. Soon we heard shouts in a strange language. Then our names were called, as a ladder was placed against the hay stacks, and a head poked above the rim of our den.

'I've found them. Quite safe up here, they are. Half asleep, I should say.' With that information given to the searchers below, the man climbed up to our level. He was a policeman – a man in blue – and there were a lot more like him down below.

'We thought you had wandered onto the beach. The sea is so wild after the storm, and very high. We've been searching for hours, fifteen of us, look you. It's two o'clock in the middle of the night, and very dark. You're both very cold, are you thirsty or hungry? Don't you be frightened now,' and the good policeman, sweating in his blue uniform, kept up this running patter as he helped both of us down to ground level.

We soon found out that since we had been missing for our evening meal, the Guide leaders reported this to the farmer. He informed the police as well as the neighbouring farms who, fearing the worst for us quickly organised a thorough search, while our group from the deflated tent were finally escorted to the cow-byre and put to bed there for a second night. Subsequently, farmer Jones had cleared an area in the hay barn for the use of our small nomadic group, very pleased that he wouldn't have to move his cows yet again.

The following day there was an inquiry into our behaviour, as well as a long lecture on being 'now at a suitable age of responsibility,' how we should make up for our sins, and the enormous costs to the police force for searching for two very thoughtless little girls. Being a patrol leader, Jane was censured for not watching out for her younger sister. I did not feel that I'd done anything wrong, except fall asleep, but apologised frequently for having done this, and vowed that I would never get into trouble again. What a vain hope.

But I will always remember seeing all those men in blue, who came searching for us through the night.

ROYALTY

While I was getting to grips with the first term at my new school in Hammersmith, I was greatly saddened by the death of my gentle Aunt Mary in October 1948. She had lived in Malaya, (now called Malaysia) in the northern part of the Malay States with Uncle Will, until his retirement as the first headmaster of the Malay College, Kuala Kangsar, in Perak, (MCKK) from 1905 until 1918, after which they returned home to England. She was widowed in 1939, and subsequently lived either with Grandfather or at our house in London just before her death.

Aunt Mary Hargreaves

She had been an avid painter, and I learned a great deal from her, watching her devise 'paintings' in silks or wools, because she excelled at embroidery, in addition to her skill at conventional painting. She had been a power of good, being a stabilising influence on my mother, recognising the similarities of temperament to her long-departed eldest sister Flo-Jane. Both had terrible tempers, but my mother's flared up uncontrollably at times, especially when other people disagreed with her.

Aunt Mary's embroidery of Bowerswood.

One of the most remembered occasions in our family concerned playing Scrabble. My father chose to use the word 'Id', which did not appear in Mother's *Pocket Oxford Dictionary*. We were obliged to consult this for reference in disputes. All six players on that day were happy with 'Id' except Mother, who consulted her dictionary. As anticipated, 'Id' did not appear and therefore did not exist. My father laughingly insisted he was correct. However, my mother, with great fury and explosion of temper, put both hands underneath the board, and with an upward thrust, propelled the board to the ceiling of the sitting-room. This action smashed the board, and scattered the little squares everywhere including behind the heavy Victorian furniture. It was many weeks before all the tiles were recovered. Subsequently that moment was always referred to as the 'Id incident', and my father was always able to laugh about it.

After a while Father decided to give up the specialist delivery service at London

Airport and looked for another job which suited his interests and intellect. He was fortunate to find work as an experimental scientist at the Thorn EMI laboratories outside London. He thoroughly enjoyed his new job and position in the design and research of electrical and electronic equipment. He told me that one of his jobs was to test to destruction certain pieces of equipment, then remodel them to solve the problems. After a short while, he became established in the business's internal education programmes, teaching the younger men, and passing on some of his accumulated knowledge. In fact he worked there until well into his eighties (by then, only part-time), a period of over 30 years.

Jim stayed at the delivery department of London Airport for a while. As a result of the special deliveries, which arrived from all over the world, on one occasion he had some unusual items to be delivered to the Shepperton Film Studios, situated not far from our house. He made regular runs to the studios at one time, and noticed that the film set for *An Ideal Husband* was being constructed. The speed with which it was progressing made it a 'must' to be seen before it was dismantled. Mother was keen to see if Jim could organise a visit to observe the progress of the making of this Oscar Wilde film, which was being produced by Alexander Korda in 1947.

There had already been a one day strike by the hairdressers union at the studio due to the use of a Swedish hairdresser for Paulette Goddard. Apparently, the hairdresser possessed a special Home Office visa, but unfortunately she was not a British member of the Hairdressers' Union. The unions seemed to be very powerful then.

Glynis Johns in 'The Ideal Husband'

Finally, our day arrived to visit the studios to watch the film makers in action. Decorated with appropriate visitors passes, pinned to our coats, we were delighted to watch all the carefully arranged shots of the actors and actresses – which included Michael Wilding and Glynis Johns arguing with Paulette Goddard, in a lavishly-built and fitted-out make-believe nineteenth century home – with no back to it. In another scene, the characters then reorganised themselves in a different part of the building, which included the front section of a sweeping staircase down to a ballroom. Now filled with elegant dancers, the ballroom was propped up with planks of wood, which of course were out of sight of the cameras. Now the cameras rolled to record the ladies sweeping down the staircase to join the dance below, although this action was repeated a dozen times until being told 'OK.' after which they all quickly melted away.

I was intrigued by the creative aspect of all this make-believe. At the filming interval, having accompanied Mother to speak with the actors, I wandered off to explore the backs of the sets, first looking at what the audience might see, then finding out how it was actually made at the back. Part of the house interior contained a table with props, to be carried on to the set, spilling posies and button holes onto the floor. I picked up one of the beautifully made silk roses, and stuck it into my broach.

When it was time to leave, and as was often the case, Mother discovered that I was missing. Fortunately for me, it was not for long and I was found riding with the cameraman on a bogey, running smoothly on a track in the floor. He had been proudly showing me the camera eye-view of a film set. In those days, films were completed very quickly, and in a record time of 66 days, I believe, for this film. Once the film was released, I went to see it several times, knowing that I had walked up and down those few stairs. I kept the silk rose for many years afterwards.

According to the newspaper reports, when Princess Elizabeth and Prince Philip were married, the producer of the Shepperton Studios films, Alexander Korda, lent them a selection of his very own guards' nineteenth century uniforms, which had been used on one of his film sets. The reason behind this was that the original Palace uniforms had been destroyed by the bombing during the war, apparently having been moth-balled and stored in a 'safe place'. Now the Royal Guards were able to be fitted out correctly to accompany the Princess's golden coach during the wedding procession.

My world of well-loved elderly relatives was beginning to be reduced during the late forties and early fifties. Aunt Caroline had passed away at the end of the war, and the two travelling Cairo-dwellers, Aunt Nona and Aunt Gee, in their eighties, now very wizened and brown, only came home in the summer months when the temperature in Cairo became unbearable. Nevertheless, I now began to meet other members of our extended family, who all lived around London. Aunt Mary's son Tony, his wife Libsie, and daughter Janet Hargreaves, my cousin, approximately Jane's age, who eventually became an actress, in London theatres and on television, were often visitors at our house.

Then there was Mother's brother-in-law, Col. Jim O'-Sullivan, almost a generation older, who had married Mother's now dead eldest sister. Mother took us to see him for a meal one day at a big establishment, the Regent Palace Hotel, Piccadilly. Here he bought us all a filling lunch, with brandy and Turkish coffee to round off the meal, but became very annoyed when Jane and I refused both the coffee and alcohol. He was a large, portly man with a droopy moustache, full of self-importance, had served in the Indian Army in the First World War, and talked exclusively about his past deeds.

Uncle Jim O'Sullivan

When we got up to leave, he pinched my bottom. This indignity made me blush, and also hurt. From that moment on, I decided to dislike him intensely, despite the fact that he was my uncle, and refused ever to see him again.

My mother's only proper brother, Stephen, (referred to in the family as the Wicked Uncle Stephen) was an accountant who had developed a reputation which went before him. During the war, he had returned from Argentina at the age of forty, to make his contribution as a recruitment officer. Once the war was over, he retired into civilian life again as an accountant, and lived for a while in Highgate, North London, with Auntie Vera. My father said he was a villain. He was – this will be explained in a subsequent chapter.

The next influence in my young life was my aunt Daisy Stuart, my godmother, who truly behaved like a fairy godmother. Born in the 1870s and christened Maud Erinvine, she was my grandfather Stuart's youngest sister, one of eight siblings. Aunt Daisy explained to me the reason behind her strange name, which started while she was young. Apparently, as a girl she had looked at everyone with large, soulful brown eyes, like the Jersey cow named Daisy in the pasture. So thereafter, her teasing brothers called her Daisy.

Great aunt Daisy Stuart.

She had been a keen sportswoman all her life, becoming the Northern Ireland Women's Golfing Champion several years running. But when the First World War put an end to many peacetime pursuits, she chose to join a group of ladies of independent means who helped run Lord Roberts Workshops for disabled soldiers and sailors who had returned from the First World War seriously injured. With no prospect of any job, many men were unable to return to their peacetime activities, due to blindness or amputations.

These workshops had been started by Field Marshall Lord Roberts VC, who campaigned tirelessly to do more for the disabled ex-servicemen. Following his death in 1914 whilst visiting the troops in France, the movement was named after him. I became aware of there being at least 11 workshops around the country. The articles produced at these establishments were then sold in Knightsbridge in a large showroom, opened for a month every year, and labelled 'The Lord Robert's Workshops'.

Through Aunt Daisy, Mother and I were asked for our services for a number of weeks every year. I volunteered my time for three weeks in the summer, to man the stalls and help generally in the large showroom, where handmade items were displayed for sale. Basket making, small furniture, waxed flowers, jewellery making, and colourful paintings on stones as paperweights were a few of the items which caught my eye. As a teenager, life was always exciting, and I was continually full of conversation, wishing to chat to anyone who would talk to me.

While at the showroom, I went off to inspect the brightly-coloured toys on the neighbouring table, and then saw the little tables with lamps, piled up on the next one, all so beautifully made. Aunt Daisy and Miss Cadogan were in charge of the needlecraft tables, with items such as sewing kits, teapot covers, embroidered table-cloths, and decorated oven gloves. The workshops enterprise proved to be very worthwhile, especially because the rich and famous gladly attended and supported financially this venture, clearing the shop of goods by the end of the three weeks.

I was soon called to order from wandering around. 'We are expecting Royalty today, so you must not speak unless spoken to, but if you do, curtsey neatly and say "Yes, Ma'am or No, Ma'am", and offer no other thoughts of your own.'

My dear Aunt Daisy spoke firmly, and because she had put a lot of trust in me, I was determined not to let her down. The Royal family were always keen to support such good causes, so I was excited to see who was coming, what they intended to buy, and I waited, hopping from foot to foot – I could not stay still through my excitement.

'Stand exactly still, or I shall have to put you in the store room.' Miss Cadogan had less patience with children than my aunt.

Londoners always seem to have a sixth sense of impending action. There was a fair-sized crowd standing on the Brompton Road, pressing their noses to the windows, as a cavalcade of royal cars glided to a standstill, carrying chauffeurs, detectives, ladies-in-waiting, and at last the Royal party, who stepped out onto the pavement.

First to alight was Queen Elizabeth in a pale blue dress with her coat edged in fur, to match her fur trimmed tilting hat, then her two daughters, the Princesses Elizabeth and Margaret Rose, and finally the old Queen Mary, widow of George V and now about 81 years of age. (George VI was otherwise engaged doing 'kingly things', according to Miss Cadogan.)

Daisy Stuart and Mother with the Dowager Queen Mary.

The Princesses were all dressed in the latest 'New Look' fashions, with hats and gloves to match, while the old Queen Mary (sometimes known as Queen May of Teck colloquially to the older generation), walking with a silver stick, wore her usual style of Toque, topping white curly hair, with many rows of real pearls adorning her neck and bosom below, but now hidden by her fur collar. I tried not to stare at her too much.

The staff were lined up, and then duly presented to the Royal party. This included my mother, and I had the pleasure of being introduced as Miss Stuart's young niece, during which time I smiled at them all and curtseyed neatly when secretly being poked by Aunt Daisy to do so.

'She is a very pretty child, and helpful to you, I hope?' said the old Queen, without offering to shake my hand, or seemingly to look at me as I stood almost behind Aunt Daisy and beside the photographer.

Aunt Daisy and Mother with The Queen and Princess Margaret.

I picked up a little needle case to fiddle with, to cover my nervousness. The visitors walked round every table, admiring all the work, and handed over items which they wished to buy, to their ladies-in-waiting. I was told that Royalty never carried money. Princess Margaret Rose, the youngest member of the party, wandered over to me, inquired my name and asked if I was enjoying the day. I managed to curtsey, and answered her questions, but forgot the Ma'am bit.

'What have you in your hand? That is a very pretty embroidery with the forget-me-nots. Can you sew?' she asked, inspecting the needle case I was holding.

Without further invitation, I told her all about Aunt Mary's work of embroidered pictures, and how beautiful I thought they were. I was just getting into the description of her work, but before my conversation progressed any further Mother intervened, and took me to attend to other matters. At the end of our visit when the last car had pulled away, Miss Cadogan came over to thank me for behaving so well and helping during the day, after which she gave me a small parcel.

'Her Royal Highness, Princess Margaret, wished me to give you this little gift she has picked out for you, as a memento of the day.' And so I have the little needle case with forget-me-nots for use even now, because I still enjoy doing sewing and embroidery. I am also very proud of the fact that Aunt Daisy was recognised for her long years of voluntary work for the disabled, by being awarded the OBE when in her nineties.

THE WISDOM OF SOLOMON

In 1947 when Princess Elizabeth married her sweetheart Lt. Philip Mountbatten, it was an occasion of great interest to the post-war public. For the first time, those who were rich or lucky enough to own the new-fangled contraption called a 'television' were among the privileged few to watch part of the ceremony live inside Westminster Abbey, albeit in black and white.

In all probability, the viewers saw far more than the cheering crowds who lined the route to the abbey, or indeed the chosen audience inside. Therefore, when I was able to watch this piece of history in the making, on the newsreel at our cinema later in the evening, I felt quite excited to be able to experience the occasion.

In the early 1950s television sets had, by modern standards, screens which were barely larger than a large book. They were black and white, often not easy to tune, and produced extraordinary hues if set up badly. Not having a television at home for many years did not pose any particular problem because newsreels at the cinema served the same purpose, therefore our weekly visits kept us fully informed and up to date of all current affairs from the last seven days, as well as the latest news about well-known film stars of the day. This reminds me of one occasion at the cinema I shall not forget...

During one holiday, I was short of pocket money, therefore took a job at the Mogden Nurseries, where hundreds of chrysanthemums were grown. They varied so dramatically with in-curving, out-curving and flat petals crying out for attention with large, small, spray and pom-pom varieties, that it was easy to see why so many casual staff were needed to disbud the unwanted flowers at the right stage. There were several permanent staff of varying ages, but also some school students like myself, all cheerful and friendly.

One young man, Dan, who had now just left school and pleased to be earning a living took a shine to me. When he arranged an outing to the cinema (or the Pictures or The Flicks, as it was sometimes called, but never the American term Movies) for the following week he offered to pay for my ticket.

'Bring your friend, and I'll bring Mike.' Dan said, but since I was only young, Father was uncertain about letting me out on my own to meet up in Hounslow for this event, especially when I mentioned a keen young man. The impasse was overcome by agreeing to take my friend Anthea with me, and that we would go together on the bus.

'He can escort you both back here to this bus stop, where I can meet you,' suggested my caring and worried father. Next week duly arrived. We dressed with care in our circular skirts and new sling-back shoes for our outing, caught the No. 37 bus in Isleworth, and alighted in the dusk at the stop near the cinema. I had only seen Dan previously with the working group at Mogden Nurseries, a somewhat cheeky, grubby, overall-clad, older boy who was also employed there, so I knew he could well afford the cinema tickets. But I was stunned by the 'elegant' creation who met me; the transformation was amazing.

Dan was now clothed in a pale blue suit, with deep blue velvet lapels and piping round his lengthy jacket, slim trousers that elongated his figure, a pink shirt showing off a thin string tie ending in metal tabs. The whole ensemble was finished off with thick-soled brown suede shoes (these later became known as 'brothel creepers'). His hair did not miss out in the grooming, for now it was greased, brushed back at the sides and carefully arranged at the front with a large quiff falling over his face.

Dan in his teddy-boy outfit.

He was so eye-catching, that he stood out in the crowd, and his friends were almost the same, in purple suits and green shirts. The teddy-boy era had arrived. It was at this time in its infancy, for only the extroverts and youngsters with money sported the new fashions that were beautifully tailored and quite expensive. (The name of teddy-boy derived from the Edwardian style of the clothes). Anthea and I greeted them, almost embarrassed by their fashionable outfits, and very glad when we soon went into the darkness of the cinema. As all girls do at the break between the films, we hastened into the 'Ladies' to discuss a possible predicament.

Anthea

'I cannot be seen getting off the bus with them, by my father. He wouldn't understand.'

"My father is worse. He intends meeting us, as well.' This was new news to me from Anthea. She had an even more difficult father to placate. So we devised a plan, and at the end of the show, asked if we could go along to the corner ice-cream parlour for some milk shakes.

This shop opened onto both streets, very handy for the shoppers, but even more so for our cowardly escape route from these two poor boys, who were busily chatting to our group of friends in the shop, and who would never understand that we were running from their carefully chosen outfits for the evening, and not from them. I explained later to Father that Dan wished to stay on the No. 37 bus travelling to Lower Isleworth and visit his Gran for the night, thus avoiding an adult questionnaire and an inspection of our escorts. I felt it was only a little white lie to cover my embarrassment.

When I arrived at work the next day, however, I had to be more inventive to my friends, pleading sickness on the part of my friend Anthea, 'She needed to be taken home quickly, and as you were both busy with our friends, we did not wish to break up the party.' I was learning the gentle art of tact, for I didn't wish to hurt their feelings.

The summer holidays of 1950 were magical days for me, because I had now got to grips with my schoolwork a little better, and had been given when we moved to the new house the little room above the garage as a study, and also as a playroom. In here I could be creative, and had started building a two-storey doll's house out of stacked orange-boxes, soon to be a three-storey house, with a working lift for my tiny occupants built up the side of it. I continued to add to it over the years. Father cut out the doorways, and I papered and carpeted the rooms before he made the light fittings out of tiny torch bulbs in holders screwed to the walls.

Although I was now a teenager, I still had make-believe attitudes, like a child. I was also very creative, and loved the excitement of making miniature furniture, pots, pans and ornaments out of a variety of materials for my house. Father taught me how to use a soldering iron to make the springs on the little beds, while Mother was persuaded to help with some frilly curtains and bedding, and my aunt Mary provided a set of little paintings for the walls that I framed effectively with some 'gold' braid. Soon I had my house well furnished.

I could also keep out of the way from the growing arguments in the main house, which broke out sporadically but repeatedly, with my sister Jane always fuelling these angry spats between the adults, with unasked for comments and opinions. I tried to ignore it all as much as I could, but found it very difficult to understand. I was sitting on the staircase outside the sitting-room one day to avoid being included in the conversation that was clearly not my business.

'Jim must go and find himself another place to live now that I am home. I am grateful for what he has done for the family, but now he really must be on his way.' Father said one day to Mother, 'You are denigrating me socially at every turn, and you are not even wise enough to be discreet about it.' I did not understand what it was about, but with the next comment I certainly did.

'If Jim goes, then I will go too.' Mother declared angrily.

'What about the girls? They are so young, and in the middle of their schooling.' Father was truly horrified at this bombshell, but he knew that mother was self-willed enough to do what she said, regardless of the consequences.

'I don't care. We managed before, and could do so again.' Mother rushed out, slammed the door and fell

Jim, Mother, Jane and I in Dorset.

over me, both of us landing in a heap on the hall carpet. She was so angry. I picked myself up and melted away as fast as I could, but when all seemed quiet later in the day, I crept downstairs again to my father's study, and knocked. I had learned quickly that nobody entered unless invited, but he said, 'Enter, do, and shut the door. Make yourself comfortable in the big chair. You and I will have a little chat.'

I wanted to help, but felt powerless, so as my tears rolled silently down my face, I let him talk about this and that, and gradually he worked himself around to the present situation.

Father started to talk about the problems of being separated unavoidably for nearly ten years; the difficulties that Mother must have had being on her own, and the cruelty now of getting rid of her friend, her prop in life, which would be too unfair to her. He was generous in his understanding of her plight at this point in her life. He also thought it somewhat unfair to Jim, who he had himself asked to act as watchdog over the family during the war, and now obviously had no home of his own.

Father in the 1950s.

'I shall find a compromise, because there is always a solution to any problem. Do not be so upset. I will put things right,' and my dear Father dried my tears and stilled my worried heart, for I feared losing my home, my family and my settled way of life. This would need more than my fairies' magic. He quoted one of his little sayings to me which I wrote down. He seemed to have one for most occasions, and I collected a little book full of them, to ponder upon at a later date.

One should be prepared to accept
Death, Loss and Disappointment,
As it were straws upon the tide of life.

I was completely unaware of the events which transpired in the next few weeks, but Jim was told to stay in his part of the house, and Father would use the rest of it. However, I suspect that a few additional 'ground rules' were set out. Mother never again tried to invite Jim to any 'Do' involving Father, and Father with his expanded social circle of friends, never included Jim.

Mother's family, including Grandfather at Bowerswood, called Jim Valerie's 'chauffeur', and would only let him stay in the gardener's quarters. The social order of things in the 40s and 50s were quite clearly defined, but the war had stirred things up almost irretrievably, chipping away at the old order. In time I realised how torn my mother must have been emotionally, and how sad Father must have been, but his solution had the touch of the 'Wisdom of Solomon' about it to share our house, because he was a caring and kind man, with an enormous sense of fair play. So he got on with life as it was presented to him.

My summer holidays in 1950 were spent at Bow-erswood, renewing my acquaintance with all my friends there. Jane had gone to stay with friends in Germany, and both Mrs Pearson, the cook, and Nellie, the parlour maid, had retired, as had the chauffeur. So now Grandfather employed a couple, the new chauf-feur Drummond, and his wife Denise, as cook, to fill these vacant positions, and with a new parlour-maid from the village.

It was just like old times, because the Cairo aunts came to stay, and I spent a lot of time particularly with Aunt Gee with painting pictures. She was a fine artist like Aunt Mary, witty and entertaining, and extremely knowledgeable, but surprisingly strict. All her em-

Great-aunt Gee.

broideries continued to be a riot of colour like her paintings, due to her advancing colour-blindness, but it didn't really matter.

I was delighted to meet up again with mother's cousin Norah, who was staying for the summer and who shared my room. I was glad to return to what I called home, and leave the London problems behind for a little while. When Drummond told me that the fair had arrived in Garstang, I instantly badgered Norah to organize a visit.

Norah requested from Grandfather the loan of Drummond, and the car for the evening; she said that she felt safer to take a man with us, so we set off to Garstang to enjoy an evening of noise, roundabouts, and side shows. Having tried out most of the entertainments offered, I settled down in front of the rifle range to win some little pink fruit bowls. I won a pair of them with my first three shots, and the show-man smiled indulgently.

'Proper little Annie Oakley, ain't she.' he shouted, handing over the dishes. But I had a plan. The stall holder did not know of my earlier training with guns at Grand-father's shoots.

Cousin Norah Simpson.

'I want to win 24 for a birthday present for Grandpa's 87th party in September' I told Norah, who, when she saw my determination, added a bit to my pocket money and detailed Drummond to stay by my side at the stall. It was three shots for a sixpence, the dishes came in pairs for every win, and I confi-dently acquired eighteen dishes, before the showman said 'Stop.' After a few more moments, he said, 'New rules – only three goes per person – you've had enough,' which was followed by 'Just go away and have a ride on something.'

Drummond now stepped up to the man, saying, 'OK, here's my money for three turns.' He had nine shots to win something, but feared we would not reach our target. However, I was amazed to see him place nine 'bull's eyes' without hesitation in quick succession on the board, thus securing the last of the six dishes. Now we had the 24 between us.

'You never told me you were such a good shot. Why not?' I asked him later, as we were returning to Bowerswood, tired and well satisfied with the birthday present for my grandfather. Norah was laughing at our joint efforts and carried them carefully in her lap.

'I was in the Rifle Brigade, then demobbed, and came to work for your Grandfather. I did enjoy watching you, handling that gun with such skill. Did you know the sights had been offset slightly to fool the punters?' He then proceeded to explain some tricks of the trade, and complemented me on my accurate eye with the gun. These skills were useful in later life.

The new cook, Mrs Denise Drummond, was an efficient and jolly woman in her forties, and when the subject of the birthday party on 17 September for Grandfather was broached, she soon came up with a

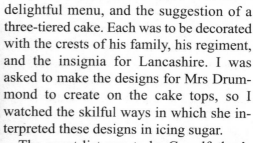

Jane in the Georgian dress.

delightful menu, and the suggestion of a three-tiered cake. Each was to be decorated with the crests of his family, his regiment, and the insignia for Lancashire. I was asked to make the designs for Mrs Drummond to create on the cake tops, so I watched the skilful ways in which she interpreted these designs in icing sugar.

The guest list was to be Grandfather's own friends of similar age. Unfortunately, since all the aunts had to return home by early September, there wouldn't be an obvious hostess for the party. However, it was decided as a solution to this impasse that Jane, now sixteen and quite grown up for her age, should play the part. She was given one of the Georgian dresses out of Grandpa's big clothes box that had belonged to Great-great-great-grandmother Simpson, which fitted her perfectly, and complemented her willowy figure. She certainly had the stature and manner to carry off the evening with style. She arrived back from her holiday in Germany a few days before the occasion, and turned out to be an ideal hostess for this grand affair.

153

Grandfather's 87th birthday party.

The long dining room table was set in the Edwardian manner with the great Epergne placed in the centre, filled with fruit and flowers, and artistically arranged. These were surrounded with gleaming crystal glasses, finger bowls and shining silverware. I even painted small place names for each guest, making them stand up by each plate and kept the list of names of the guests when I returned home.

The list included Sir William and Lady Ashcroft, Mr and Mrs William Goodair, Captain Dudley Foster, Mr and Mrs Redman, Capt. and Mrs Lawford, Mr and Mrs Walmsley, Mr Langton Birley, the two Miss Healeys, Stephen Simpson (grandfather) and Jane, but apart from the last two named, I cannot now put the right faces to the names.

I had hoped that I could stay, but was firmly sent back to school in London at the beginning of September. Having helped with all the preparations, but now missing out on the grand occasion, I was really upset by the injustice of life. I thought about my grandfather a great deal, and missed him when I was in London, wishing that I was back in Bowerswood with him. I still considered the place as 'my home', not the new one in London.

One morning at the end of September, when I woke up, I had a premonition that something was wrong with Grandfather. I had dreamed he was ill. I dressed for school in an agitated manner, then refused to set off for the bus, telling Mother of my worries about my grandpa, and that I feared we would now be too late to see him alive.

'Can we go now to see him?' I pleaded with her.

'It's all in your imagination. You do say some silly things, Wendy. Set off to school now, or you will be really late. You've already missed the first bus," she scolded me.

At that moment the telephone rang. When Mother answered, she stood transfixed to the spot for ages digesting what she had just learned. She was horrified to hear that Grandfather had just died – just ten days after his birthday.

'How did you know? You must have answered the phone before. Who told you? You're hiding something. Who rang us earlier?" Mother demanded explanations, but I had none to give her, however she ques-

The pine tree at Bowerswood.

tioned me, and I was reduced to great tears of anguish at my loss, also fuelled by my mother who kept on accusing me of lying.

In due course arrangements were made for the funeral, to which I was not allowed to go as punishment for my perceived selfish behaviour at the time of his death, so I mourned on my own. I was glad that I had been able to spend my summer holiday with him, and share in little things like digging the dandelions up together with his digger. We had been very close despite the enormous age gap, and I knew in my heart that he had been saying goodbye to me privately across the ether, that sad morning.

When finally Bowerswood, the rose gardens, the estate and two farms were auctioned to the highest bidder, I felt that my whole world was sold, so what was there left to live for? My father wrote out a little card for me to keep, kissed me gently when he gave it to me, and said it might help.

> *Time that is past, thou never canst recall;*
> *Of time to come thou art not sure at all.*
> *The present only is within thy power,*
> *So let you now improve that present hour.*

After a period of time, I started to understand the meaning of my father's words of wisdom – that looking forwards, and not glancing back was the only thing to do…

TIGERLILY

Up to this point in my life, I had not really had to deal with the shocks and fears of losing someone really close to me. At fourteen I was a fairly self-contained but quite immature teenager, and I do not think that I knew how to 'handle' the death of my beloved Grandfather, and the attendant loss also, of my home and friends in Lancashire.

My only photograph of my first cat, Smuts.

My father's homespun wisdom of 'One must expect death, loss and disappointment, as it were straws upon the tide of life' at that moment was no comfort, so I settled down to my schoolwork with an ill grace, not concentrating on what needed to be done. I spent months dreaming unhappily of the loss of my past life, and saw no pleasure in an uncertain and unknown future, because the one thing that had been apparently stable in my 'nomadic' life had now gone, my home in Lancashire and Grandfather.

Resignedly, I followed Mother's lead whenever she suggested any activity, which gradually did help me to move on to another phase. To this end, a neighbour gave me a small long-haired black cat to play with, called Smuts, who was cuddly, friendly, and purred a lot. Very shortly thereafter Smuts produced three little kittens, all short haired brown tabbies. Sadly, I had to give two of them away as they grew older. But I kept one, Tigerlily, and his mother, Smuts, of course. Father insisted that the kitten and mother were both neutered, with the result that Tigerlily grew at an enormous rate, becoming the largest and friendliest cat ever seen, with short, thick, springy fur, and the classic markings of a brown tabby cat.

Some months later, Mrs Dukes, a friend of my mother, came for coffee one morning and was intrigued by my very large cat, still growing – not in any way fat, but proportionately long-limbed and also with a lengthy tail. In time, there was to be more to Tigerlily's story, because Mrs Dukes was a judge at the Hertfordshire and Middlesex Cat Club. She realised that I had an extraordinary animal, unlike any other that she had ever seen. She kept in touch with me over my cat, as he continued to grow in length and height. Through this time, occasionally I went to help Mrs Dukes at cat shows.

Mother organised a visit to Olympia, in the late autumn of 1950 to see the Ideal Home Exhibition which was held just five years after the end of the war. It opened our eyes to a great many very modern homes, unimagined by us, but commonplace

Tigerlily with Mrs Dukes.

to the average American. Demonstrated also at Olympia were diverse, newly-developed materials, along with numerous domestic appliances and equipment, many of which had evolved from the technology created during wartime. As a consequence, we wandered around this vast show quite amazed. Unfortunately, a day was not enough to see it all.

At home we had no fridge, only a cold larder with stone shelves, and fine-wire netting over the grill to the garden outside. But here at the exhibition were electric refrigerators, within the bounds of financial possibility, gas and electric irons to drool over, replacements for the old flat irons and negating the need for a hob on which to heat them up. Washing machines with wringers attached caught everyone's eye, without the need now for a mangle, and even more revolutionary, a spin drier. But the height of modernisation was the new twin-tub washing machines, designed for small modern kitchens. It seemed that the external wash-house of old would soon become superfluous. Electricity had revolutionised the whole washing day experience.

The latest pressure cookers were shown off to amazed onlookers, and new labour-saving food mixers, table-top variety or hand held, churned out tasty titbits to tempt the crowds. Having feasted our eyes on the wonders of 'the modern kitchen', we then strolled around the new furniture designs, where tubular steel chairs, moulded plastic seats, and Formica tops vied for position with the new all-in-one kitchen cabinets, heralding the start of an era of built-in furniture. Even modern materials for soft furnishings and clothes had not been neglected, because the new polyesters (i.e. brands such as Terylene or Dacron) with bright and modern coloured designs, advertised as non-iron and easy-care, were presented at the fair. Wallpapers were also matched up with these materials.

Father had accompanied us on this trip to Olympia, because it was nearing Christmas time, and he thought he might buy some Christmas gifts. We soon found him engrossed in the electrical section, discussing with the salesman the benefits of new televisions, which were unbelievably expensive. He was also shown new transistor radios, because the older valve wirelesses were being phased out. He was keen to see record players too, and bought for me a Fidelity Portable Player, mounted in a lightweight suitcase. When switched on, it would play three speeds, the 78s, 45s and 33s. It was an unexpected Christmas present. I was delighted with it, because I had been using an HMV cabinet which one wound up with a side handle. This had belonged to my cousin Norah. I had quite a lot of old 78 speed records, but only three new 45 speed ones, because I couldn't afford any more at the time.

He bought Mother a new leather-covered Roberts transistor radio to put on the kitchen window sill, so that she could listen to 'Dick Barton, Special Agent' each evening at 6.45, a ritual which continued for some years. Likewise the new daily serial 'Mrs Dale's Diary' (the life of a country doctor's wife, according to the adverts) every afternoon, held my mother captivated by the imaginary Dr Jim Dale's family activities for the next 21 years.

New plastics and stainless steel were revolutionising so many domestic goods, previously made from more traditional materials, that it seemed we were being transformed into a new 'space age home'. The designs, materials and colours were so alien to our eyes, and not always so acceptable to older people. For example, Mother did not care for tubular steel furniture.

I wandered over to the side shows, where I strolled round a walkway which surrounded a beautifully built, but giant-sized living-room about fifteen feet below us. Everything in this room was scaled up to be twice the normal size, and was fitted out with sitting-room apparel and items such as books, writing materials, crockery, bottles of beer and glasses. There were comfortable chairs, covered with cushions and rugs, but in every instance, everything was enormous. There was even a giant-sized bicycle standing in the corner of the room. Suddenly I realised the reason why – I now spied the tallest man in existence, sitting by his table eating a sandwich.

According to the explanatory notice nearby, this man was called Ted Evans, from Derbyshire, born in 1924, who was 7 feet 8.5 ins (2.35 m) tall. He had been trained as a boxer, but was now earning a living as a curiosity at various shows including at Olympia. This well-dressed man was very slim, tall, bronzed and good looking, and spent his time mostly reading and ignoring the watching crowds, while stroking a small adult cat, which seemed like a kitten in size to the man. He occasionally waved to one or two people who spoke to him. I immediately wondered whether my Tigerlily had somehow eaten a similar diet to this man, for he would have fitted in to this large-scale environment perfectly.

This occasion forever stuck in my memory, as being a 'one off' moment in my life to see such a unique person. I felt very sorry for him too, because he would not have any companions his own size. I heard of his death some years later when he was aged thirty four, in 1958.

I wandered on to watch the sewing machine demonstrations, where a miniature version, designed for the 'Junior Miss' was being advertised, producing basic stitches, backwards or forwards, powered by the handle at the side, and all was packed into a little carrying case which was pink. Mother bought me this as a Christmas gift which I prized for years, feeling I had moved into a new age.

The only survivor now of this happy visit so many years later, was an item bought from a jewellery maker, who cleverly manipulated silver gilt wire into name broaches. I had just enough pocket money left to buy my name 'Wendy', beautifully scripted in gold, before we set off for home, tired but well-satisfied with the trip.

Our house was always a hub of activity within our family, many of whom lived in the south east region at that time; aunts, uncles and cousins regularly appeared for meals, or were invited to stay a few days. My father's youngest brother, Lt. Colonel Robin Stuart had two children now, Charles and little Rosemary, but the whole family lived in Germany, where Robin was still on active service with his regiment, the Royal Signals. Not surprisingly, he looked remarkably like my father.

When the subject of school for ten year old Charles came up for discussion, my father agreed to act as his legal guardian in this country, and suggested that he should stay at our house, so he could attend prep school, then go on to a boarding school.

Uncle Robin back from Germany.

The aim was to send him to Pangbourne College, a naval establishment for 11 to 18 year olds in Berkshire, to train young officers eventually for the Merchant Navy. This was not far from where we lived.

The college was established in 1917 by an ex-naval schoolmaster, and was run on the lines of 'a large ship on land', with naval terminology used, such as 'cabins' for bedrooms, etc. The headmaster, Dr Kenneth Grieg, came one day to see my father to discuss Charles' future education, and I thought he looked like a typical sea captain of old that you could see on the Players packets of cigarettes, surrounded by a life-ring.

The arrival of my cousin Charles at our house caused quite a reorganisation, but I was pleased to have a younger 'brother' to share my activities with. We got on very well, because he was a friendly boy and as inventive and artistic as myself. He arrived with a large cage housing three hamsters, but they did not last long, escaping when Charles was cleaning out the cage in the garden. Mother was terrified of meeting them, having a pathological fear of mice. The hamsters were so small, that I worried for a while about their welfare, hoping they were happy in the greater world. With his wide blue eyes, round freckled face and broad smile,

Charles's family likeness to all the other Stuarts was there for all to see, so he fitted in well with our family.

My sister Jane now had two younger siblings to boss around, and we took a delight in foiling her attempts to rule us so authoritatively. She treated us with the contempt she thought we deserved for being noisy, gleeful and high-spirited youngsters, but this fun did not last when Charles was sent off to boarding school, and I lost my companion. Jane had other issues on her mind.

'Why can I not stay on at school, do my A level exams and go on to university?' Jane asked Mother. She was nearing the end of her spell at St. Pauls School, having done well academically. I can still remember hearing Jane plead with our parents. It seemed a reasonable request to me, but Mother had a surprising and truthful answer. This financial side of life had never entered my head.

'We cannot afford to keep you on at school. Your Grandfather's Bursary fund has nearly run its course, lasting until you are both sixteen.'

So Jane had to rethink her future. Gone were her grand plans for being a Debutante, following Mother's and Aunt Melene's route into society ('We cannot possibly afford it') so she now prepared her-

Jane in her nursing uniform.

self to attend a secretarial course for a year, before training as a nurse when old enough.

She made friends with an older lady in her late thirties, Pauline Moran, a widow, who attended Jane's course at the same time. She had a small flat in Richmond, shoebox-sized but tastefully decorated, to which we were both invited at times. Father took us there over at Christmas, and we admired her little 'tree' made from silver painted twigs and dripping with glass baubles. We laughed a lot at her humour while drinking some sherry, for the first time in my life. Fair curly haired and pretty, she had been in the forces during the war, and had a precise veneer of army organisation about her.

Jane still tried to needle Jim in whatever way she could. After a terrible row with him at our house one day, Jane rushed off to Pauline's house, declaring he was impossible, exaggerated the situation greatly with an embroidered story, and begged to be allowed to lodge with her new friend. Pauline, a caring and kindly woman, now felt boxed in, but under this great pressure said, 'Yes, you can come, but just for a couple of weeks until the heat of the row has evaporated.'

This state of affairs, however, drifted on and lasted for more than a year until Jane went for her nursing training at The Middlesex Hospital, so she never returned home for long spells to live again. Bossy though she was, I admired and loved my sister whom I missed greatly, and my loneliness returned. For the next fifty years, our paths rarely crossed because, when she finished her training, she went to Kenya. Her story would probably be sufficient to write another book. None of those grand ideas of Jane's entered my head yet. I still had less than two years of school to attend where nobody thought that I was remotely academic.

The festival of Britain brought a great many visitors to London in 1951. This was to celebrate the centenary of the Great Exhibition of 1851, and many new buildings were erected to house new exhibitions and activities. It was like a vast trade show, the centre-

A keepsake piece of soap from the Festival of Britain.

piece being the 'Skylon', which was a statue created in an angular fashion, very tall and impressive, dominating the London scene. The Festival Hall, an enormous edifice of concrete, now housed theatres for plays, festivals and concerts, drew in a different audience from all over the world, and those of us who lived near enough to these activities, benefitted greatly from our proximity to the action.

Mother put her name on the 'Welcome to London – Bed and Breakfast' list for visitors, bought a large box of festival soaps to give one each to the guests, and then sold them for 'home presents'. Very soon we had a regular stream of paying guests from abroad, who thereafter came back for their yearly London visit. Mother was always very enterprising and managed to make it pay well.

Mrs Dukes suggested one day that I should take Tigerlily to the Hertfordshire and Middlesex Cat Show and enter him in the neuter class. Here it did not matter that he had a questionable parentage, but was judged only on his own magnificence, not as a breeder. There were several hundred cages there, and I learned for the first time of the wonderful variety of breeds of cats, such as long haired Persian animals with squashed-up noses, Siamese cats that seemed to talk loudly, or Russian Blues who were grey with very short thick coats, and deep orange eyes.

Many others were there, placed within their own breed groups, all brushed up and in their 'Sunday best'. The blue eyes mingled with the yellow, and orange with green-eyed felines. The cats had beautiful coats, long or short, of black, white, ginger, tabby, tortoiseshell and karomac, with all shades between, and all were lined up for inspection by the judges. Mrs. Dukes gave me a white coat to wear, a badge to clip on, and we settled Tigerlily into his cage, now labelled with his official name of 'Tigerlily-Smuts'.

He was such a softy, and seemed to be happy to sit there in the warmth with water, food and a soft cushion to roll on, ignoring all passers-by, who often stopped to talk to him in what they thought of as 'cat language'. He just yawned and shut his eyes, no doubt dreaming the day away; he behaved impeccably when the judges lifted him out and placed him on the table for inspection, arching his back with pleasure when stroked, and purred loudly in his very best cat-talk.

All the owners and visitors were removed from the hall while the judges deliberated on their decisions, and eventually they placed their cards around the hall for awarding the firsts, seconds, thirds and the champions. There were even a lot of the very highly commended groups, so that owners were not too disappointed, for every cat was somebody's angel.

I hastened back to Tigerlily when the hall was again opened to owners and was amazed by the result from the judges. The card tucked into the bars of the cage was bright red, and gold edged. It said, 'Champion, winner best British short-haired brown tabby (neuter)'. I was so proud of him that day, but I don't think he cared one way or another.

SOUNDING BRASS

Memories of events during my teenage years seem to crowd my mind sometimes, occasionally as little flashbacks, with clear moments of either pleasure
or pain, or with regrets of nostalgic dreams, all mixed up like a bag of 'Liquorice
Allsorts.'

I had no control over my time at school, because as with everyone it was an established process, set out in an ordered fashion, so I accepted this and was content
with school. Nevertheless, I was still struggling with my propensity for reversing
letters, sometimes words, and many numbers. My form teacher Miss Higginson,
had long since made allowance for this habit, saying it was 'the way I was made',
and with her continuing encouragement I worked hard, with average results.

In great contrast to this, on the home front I felt very unsettled during my teen
years, with my grandfather having died at the end of September 1950. Now I could
not clamour to go back for my Christmas holidays to Bowerswood, which had been
sold. Even though I had reached the grand age of fifteen, I was below average height.
I was not yet at the stage of puberty, which started a year later, and still cried in
secret when on my own, pining for my old home. I had not yet passed the threshold
of leaving school, thus continued to be considered a 'Young Lady', or, as the older
generation in my family would have put it, I had not yet 'Come Out.'

There were many different undercurrents of discontent in my newer home, and
sometimes open conflict. My sister, who was still my role model, showed determined attitudes, and had grown into a beautiful, but troubled brunette of sixteen and
a half. She despised poor Jim for his working-class roots, that kindly man who kept
a very 'low profile', occupying mainly his own room, the garden or workshop in
turns, or went out to be 'invisible'. He also went regularly to Kneller Hall to meet

up with his bandsmen friends and played with a group of
them some evenings, at what was known as a 'Jam Session'. He liked to keep his hand in with his musical skills,
either on his euphonium, or with his stringed double-bass
in the five-man dance group. He missed the military band
so much.

Father got on very well with Jim, as they shared some
of their hobbies, building together extensions to the hydroponics greenhouse. Father also acquired some long,
thin, springy metal rods, maybe aerials of a kind, and Jim
creatively made them into three fishing rods, binding eye-
holes along their length, and clips for the fishing reels,
then glued on cork handles for firm grips in rainy
weather. Now having bought three reels, a box of worms,
and equipped with the wherewithal for a day's sport, we

three went off early one day to Feltham Gravel Pits; the site was now closed, but had filled with deep water. Local fishermen had stocked it with fish, so we looked forward to a bit of coarse fishing there.

We bought pies for lunch at the local shop, and came back at the end of the day, very content and happy that we had participated a little in another new sport, escaping the demands at home. On our return, we resolutely turned a 'deaf ear' to Mother's annoyed cries of complaint.

'Wherever have you three been today? I needed you here. You had no business to go like that.'

Inevitably there were conflicts with Mother, who wished ever more to control everybody's activities, particularly whenever we showed any signs of having the slightest independence from her. She continued with her controversial friendship with Jim, although my aunt Melene had

Mother at a party.

other words for the situation. But I was beginning to suspect that Jim was now so caught up in this 'spider's web', that he did not know how to extricate himself from the relationship.

Known as Val to all her friends, my mother was either loved and admired for her energy, kindness and drive, or was to be avoided if one did not want to be drawn into her devious plans. Father took a much more kindly and understanding view of my mother, with her needs, and ignored the situation, realising it allowed him to find other interests that suited him better. It also took the pressure off him to deal with her recurring tempers. He had his scientific work with Thorn EMI, read extensively, studied a great deal, and created experiments in his own home laboratory.

In time he became Chairman of the Regimental Association, enjoying the challenge of organising events for past members of his regiment. As some of these were social 'get together' nights, we eagerly supported Father and attended most of these occasions.

At the regimental dance, wearing my first evening dress.

Each year as I grew older and

taller, I regularly wore Jane's last year's evening dresses, which often suited my blonde colouring better, while she floated around each time in a stunning new creation. On one of these occasions a young ex-officer, wanting to dance, said to me, 'I do so admire your lovely green dress, which you wore last year – it suited you then, and it does even better now. But you have changed your hair colour. You are prettier than ever.'

The green evening dress.

Hollow compliments flowed from glib lips. He had only remembered the dress, and not the girl inside it. I did not bother to correct his mistake but basked in his brief admiration instead. Such moments were fun, as we learned to be sociable young ladies for Father's sake.

Mother could be very caring of us both, and it pleased her to have two girls around that she could dress well and show off at different functions. At this level she was amusing and entertaining, and loved attending these social engagements as the Colonel's wife.

Yet with all the inherited style and poise she possessed, her temper still surfaced regularly if she was ignored or crossed in any way. I hated being in the firing line, and on many occasions it was much safer to keep my head down, avoiding much trouble for myself by offering no opinions, no actions, and no plan that would raise the slightest eyebrow.

I often pretended that none of this was happening – I was the proverbial ostrich with its head in the sand. Metaphorically speaking, I crawled back to safety in my hiding-hole of memories with my fairies, which I still occasionally peeped at for comfort, as they represented a past stability. They were then replaced in their battered old envelope, which had been repaired many times with strips of gummed paper- then hidden away again.

However, Mother had her good side too, and her parties were well known, because she was a superb organizer and everybody flocked to attend them. It was 1950, and the Yuletide season approached. With great energy and determination she organised some staff. She unpacked all the decorations that had been carefully wrapped in layers of tissue and brought from Bowerswood, and these were put up with loving care, as a reminder of times past.

Aunt Gee from Cairo.

Our house then filled that Christmas with friends and relatives, perhaps deliberately, as an antidote to the loss of Grandfather and Bowerswood. The Christmas feast was a triumph of pleasure for everyone that year. Norah joined us, and even the Cairo aunts came for a few days, because they were now staying at their 'Sesame Club for Overseas Patriots' in London. Also our cousins and related uncles, living in the London area, made an appearance for the day. We all drank a toast to my recently departed Grandfather, which somehow made my sadness a little more bearable.

It was a warm winter so far, the balmy spell continuing well into January, which augured well for the New Year celebrations. There was enough food for our guests to continue over the holiday period, during which time various forms of entertainment had been planned. Everybody had a job in this scheme of things.

Coloured fairy lights twinkled everywhere, and rooms were prepared, beds allocated for staying guests, silver polished and glasses placed in rows by the liquid refreshments, which arrived from Threshers, the wines and spirits shop, in good time to be inspected. A large tree was placed in the front gar-

Great Aunt Nora.

den and decorated well in advance of the coming party. The whole place flickered with colour, and seemed to be lit up better than the Blackpool Illuminations. I twirled about in my new long, pink taffeta dress that rustled like autumn leaves, pretending I was a princess. For once it was not a cast-off from Jane.

Mother had invited her friends from Lancashire, and with a truce being declared some time ago, Father asked if Jim would like to invite four of his friends. All the musicians at Kneller Hall were student bandsmen-conductors, who had come from bands all over the world, studying at Kneller Hall. In fact his friends offered to play with Jim as a quintet for the New Year party, so they happily joined us for the meal beforehand, stowing their instruments in Father's study for use later. What an international group we were. They were all first class musicians, studying their final exams in England for a year – a Scotsman, a Norwegian, a Ghanaian, and an Egyptian.

These four jolly musicians, Andy, Lars, Obar and Mustafa all helped us in the kitchen, taking out of the oven sausage rolls and other delicacies, and placed them on trays to be carried upstairs. It was all hands on deck and the party started to gather momentum as people arrived, divesting themselves of coats and wraps, greeting old friends, as the food trays appeared, while the wine flowed. Being curious, as always, I was fascinated by our visitor from Ghana, because it was the first time I had ever seen a coloured man, who seemed to me to wear beautiful black woolly hair.

'Please may I touch it? It feels like lambs' wool.' This caused ripples of laughter from the men.

'Look, I have another trick for you.' He turned over his hand to show the white of his palms, and laughed with fun. The English population in the fifties was still generally white, and I was delighted with the novelty of these new friends. I remember it well, because it was the very first time I had encountered anybody from another country, of a different colour.

I had asked my friend Anthea, and the two older teenage boys from next door, David and John

Jane and Peter van Zyl.

Harold, to join us for the New Year's party. Jane had decided to come home for the New Year celebrations, bringing Pauline and a friend of hers, Peter Van Zyl, a fair-haired, well-dressed young student of about 22 from Capetown who was studying medicine. They all joined in the merrymaking in the drawing-room upstairs. At first all the young men were friendly towards each other, as food and drink circulated, and the good spirits of Christmas prevailed.

David Harold.

Suddenly the loud, clipped tones of Peter could be heard clearly and authoritatively, above the laughter and merrymaking.

'What is that Kaffir doing, feeding in this room here with us?'

There was a sudden and complete silence in the room..The Christmas spirit evaporated in a swirl of puzzlement and instant shock. David Harold and John shouted almost in unison,

'We don't believe in Apartheid here in England. It's wicked. We get on with everybody here. We are all friends in this country, wherever people come from.'

'We don't have slaves here.' Everybody now joined in, expressing their outrage.

What was Apartheid? I had not heard that word. What did it mean? I did not understand it at all. What was happening to our party? Many people started talking at once, as the angry exchanges with Peter grew louder. Father immediately apologised profusely to the bandsman, then turned and firmly took hold of Peter, marching him out onto the porch, without giving him a chance to refuse.

What he said we never knew, but Peter, now angry and shouting loud, abusive words, leapt down the steps and disappeared into the night. Later on I heard Father saying quietly to Jane that he had told Peter not to return, he did not approve of his politics, and anyway he was not an ideal companion in this changing world. Jane looked a little chastened for once and disappeared upstairs to comb her hair, smooth out her new dress and swallow her pride.

Suzaphone.

Father and Jim now set up an area for the band with chairs and music-stands in the large hall, while the musicians prepared their instruments, because they had brought a selection. All the students at Kneller Hall played most brass instruments, as well as stringed and woodwind varieties. Carpets had been rolled back in both drawing rooms, and the guests now enjoyed a house party ball. David and John, in party spirit again, prepared the fireworks in the front garden, waiting for midnight. It was the kind of ball in miniature that Jane had craved as a coming-out ball. I think it was the best party that I ever enjoyed, and certainly totally different. There was more to come.

As the hands of the clock crept on to midnight, the five

musicians opened the front door and took their seats on the top porch steps, opening their trumpet cases. As the clock struck twelve, they rose and played a magnificent fanfare, the sound reverberating around the neighbourhood to reach everybody within earshot. The clear notes mingled with the peels of the mellower church bells, now ringing in the New Year, and created for me an intense excitement, with the sounds of these trumpets in unison reaching far into the starry night, the exploding fireworks transporting these shining notes far away to reach the stars.

Warming up the instruments ready to play.

As more neighbours now joined us, the party continued all night. We did things like that then.

ETTERSGILL FARM

As time passed, I was beginning to develop adult views and opinions in life, and a personality that was very much at variance with Mother's view of me. She continually maintained to her friends that I was so young.

'She is still very much a child, a sweet thing and a bit of a dreamer, with not an intelligent thought in her head; not very clever either, like her elder sister, but I expect she will find something to do in life.' As always, my mother made her sweeping statements, without thinking. My self-esteem was fairly low. It did not help that I often heard these comments which were spoken to her friends, when she had forgotten I was within earshot of her conversations.

Father, realising my misery at that time, decided to redress the balance a little. He asked his friends Percy (Pop) and Helen Ridley in Shildon, County Durham, whether their offer of a caravan holiday was still possible on a farm in the Teesdale valley, where Helen had offered to take me a few years previously. This had then been postponed when I had broken my ankle falling down the mine shaft. But now the holiday idea was soon resurrected, and agreed upon for the Whitsun holiday month, so I was duly put on the train bound for Shildon.

Helen Ridley.

While travelling north from Kings Cross Station, as the train regularly crossed the joints in the railway lines, it offered a sound like a feverishly working woodpecker, or the tapping of the Morse code for 'V' – diddly-dum, diddly-dum, diddly-dum. The train sang out its repetitive mantra like a lullaby for passengers swaying and daydreaming in the sunshine through the carriage windows.

The landscape gradually changed from the springtime warmth and the multi-coloured displays of flowers and blossoms in the south, to the softer tones seen further north, of a landscape just awakening to a later spring display. For the first time I was very much aware of the differences between north and south. Whole areas as we passed, showed the gradations of green, becoming yellower the further we travelled, and through the ploughed and harrowed fields that were still brown, without the cover of new crops peeping through to clothe them.

It was a late spring that year, with slivers of snow and glistening ice patches that were scattered about in the sheltered corners of North Lincolnshire, Yorkshire, then County Durham, creating noticeable winter patterns over the landscape. When we finally arrived, the breeze carried with it a hint of distant snow and it had a freshness untainted by the clinging smells of smoke, smog and chemicals, which saturated the London environment that I had just left.

It was a delight to meet up with Helen and Pop again, and I soon fell into a pattern of helping her with all the chores, and making the bread. Her walled garden provided a good protection for the determined spring plants and vegetables bursting forth, and covered it with new growth. Her cheerful hens, now a new younger selection, as usual with variegated colours, and just as friendly, greeted me with chortling curiosity to see whether I was the bearer of corn titbits.

I collected the eggs, and thought how very recently we had been short with our food rations, sweets still being rationed. Bread had just come off the ration list, but other foodstuffs requiring sugar were still difficult to get, and eggs were much sought after.

Nora, Pop's maid-of-all-work!

Pop, still the manager of the Midland Bank, used his hours of relaxation to tend his vegetable plot, proving more useful than many of the beautiful roses he had previously grown there, but still kept a few flowers among the vegetables. Now, after the war, the habit of providing home grown food had taken hold of the nation's gardeners and he was no different. Nora, the maid-of-all-work, was still there, and just as happy to do a little garden tending.

Helen, being logical and practical, was making a list for our stay in the caravan, in quite an isolated spot, but near a farmhouse in Ettersgill, in a field opposite the buildings.

'We must take enough warm things and bedding with us for our stay in the caravan, waterproofs and wellingtons if it rains, you'll need your bag of painting things and a book to read. And we'll pack plenty of food,' she said, ticking off the items on her list.

Pop drove us there in his small car, but did not intend to stay, and arranged a collection time a couple of weeks away. The little caravan was well placed in a small

field, and next to a busy stream, that chattered noisily with the force of flowing crystal-clear water from the fells. We unpacked our belongings and stowed everything away before exploring the immediate area. The caravan was a two-bunk van, cosy and clean, with a paraffin cooker, and other necessities. I was glad we had also brought an oil stove, for extra warmth, with a cooking ring on its top, and a

The caravan at Ettersgill.

can of paraffin fuel. I thought it might be colder than we had planned, although Helen seemed untroubled by this thought.

We were indeed not far across the field from the farmhouse. We were welcomed in by Mrs. Allinson, and her sister Mrs. Nattress, both middle-aged country-spoken ladies with wiry grey hair and strong local accents, who sat us both down in the warm kitchen, and then supplied us with a home-baked tea (the north of England expression for an evening meal). Several small black and white farm cats were basking with half-closed eyes near the warmth of the range, stretching out on the home-made multi-coloured rag rugs.

Mrs Allinson, Ian's mother.

The farm covered many acres of lower-lying fields, but also had access to several thousand acres of common land known as Ettersgill Fells, and was run by Mrs Allinson's son, Ian, with the help of two farm workers, George Brough and Allan Beadle, and four keen working collies.

The farmhouse was a whitewashed building attached to a barn and other farm outbuildings, with all the doors painted red, in the middle of which were steps to an upper barn. The surrounding area of fields and moorlands stretched for miles, with

Ettersgill Farm

few trees to interrupt the view, just a winding road up into the hills beyond. Outside the gate were three milk churns, indicating the presence of a milking herd, a fair scattering of hens who were roaming at will, and mixed in with a few sheep in the nearest small field. But this proved to be only 'the tip of the iceberg'.

'The men are arl oot up on't fells, roonding up stray gimmers an' hoggets. Y'll meet 'em at tea time, and y'll stay for tha meal?' Mrs. Allinson inquired.

We were soon greeted by four wriggling, panting wet collie dogs by the back door, heaving from their exertions on the moors while rounding up flocks of Swaledale sheep, numbering about 250. We watched from the window as these horned animals were penned into the 'inbye' field beside the farmhouse. I soon found that there was a whole new language in the shepherding business, and I listened carefully to learn the meanings of the most often used words. The dogs had preceded the farmer, Ian Allinson, to the door, and then sprawled down outside, while he entered the house, shed himself of his boots, then his cap, jerkin, coat, scarves and gloves, so he could quickly thaw out.

He greeted us cheerfully as he warmed his frozen hands.

'Tomorrow we'll be bringing another 500 sheep down, they've had a hard winter, and the lambs need checking,

Ian Allinson

also the ewes with bad feet.' He explained to us the reasons for this work. When I asked him how many were left up on the fells, he said, 'About 1700, I'd say. We'll be counting 'em soon with their new lambs.'

Ian was tall, with sandy coloured hair, a jovial smiling expression and seemed well-built and tough, a necessity for his job that required much strength. About 30 years of age, his positive actions and thoughts revealed a purposeful man determined to organise his farm to its best advantage and he was definitely in command.

For such a large man, he moved delicately around the small farmhouse kitchen almost like a ballet dancer. He was gentle with his mother and aunt, and courteous to ourselves. I was mesmerised by this likable hill farmer, but even more so because he had one strange and different feature.

He had two expressive orange eyes. These I will never forget. I am very well aware of colour. I know that blue-eyed people have colours ranging from grey, to light then dark blue, and also encompass all the shades of green. On the other hand, brown-eyed folk sometimes have dark brown-black shades ranging through to light brown, so I must assume that at this end of the scale, the lightest brown must also appear to be orange. But it was indeed very unusual.

Ian suggested that we might like to visit High Force waterfall the next day before we did other things, and he would drop us off by High Force Hotel, on his way up to the fells. He also offered to take us to the sheep sales in the market town of Middleton-in-Teesdale the day after, for selling some 'hoggets and wethers', which in common parlance meant teenage sheep, both sexes, and castrated young males.

So we took up his offer the following day, and hitched a lift in his truck to High Force Hotel, from which point we started down the trail to view the magnificent and celebrated waterfall. It meant walking down through woods that bordered the River Tees, over boulders, and through gaps in the under-

My painting of High Force, Teesdale.

growth, until we arrived at the edge of the water, flowing over very slippery pieces of rock. It was wet, because the thunderous waterfall covered the area with a fine mist of spray as it fell, creating several rainbows within a damp white halo. I had never seen before such a large cascade of water tumbling over a cliff face, from about 22 metres high (71 feet), and plunging into the pool below, almost as deep. There was a smaller waterfall to the right hand side which dried up in times of drought, but it was now there for us to see in full spate.

We sat there making some sketches of the falls, then eventually started back up the sides of the ravine to the hotel. Helen struggled over the rocks, then scraped her leg on a tree stump, which made it bleed, and caused her much pain. We took a long time, with many stops for rest, finally reaching the top, and walked over to the hotel for a cup of tea. The proprietor, seeing Helen's distress, offered to run us down to Ettersgill House Farm, which he said was at least two miles south of the hotel. So we arrived back in reasonable comfort, where Mrs. Nattress dressed the wound with creams and an enormous bandage.

'Into bed now with you,' she said, 'it will soon be better.'

So Helen read her book, kept herself warm, and soon felt much more comfortable. By the following morning she hobbled about in the van, with less pain. But now she did not feel strong

Group of young Swaledales.

enough to go to the cattle market. Once Ian had loaded his sheep to be sold, I clambered into the van with him and George, well wrapped up in warm clothes.

We travelled down the valley for about five miles to Middleton-in-Teesdale and into the stock market, where Ian off-loaded the animals divided into two pens for the hoggets and the gimmers. Our pens were numbered, and the other pens soon filled up with sheep, of different breeds and ages from other farms. We had taken one dog, Jess, who had helped the unloading, and now stood quietly next to Ian, as he wandered around talking to his neighbours.

Swaledale sheep are classified as a small, hardy hill breed. They all had curly horns, with thick off-white rough fleeces, strong stripy white legs and dark grey faces, that showed up their white muzzles and distinctive white rings round their eyes, as if they were all wearing sunglasses to show off their knowing yellow eyes.

It was often the preferred breed in those parts, because their toughness was proven in the harsh areas where they lived. Usually the flocks ran with a larger, heavier ram of a different breed (known as a tup), often a Border Leicester, to produce bigger lambs for the table market. This much I learned about sheep that day.

Soon buyers, sellers and spectators lined up around the large selling pen, made of close laid rails, the farmers resting their arms on the tops with a foot apiece on the lower ones, and there was a hush as the first batch of sheep entered the ring. Auctioneers have a language all of their own – a smooth joined up roll of strange words would be uttered, be it for cattle, sheep or even furniture, whatever the merchandise. The speed with which this auctioneer talked, sold, and moved on to the next lot was truly amazing, and I did not understand a word of what he was saying.

The sheep were excitable, and wild as deer. The stockman kept moving them around for the viewing farmers to see, which made them leap over each other in fright. The farmers stood shoulder to shoulder viewing the stock, where I also stood, at least a head shorter than the smallest man around the ring, watching the farmers flicking a finger, giving a small wave or a discrete nod, to secure a sale when the preferred lot came into the ring to buy.

Then the seemingly impossible happened. Suddenly one big young animal, no doubt spying a lower gap in the wall made by this mass of farmers' caps and faces, took a leap at my head which was indeed very much lower. In fear I

Swaledale sheep in the market.

dropped instantly to the floor behind and below the fence, regardless of the straw and dirt into which I fell, as the sheep rose up like a champion hurdler and cleared the barricade and me, with one bound, followed closely by two more agile animals in tow (as sheep are known to do.) and raced down the vast shed, before the sheepdogs had them cornered again. I was thunderstruck at the speed of the actions of these sheep, which can apparently leap stone walls twice my height.

After this experience I felt a bit shaken, so I abandoned the auction pen. Ian suggested that I wait for him in the café outside the mart, where he would meet me after visiting the farm stores for supplies. I wandered around the few shops, with only pennies in my pocket, and entered a junk shop with a variety of bric-a-brac in the window. I had spied a small carriage clock with a window through which you could see its movements, and asked its price. Unfortunately, it was out of my league at three shillings, so I regretfully left the premises without it. As I walked to the teashop, I met Ian going in, who asked in a concerned way if I now felt recovered,

and felt my heart pounding at his interest. So we had our cup of tea, while I told him of my 'find' in the shop, and that I didn't have enough money to pay for the little clock, and the reason for wanting to buy it. After a few more purchases, we climbed into the van, with Jess leaping in effortlessly, and headed back to the farm.

Ian had explained that all the local farmers used the Common fells for their flocks of sheep, which roamed at will for miles, mixing with the others as they grazed. They tended to stay in their own territory though, being 'hefted' sheep, which means knowing their own home ground from which they do not often stray. This homing instinct is bred into them for generations. The canny dogs also know the sheep on their 'home' farm, and only gather up their own animals.

Jess the sheep dog.

When he told me that he was now gathering up his flocks to take to his lower fields for checking and sorting, I asked if I could go to help, to which he answered with a friendly smile, 'An extra pair of hands wouldn't go amiss.'

So the next day I went with the three men and four dogs on the trailer behind the tractor. It was exciting to be thought useful and a member of a team. It was cold, and flecks of snow started to appear. This was falling on deeper un-melted snow from previous weeks. By the time we reached the higher levels of the land, the snow became more persistent and lay thickly, creating a completely white landscape. George and Alan, with their dogs dropped off the trailer to start the gather, guiding their eager animals with whistles and calls, ignoring the thickening snow flakes. Old George counted sheep in a shepherd's tongue.

'Yan, Tan, Tether, Mether, Pip…' he intoned, continuing with 'Lezar, Azar, Catrah, Borna, Dick…' twice, and adding 'Jiggit' for twenty, before repeating the mantra. This was the way that George counted sheep, in similar vein to his father and grandfather before him. At every Jiggit he transferred a small pebble from his left to right pocket.

Ian took the trailer a bit further on, explaining he was going to search for injured sheep, then set Jess on to guard me. This was a first for me to be guarded by an intelligent dog, but soon I saw the necessity of the trailer when Ian started filling it with lame or injured animals. He lashed ropes round injured beasts fallen in deep holes and hauled them out, placing them in the trailer. I made sure they did not roll onto each other and were securely tied on, where necessary.

'Many 'ave snow-blindness, and 'ave wandered int' gullies, an' cannut climb oot by themselves. Tha'll be al'reet in' t'warmth o' t' barn,' he told me.

There were also disused entrances to old lead mine shafts, once owned by the London Lead Mining Company but long since abandoned, and a constant danger for unwary sheep. So the afternoon progressed, with all of us doing our part. George and Alan continued to move the flock down to a lower level; Ian, with his dog, searched and found needy sheep, and I, with Jess, looked after the injured. Soon all the inbye fields were full of bleating sheep, usually from mothers who had mislaid their lambs, now half grown, and we penned up others in neighbouring fields. The injured sheep were placed in the barn together with sickly mothers and lambs, because it was now snowing heavily.

'Have we gathered up all of them?' I asked, as we all eventually sat down to a welcome stew prepared by Mrs Allinson. Helen had come in to join us, and told me she had spent a very restful day, with her leg now improving.

'We will know when we have done a head count tomorrow,' Ian murmured tiredly by the fire. Seeing that the falling snow had finally ceased by the end of our meal, and the moon was shining on the glittering ground of a settled night-time scene, we went back to the caravan with its thick blanket of snow on the roof as insulation,

My painting of Ettersgill Farm, County Durham.

and slept soundly in our sleeping bags. The following day the men went back up the fells to search for any more lost animals, before starting to divide up the various flocks in the home fields.

For the next few days while the sun continued to shine brightly, there were no more snow showers. The snow lay thick and crisp to walk upon, so we all helped by sorting out the various sheep, and took another large load to the market in Middleton. This time I avoided standing round the ring, but did a little shopping instead for Mrs. Allinson, finding things that she had requested. Helen came with us, and enjoyed doing her own shopping, fulfilling some errands for Ian at the farm shop, and other tasks, so that we all met up again at the end of the day minus the sheep, for the return journey to the farm.

It was nearing the end of our holiday. This really saddened me, because while I had worked so hard for two weeks, I had also grown very attached to Ian, who had treated me as a valued adult with responsibilities. I could not have told him so, but he also made my heart leap strangely, which for the first time made me acutely aware of the attractions of the opposite sex. What very mixed up feelings I suffered. The object of my desire was at least fifteen years older than me. I could not tell Helen, for fear of being ridiculed, so held my peace.

We packed up our belongings, in preparation for Pop's arrival at two o'clock, then went over to the farmhouse for our lunch. Helen wished to thank the two good ladies for their kindness. Ian also came in for his lunch, accompanied as usual by his dogs at the door step. We handed over two packages as presents for Mrs. Nattress and Mrs. Allinson to show our appreciation, while they served a hot lamb stew to us all. Then Ian asked Helen, 'Did you bring in those parcels of mine?' and spying them laid in the armchair, he picked up a small square one, and placed it on the table in front of me.

'Y've bin a great help during yer holidays. I cannut pay yer what yer deserve fer all yer hord work, but mebbe in yon li'le box, yer'll be reminded of us and m' thanks, fur a long time t' come.' He looked into my eyes and smiled, as I felt a blush on my cheeks. So I opened the box and there lay the carriage clock that I had admired in Middleton-in-Teesdale, and it did indeed remind me of those happy moments – for a very long time.

YOU WIN SOME, YOU LOSE SOME

One of our frequent visitors during the early 1950s was my Uncle Stephen Simpson, often dropping in for lunch or tea, and to chat with Mother. As her older and only brother, they had a great deal in common personality-wise, because they both liked their own way, both behaved deviously when beneficial or advantageous to themselves, and were utterly charming while manipulating others. Stephen was very tall, with enormous feet, a scattering of fair hair, and wore thin horn-rimmed glasses which seemed almost to rest on his little moustache. My mother was barely five feet two, less trim as she aged, but always well dressed.

Uncle Stephen was the last in a long line of the 'Stephen Simpsons', born in February 1903 into my grandfather's wealthy family. He was expected to do well with education, and this was aimed at preparing him eventually for taking over the leadership of the family embroidery and wire-drawing firm in Preston. I heard much about his early life from my cousin Norah, who was a little younger than Mother. She met Stephen when they were both young, did not like him much, and this no doubt coloured her views of him. Grandmother died in the 20s, and he soon became a wild young thing without her restraining hand, as did my mother, who was by then nearly fourteen.

Stephen as a boy with his eldest sister Mary.

Stephen was a good looking boy, much sought after by the girls, which he readily reciprocated, with piercing blue eyes, and a charming manner, always seemingly to have money to spend, but not too keen on working for it.

Having attended Trent College as a boarder in Derbyshire with average results,

Stephen as a teenager.

he was then apprenticed to my grandfather's company Simpson's Gold Thread Works in Preston. He was given a large allowance, where his 'rich playboy' attitudes soon caused problems as he grew older, but certainly not wiser. He gambled with his friends, becoming addicted to the thrill of horse racing, because he won many thousands when on a good run, thus fuelling his thirst for more easy money, yet ignoring the reverse effects when on a losing streak. Between the wars he studied accountancy, then acquired a commission in the Royal Field Artillery in 1921, thus gaining status, and an officer's pay that soon disappeared by the same route via the horses.

Cousin Norah remarked that in the 1930s, Stephen's undoubted downfall was 'fast women and slow horses', but the final crunch came when he caused a young society lady to become pregnant, and at the same time 'borrowing a large sum' from the Simpson Works funds, to pay off his mounting gambling debts. Grandfather was furious, re-placed the money out of his own account, and provided a hefty sum for the young lady. He finally settled the matter of his errant son swiftly and very firmly, by making a drastic decision.

'The boy has turned into a blaggard, and not to be trusted,' he told his works manager, 'I shall send him to my business contact in South America, and see if he can prove his worth as a representative for the firm there and

Stephen with my parents showing how tall he was.

drum up some trade. Away from his friends and the horses he might turn over a new leaf.'

He was sent to London to the works manager there, Leonard Cleaver, who, under instructions, fitted him out with tropical gear, a case of samples from the Gold Thread Works, and enough remittance to fund his first month, which was to be re-peated monthly on the assurance of his good behaviour. He was then put on the boat bound for Argentina.

He made a poor agent, but his bookmaker's mind and accountancy skills proved useful, earning extra money, while sampling the excitements of the Argentinian horse racing courses, spoken of as second-to-none in the racing world. He was kept there, by Grandfather sending him his monthly remittance, but as before, Stephen became entangled with a horse breeder's daughter, with the resultant offspring forc-ing him to beat a hasty retreat to Mexico for a brief spell.

Years later I found a letter that Grandfather wrote, explaining lengthily to his cousin in Exeter that he flatly refused to pay his return fare on a passenger ship to England. Stephen would have to make his own way home, but secretly he hoped that he would be unable to do so.

The Remittance Man, as the family always called him, was finally recalled to his regiment's reservists during the war, so he had to pay steerage on a very rough sea passage across the Atlantic. He took a bunk in a trader, full of cod, herrings and whale meat, dodging the enemy shipping, and finally joined his regiment as a non-combatant member of the battal-ion, due to being in his mid-thirties.

Bringing him up to date and into my era, Stephen married Auntie Vera in the early 1940s and settled with her in Barnet, unchanged in his ways over the years. Still very charming, extremely tall, good com-pany and entertaining although somewhat over-weight and a heavy smoker, he was ever a wheeler and dealer to make money by straight or questionable

Stephen and Vera's wedding.

means, but he mainly relied on horse racing, insisting that he would have yet another big win. I was still too young to understand my uncle's great foolishness.

I went one autumn weekend to stay at their house in Barnet, and he took me to watch a cricket match at The Oval, but it was not to my liking because I was cold. When we returned, Uncle Stephen became glued to horse-racing on his new television, so Auntie Vera and I kept warm making a large bonfire in the garden with fallen leaves. I admired the different colours of several Michaelmas daisies which she grew amongst the autumn crocus and late flowering shrubs. She was a good gardener and a kindly, shrewd

Vera in her garden.

Welsh woman with sad brown eyes, so I enjoyed her company, because she had a good sense of humour, and told me a great deal about him, and of his earlier life.

'I met your uncle on a train travelling to London, where he insisted he polish my cutlery before we ate our lunch on board. I wish he had not bothered. Soon he will wish he had not bothered either.' She laughed as she brushed her straggling grey hair out of her eyes, and smiled at me. She did not put up with Uncle Stephen's questionable dealings for much longer after that.

Eventually, she threw him out, living more happily and securely by her own means. He then had to find a small flat for himself. After quite some time, with no-one having had contact with her, the police came to see Mother, having found her address on a Christmas card in Vera's house. They told Mother that my aunt had been found dead in her bedroom. She had suffered a heart attack and had died three months previously, with nobody having been aware of the occurrence for all that time. I cried a lot during the modest funeral for the passing of that lovely lady, and insisted that we decorate her grave. I was beginning to recognise the pain of death only too well.

Vera when much older.

One day Uncle Stephen had a suggestion for my mother. 'Would you like to come to Ascot with me next month? I'm hosting a business group and have booked a box for them. Lunch will be served, and you can bring Wendy too. You can also be my hostess for the day – you are always so good at that role, organising people.'

On this particular day, when he dropped in to see us, I knew he had wanted something. And that was not all. He had seen a portrait which I had painted of Grandfather, and two portraits propped up which were completed commissions for Father's friends. I might not have been academically minded but was honing my talents in portrait painting. It was a way of earning some much needed funds while I was at college.

'Those portraits are extremely good. How much do you charge?'

'Twenty five pounds, and two pounds for the frame,' I replied. It was quite a lot of money in those days, but not too much for a portrait.

'That's very reasonable. Can you paint one from a photograph for me?'

Thereupon Stephen pulled out a set of ten prints, and requested me to choose one, asking me to complete the painting by the time I saw him at Ascot, if possible. I had a month now for this commission, and I worked hard to perfect the painting. When finished, Father said it was a very good likeness, and helped me choose a frame for it, after which the finished article was wrapped with great care for transportation to the races.

A snapshot of Uncle Stephen

Royal Ascot is a grand occasion for dressing up in beautiful clothes and fancy hats, and most of the men wore tail coats and grey toppers to complement the ladies' elegant outfits. It was a warm June day, sultry, cloudless and still. With small labels attached to our frontages, and dressed to kill, with our chosen headgear firmly pinned on, we entered the member's enclosure to the boxes, seeing the colourful flags fluttering like flowers in a mixed border waving in the wind.

We smelled the mown grass being trampled by the urgent feet of excited crowds, milling around the turf accountants, as the line of bookies liked to call themselves. We could see the tick-tack men waving their arms with secret signals like semaphore flags, and heard the bookies' barkers trying to out-do their rivals in attracting customers, while the great roars of the crowds swelled to a climax as a race reached its winning post, and was topped by deafening cheers.

We had stood excitedly by the rails to watch, as the gleaming carriages, pulled by matching steeds, swept past us and up the main racecourse, carrying the Royal entourage to their box for the day's racing, all dressed in magnificent finery.

We stood by the parade ring and studied the form of each of the runners, magnificent horses who were quivering and snorting, as they pranced around, never for a moment still, carrying their colourful jockeys. These small, thin, men were listening to the top-hatted owners and trainers, who were offering their jockeys last minute instructions just before the moment arrived for the participants to line up at the starting line. Then they were off.

We then talked and listened to advice offered by the regulars, who were keen to share their knowledge of betting, and their schemes to make money. All of us enjoyed the experience of placing bets with the bookies, and sometimes we were lucky enough to collect small winnings.

Later on as lunch was served, Mother carefully unwrapped our package, and lifted out the portrait for Stephen's inspection. It was much admired by all his friends, inspected minutely in detail and compared to the subject himself, who was preening like a sleek cat in an offhand kind of way by all the attention that was being lavished upon him.

My oil painting of Uncle Stephen

'The likeness is perfect, Stephen. It captures the very essence of you, and makes you better looking. How happy you must be to have such a very talented niece. I hope you paid her well.'

All his friends spoke enthusiastically. When I heard that remark, I decided to ask my uncle for the money so that I could spend a little that day.

Flat racing, watercolour by W. Stuart.

'Uncle Stephen, can I have my £27 for the picture? I've completed it in time for you,' I asked, as the group were just descending the stairs in the stand to join the book-makers row of tables by the track perimeter, and place their bets for the afternoon races.

'Later, later … would you like a bet on anything?" he asked as an afterthought and impatiently, as he was going down the stairs, only then pausing to take the proffered money for my bet with my instructions.

'Yes, please can you put three shillings on Early Mist to win?' Twenty shillings was equal to £1 in those days. It was a lot of money for me, and I felt I was being very bold, but I had been watching the horses with interest in the ring, and heard a trainer say this magnificent grey had stamina. It looked such a beautiful horse, so lively too. I returned to the box where the view of the racetrack was ideal to follow the race.

My excitement was overflowing when my horse won by a short neck at six to one, giving me back an eighteen shillings win, plus the stake money of three shillings, making a grand total of 21 shillings. That was a whole guinea. I waited expectantly for some time for Uncle Stephen and his friends to return upstairs, so that I could collect my winnings from him, but was horrified to hear his comments when he finally returned.

Stephen going to the races.

'I collected your winnings. Then I proceeded to put a bet on Monet's Palette. A painter's name for a horse, a good omen. So I put your winnings on it, and the money for the picture too, making a decent stake. You should win a hefty amount.'

'You shouldn't have done that. I needed my money. I didn't want to make a second bet. I wanted my money back for something else.' The total was a great deal of money for me to lose.

I shouted at him, but the roar of the crowds for the next race drowned out my protestations, and after watching Monet's Palette fall back in the field to fifth place, tears started to roll down my face. I was really angry.

I never recouped my money for the race which I had won, or the fee for the painting of my uncle, but learned the bitter lesson of never, ever trusting a gambler. My good father however, recognising the dreadful injustice of the crooked transaction, and later on after having strong words with Uncle Stephen, put the full amount himself for safe keeping into my Post Office savings book.

'You win some, you lose some. Better luck next time.' Stephen's laughing comment kept ringing in my ears for years to come.

HORSE SENSE

At home, the unease between the adults was evident only occasionally, as neither parent wished to abandon their home. They had settled down to the realities of life and more often than not, were both absorbed in a plethora of activities. Father appeared happy in his sphere of scientific work, garden, hobbies and had his own circle of army friends with whom he socialised, while my fun-loving mother had her fingers in many pies and was extremely popular. She supported her political party, sometimes using our house for committee meetings. She also had a large circle of party-loving friends, who were theatre-goers and musicians, an eclectic mix of interesting people.

Mother in party mood.

On one occasion she organised a fancy dress ball for charity. The theme was Carmen Miranda, so Anthea and I had to work hard to create suitable outfits. All my friends from the choir joined in because it was a worthy cause, great fun, and was hailed as a huge success. I enjoyed meeting other people on these occasions. Father supported Mother's efforts at times if it did not interfere with the more serious business of golfing.

Jim fitted into Mother's group of friends in the main. Together, Jim and Father seemed to be civil enough, even friendly, often enjoying each other's company. They side stepped various conflicts, because both were now trying to avoid Mother's tantrums which happened less frequently. In modern terms she would be known as a 'control freak'. Sometimes there were indeed undercurrents, mainly sparked off by Jane when she returned home, openly telling Father to eject Jim from our house, while shouting at him, 'Go, nobody wants you here.' which was obviously not true.

I loved my father for his gentleness, goodness and understanding. He was a peacemaker. I loved, but really feared my mother's unexpected tempers. I had an easy friendship with Jim, whom I liked as my friend, therefore I did not agree with his being criticised so unfairly, especially when he had done so much for the family during the war, and in more recent troubled times. I could not yet see the wider

Fancy dress at the theatre group.

picture with adult eyes, or understand the class differences.

My sister had a lot of my mother's drive, and still wished to climb the social ladder of life which she thought was her due, wishing to capitalize on our deceased Grandfather's undoubted wealth, which was now tied up elsewhere, as well as the connections through Father's rank.

Jane in her nursing uniform.

I started confiding in my great Aunt Daisy Stuart, who was within easy visiting distance when travelling to and from school. It was to be my last year at school, and I had no idea what I should do, unlike Jane who still had visions of a great future, of being a nursing sister and having a career in medicine, or with her delusions of grandeur, marrying well 'into money', as the saying went. She seemed so sure of herself, tall, good looking and never wavering in her beliefs.

'If the troubles that your sister creates at home have nothing to do with you, and are not of your making, do not involve yourself, instead simply keep your own council.' My aunt spoke with ideals which were fashioned much like my father's, and I realised that she had the same kindness of spirit and thoughtfulness. He said that she had talked a lot of 'Horse Sense' during his lifetime, and her opinions were worth taking note. I'm not so sure what he meant, but nevertheless I listened to his advice.

Aunt Daisy my 'fairy' godmother.

Small in stature, with hazel-coloured smiling eyes, Aunt Daisy peered through her circular tortoiseshell spectacles; her grey hair was parted in the middle and gathered in a neat bun at the nape of her neck. She did not have the usual 'fairy godmother' image, especially wearing her home-knitted navy suits, but I loved her, because she fitted the role perfectly for me. She lived on her own in a small semi-basement flat in Holland Park, but always seemed to be busy with 'good works' for other people. She was in her seventies by then, somewhat lamed by arthritis, and used a walking stick, but was still very independent. However, she could always be relied upon when I called, to stop for a cup of tea and magically produce a good selection of fancy cakes. She listened to all my comments and uncertainties, and I even managed to explain to her a little bit of my strange attraction to my sheep-farming friend earlier in the year.

'It is better to take each year as it comes, my child, because opportunities will arise which you know nothing about. How about applying for a bursary to an art college when you have left St. Paul's? I will get a suitable application form for you,' she offered.

Within a couple of weeks she had applied for a bursary on my behalf to go to St Martin's Art College in London, to start the following year, after I had finished at St. Pauls. I filled the form in and delivered it personally, along with a portfolio of work. I was delighted to be awarded the bursary. It concentrated my mind wonderfully on my work with renewed purpose, giving me a direction to aim for, and settled me down to press on with my education.

One Saturday, she took me to celebrate, and we went to visit the 'Derry and Toms' Roof Garden in Kensington, for a meal. This large department store, built in 1933 and designed by Bernard Shaw in the Art Deco style, had re-opened after the war

Derry and Tom's roof garden, 1930s

following repairs and renovations. It was famous at that time for being the only building in London to have a large and beautiful garden on its roof, with full scale trees, and a stream running through.

I believe that landscape architect Ralph Hancock had designed this marvellous place; a curious fact, which has lodged in my mind for so long. The meal there was such a treat. I remembered having a Knickerbocker Glory, a colourful pudding in a tall glass, until then unobtainable, but the Ministry of Food still stipulated that a meal must not cost more than three and sixpence, with only one protein in it. With the starving millions in Europe to attend to, they were assisted with food supplied by the Americans, whom I'm led to believe, thought that Britain had turned communist with the new Labour government installed.

The food support to England remained restricted, therefore we continued to be quite severely rationed for many of our basic necessities, simply because the country was still not able to supply its own needs.

My penultimate year at school was full of interesting events. I was not destined to take my A-level exams but instead only work towards O-levels. I became involved in the production of Shakespeare' plays, and only once had a speaking part with one line. More often than not I was cast in the role of scenery painter, props deviser and costume designer.

St Paul's Girls School dining room.

I did not mind so much, because I knew that in these activities there was room for me to shine, and bask in a little glory, even momentarily – these were skills which did not rely on the arrangements of letters and words. I also painted two large wall-sized illustrations, one being of The Lady of Shallot on the dining room walls, because at that time it was still a grey concrete re-enforced air-raid shelter, with nothing much else to recommend it except the proximity to the kitchens.

So I acquired a taste for large-scale scenery painting, and being now somewhat ambidextrous, I found this useful, because it enabled me to reach distant points on the pictures with either hand. In later life, I did indeed design and create many sets for a variety of theatre productions, painting large drop-cloths, using my own designs and experience from these earlier years.

My holiday which had been taken in the May of 1951 heralded the way for expanding my horizons a little further. Having once tried this out, my parents realised that it was beneficial for me to travel. It helped to offset my deep feelings of mourning for Grandfather, and the loss of Bowerswood. I was still not considered old enough to be taken on Mother's next jaunt on a cruise ship to the Mediterranean in the summer.

Cruising on the high seas just after the war was becoming a popular, but somewhat exclusive holiday for those willing to pay. Mother had always had a certain amount of her own funds, which had increased greatly since Grandfather's death. On this occasion, she decided to go with her friend Lucy Green, a regimental widow, and joined the foursome of Mr and Mrs Winterbourne with Alec and Tina Pickton, a local nouveau riche couple. They took their friend Len, the owner of the local newsagents, and needed another person to share his cabin, because his wife had suddenly died. All the cabins were twins, so Jim was elected to be the spare man to fill the empty space. This move had unexpected consequences.

Cruising was not to Father's taste, after all his travels and he was grateful for the sudden peace at home. He was now Captain of his golf club, and was knee deep with summer tournaments. So with Jane now away at a secretarial college with Pauline for a year, he saw a somewhat lonely eight weeks ahead for me.

He had always been a good correspondent with friends, and had recently received a chatty letter from a Mrs Wrigley, the lady with whom he had billeted when the many hundreds of troops had returned from Dunkirk in 1940. The exhausted and injured forces who landed back in Britain had been dispatched initially, and arbitrarily, to all parts of the country, regardless of their regiments. As a result, a great many men found themselves temporarily in strange areas, where accommodation had been offered freely and in haste, particularly by many northerners.

My father had found himself and some of his men billeted in various houses in a small village in Yorkshire, just outside Northallerton. His placement for accommodation was in Warlaby Lodge. This was owned by Mrs Wrigley, a somewhat autocratic, but very kind, grey haired 'Lady of the Manor', who was tall, thin and energetic. Her home was an old-fashioned, Georgian house, square and stone clad. The village of Ainderby Steeple and its adjoining hamlet of Warlaby seemed almost untouched by the war years. The area was steeped in a pre-war essence of old world charm, where the farms were still using many kinds of old-fashioned farming machinery and methods. The letter she received from my father now set off another long-reaching train of events for me.

My father went for a few days to visit her, and while there, Mrs. Wrigley suggested that I might like to spend my summer holidays with her at Warlaby. When he returned and told me of the plan, I was excited at the thought of travelling to somewhere new. By the end of term I was already packing my summer clothes, my paintbox and drawing things. Mother bought me a small suitcase for this 'new adventure' as I liked to think of it. Father organised a bus ticket from Victoria Bus Station, to travel north to Leeming Bar, on the A1 Great North Road, near Northallerton, Yorkshire. This was where Mrs Wrigley would meet me.

In 1950 there were no motorways, very few road signs, and definitely no yellow or white road markings to spoil the harmonious grey curves of the winding roads with only their white dots down the centre – also there were very few cars.

This was a bus trip which I came to know quite well. It seemed like a leisurely journey of discovery, with time to see the passing countryside, in stark contrast to the much faster train, taken in the springtime, which had whisked me along to Shildon. For me, the train seemed to have little time to dawdle, instead would puff noisily through briefly glimpsed stations, and then race on, like a startled horse trying to beat its own record.

At the beginning of my journey I remember travelling through green urban areas of houses and trees in their hundreds which surrounded London. Later the views were of flatter, uniform land, as we continued north through Hertfordshire, Bedfordshire, Cambridgeshire, and Lincolnshire towards the southern parts of Yorkshire, following the old Great North Road. From this journey I changed my long held belief that all the counties had recognisable borders, and adjusted it, by realising that the county borders were only lines drawn on paper maps.

Taken in high summer, this journey was soon dominated by many shades of yellow, with occasional patches of red where the poppies held sway. As we travelled along I was entranced by acres of ripening corn, wheat, rye, barley and rape-seed flowers, which made the countryside glow with warmth. It smelled so strongly of summer flowers, nectars and corn crops, that it reminded me of the Bowers House harvesting behind Grandfather's house. The buzz of midsummer bees and insects competed with the hum of the huge harvesting machines and many coloured old tractors which were  visible. Crops were now grown in such large fields that several harvesters were working in the same fields, side by side.

This was farming on a grand scale, all working diligently to make up for our deficit of home grown food. Quite often I spotted a horse pulling an old binder, or a pair of Shires ploughing the stubble. In many fields the men were stooking, or following and loading the trailers high with sheaves of corn, pulled by powerful Shire horses, which paused then continued almost without instructions. There were the Suffolk Punches with deep russet coats, and larger black and white Clydesdale horses, sporting their 'long white fluffy socks', and even some Cleveland Bays, big brown horses with black manes and no 'socks'. They were all capable of pulling enormous loads, and indeed they did. These beautiful heavy animals could be seen everywhere being used for farm work, as of old, because of a lack of fuel for tractors.

There were still a fair number of riders and traps being pulled by lighter horses or ponies, using the roads for the same reason. Reluctantly, these horse-drawn vehicles were having to give way to the ever-growing volume of motor traffic, as very ancient cars gradually started reappearing out of their pre-war 'mothballs', and new cars such as Austin A40 cars appeared, sporting a selection of bright colours. Road signs, which had been taken down during the war, now reappeared, repainted, redesigned and redirected for the benefit of new travellers.

We stopped for a break in our journey at Stamford, then on to Grantham and Newark, to stretch our legs and have a drink, and at this point we saw a string of tall, shining horses, walking with springing steps and carrying colourfully-clad riders, out for their daily exercise. We were now passing near some well-known stables of the racing fraternity. As we re-boarded the coach, we saw a string of about thirty horses racing up a long incline, with their riders balancing aloft in their saddles, standing on spindly legs, and swaying with the movement of their steeds. It crossed my mind that maybe I had seen some of these horses when I had gone to the races with my Uncle Stephen. Doncaster was reached before I realised that we were now in southern Yorkshire, followed an hour later by Wetherby, to the north of the county. Eventually, we arrived at Leeming Bar on the Great North Road.

When I collected my case from the boot of the coach, I looked around to find my transport from amongst the waiting people, who had gathered either to board the coach, for onward travel to Scotland, or to meet alighting passengers. But as the crowds quickly dispersed, the only one left still waiting was an old lady sitting bolt upright in a lightweight trap with a rug over her knees.

The pony, of perhaps fourteen hands high, stood motionless in the warmth of the late summer sunshine, flicking her tail at the buzzing flies as they circled around her. She lifted her sturdy legs in turn now and again, in boredom. The old lady jumped down from her seat and strode over to where I stood clutching my case and feeling rather uncertain.

'Hello, you must be Wendy. Emily Wrigley, from Warlaby,' she announced positively and briefly, as she gripped my proffered hand firmly. We climbed into the seat of the trap with my case placed on the floor behind us, which was littered with other parcels, some farm implements, and animal feeds. She laid a rug over our knees, although the weather was still warm, saying that one's legs tended to feel cold when driving.

A similar trap to that at Warlaby.

Then she said briskly, 'You can take the reins if you like.' On this occasion I declined the offer, because I had only ever been in charge of Grandfather's pony and trap, and this one seemed much larger – I would keep this experience for later. So she expertly turned Patsy, the pony, around in a small circle. With a flick of the whip that was barely discernible to my eye, Patsy now set off down the side road towards our goal with a brisk trot, knowing exactly where she was going. Here was 'Horse Sense' in a more recognisable form.

The trees hung low over the road, and I could catch hold of the leaves as we sped along at pony speed, while I watched the fields through the ancient hedges. The sound of the clip-clopping hooves on the metalled road was as repetitive as an eager song bird, with a pleasing soporific effect on one's tired senses after the long journey. After a while we eventually passed a large paddock, and turned into a wide entrance, bordered by white fencing, then stopped in front of Warlaby Lodge. We had now arrived into a kind of nineteenth century world of horses – or so it seemed to me.

A TASTE OF YORKSHIRE

Warlaby Lodge was a square Georgian house, with at least six bedrooms and was fronted by an enormous beech tree. It was surrounded by a spread of other species of trees within its grounds, with many outhouses and stables, which exuded the nineteenth century ways of gracious living.

The three acres or so of field in front of this lovely house had several horses in it, cropping the grass with eager intent, as they walked slowly to the next tempting patch. Later, at the end of the next month I walked over this field, picking tasty mushrooms, as the autumn mists and chillier weather of late September rolled in.

I was given a little room overlooking the porch, with a door which folded in half, and enough space for a bed and small chest, where I put my things. I looked out onto the paddock through a tall multi-paned Georgian window, enjoying the peaceful scene. The house smelled of the beautifully arranged flowers in the hall, and was so quiet. Mrs Wrigley, tall and wiry, purposefully strode in carrying a candlestick, with a stump of a candle in it, and gave me another piece of new candle lifted out of her small basket.

'You will need this tonight – half a candle per night – you don't need more for undressing. Find your way down to the kitchen when you're ready. We'll have supper – no maids.' She had a very staccato way of speaking with an economy of words, but not unkindly meant.

There was neither gas nor electricity laid on to the house, and having noticed oil lamps in all the rooms, I was intrigued to find out how she cooked. I went down to a lower, basement floor, below the main hall, following the noises of clattering plates, and found Mrs Wrigley in her kitchen, lifting out a steaming dish of food from a large wood-burning Aga. The kettle was boiling on the hob.

'Janet's day off. Girl from the village. Helps me four days a week. Hope you eat anything – food's dashed short. When we're finished, go outside, meet Henry. He'll sort out a suitable saddle for you.'

Mrs. Wrigley, her son and my father.

191

So she chatted on, in small statements, like a kind of shorthand, and I listened bewitched by this lady with twinkling eyes. She obviously had plans for me, and knew that I could ride. After the meal, as requested, I went to find Henry in the yard where he had stabled the pony and housed the trap. He was about as old as Mrs Wrigley, with a weather beaten, lived-in brown face, bird-bright eyes and a smile as bowed as his bandy legs. He was busily setting up some fearsome looking contraptions in the provender shed.

'What are you doing that for?' I was always asking questions, and sometimes received strange answers. But Henry was happy to oblige with explanations, and proud of his endeavours as he clattered over the cobbles in his iron-shod clogs to show me his haul. He had carefully clipped a lot of rats' tails onto the back fence like a row of thin prize parsnips for all to admire, spaced out regularly, a grim sight to behold.

'A'm catchin' rats for't bounty. Guv'ment's payin' owt thrup'nce a tail. A've dun reet weel theer. Jist think, two fer a sil'er tanner.' The thought of gaining a multitude of silver sixpences made him grin widely.

He spoke slowly with a Yorkshire accent, as he proudly showed me his long row of rats' tails. Food was so short at that time, and rats were such a plague, contaminating and destroying so much precious grain all over the country, that the Ministry of Food and Agriculture offered a bounty for every rat that was killed, trapped or poisoned. Their tails were needed as evidence of destruction to claim the bounty.

He then picked out, from a row of saddles on pegs in the tack-room, one which he thought suitable for my size and laid it on the table with a bridle.

He added, 'This'll bi you'rn whalst yer 'ere, an' tek' this ridin' coat an' hat an' all, it'll fit thee weel. Don't want thee catching cow'd in't rain.' Thus fitted out for riding and possible poor weather by kind old Henry, I returned to the house to thank Mrs Wrigley, having learned the wisdom of dressing warmly when riding, even on sunny days.

That evening I started exploring my new environment. Among other beautiful and intriguing items in the well-furnished house I discovered a full-sized harp in the drawing room, next to a grand piano which I immediately sampled. Mrs. Wrigley came into the room to light a couple of oil lamps and saw my interest in the harp. Thereupon she sat down to play for a while, taking me in my imagination back to the nineteenth century – no modern power, no wireless, no cars, no harsh lights, only wood fires to create warmth, and home music playing for amusement.

I was aware of the passing of time at that moment, of the effects that the war must have had on Mrs Wrigley, who had lost her husband and two of her three sons in the conflict, and yet here she was, at her advancing age, running the local 'help agencies' such as the Women's

Institute, repatriation schemes, and the Women's Land Army, to good effect and with great spirit.

Soon I learned how to manage with only horse power to go for a shopping spree. Patsy, placed again between the traces in the trap, took us both into Northallerton for shopping, where she was tied to a hitch rail, several of which were placed along the main street, for the convenience of other riders and shoppers, with horse-drawn vehicles. Once we had completed our tasks, we trotted back through Ainderby Steeple, where Mrs. Wrigley showed me Blacksmith Joe's yard, warning me to re-member where it was for the next day's task.

'Patsy has a loose shoe. But you can still ride her. Go and visit Joe. He'll fix it. It's not far. She's very quiet,' and with her barely connected sentences, I got the message for the following day's activity.

'You can then do an errand for me. Here are directions to Broom Close Farm. A WI member there is having a baby soon; needs these baby clothes. See if she needs any help.' I was given my Morse code instructions in Mrs. Wrigley's usual fashion.

Early the next day in Warlaby Lodge's yard and with Henry's help, I saddled up Patsy and rode her round the paddock a few times, until I realized that she was a very well-schooled horse, because she would not do anything wild. So I set off to the blacksmith's yard, not really needing directions, because the wise horse knew where she was going.

As we approached I could hear men's voices, laughing and chatting as they worked, and noticed the acrid smell of burned hooves, a smell which I was not fa-miliar with. I dismounted and handed the reins to Joe's assistant, peering around a packed smithy's yard. It was crowded with metalwork items of all kinds, iron wheels, agricultural implements to be mended, gates, barrelling hoops, as well as a large range of half-finished horse shoes, pre-prepared for their final touches when fitted.

Inside the open-sided shed it was extremely hot. Two men wore heavy leather

aprons, and metal covered clogs. One stood with tongs holding a piece of metal in the open coke fire, encouraging the flames into a white heat by heaving on the long handle which operated the bellows. As soon as the metal piece was white-hot, Joe fashioned it into shape on the anvil, with rhythmic hammering and continual turns, causing a great many sparks to fly in all directions. Nail holes were punched into it, after which it was

plunged into a barrel of cold water. The resulting hissing of the steam created the feeling of being in a hell hole, and this image was further added to by the general commotion of noise, heat and smell.

Patsy was led into the middle of the yard where Joe bent down, lifted her foot, and deftly trapping it between his knees, proceeded to remove the old shoe. My horse was completely acquiescent in Joe's hands. I learned a lot that day – for example, that the hooves are a horse's finger nails and grow continually, so Patsy's hoof needed filing into shape ensuring a proper orientation to the ground; the new shoe was placed on the hoof for measuring, and then adjusted to fit. Finally, it was nailed into place, with nine square-headed nails, which passed through the hard outer-edge of the hoof. A blacksmith was, generally speaking, a producer of artefacts in forged metal, whereas a farrier was a man skilled in shoeing horses but also had some veterinary knowledge – Joe was renowned for his skills in this field. He gave me the spent horse-shoe to take home, to 'hang it up for good luck' he said.

We set off again now firmly re-shod, with Patsy happy to be on the move once more. We followed Mrs Wrigley's directions, past the Yafforth railway crossing gates, and turned left into the farm lane, which I was searching for, following it down to the farm buildings. Men were working in the nearby field, and as I dismounted, I saw a woman, (later introduced to me as Lucy McLaughlin), heavily pregnant, feeding about nine cats outside her door while her small daughter, Jennifer, was playing with them. Greeting them both and explaining where I had come from, I lifted down the parcel from Mrs. Wrigley for her. I then turned around to admire the fields in front of us, and got a bit of a shock.

One of the men working in the field stood still, looking strangely at me, as if I was a ghost. This young man, Bill Joynson, was the farm foreman of Broom Close Farm, in his mid-twenties, very tall, good looking and pleasant to chat with, and had a well-informed slant on many things that he spoke about.

The explanation was soon forthcoming, because I looked so much like his recently deceased younger sister of nineteen, five years his junior, and riding a horse similar to the one she rode, that he nearly fainted. She had been looking after a riding stable near Redcar before her death. Having got over his initial fright at seeing this living 'ghost', he went back to work with Wilf McLaughlin in the field, while I tried to be a help to Lucy in the farmhouse. I rode over several times that month to assist Lucy, because she suffered from a type of asthma and had breathing difficulties.

Bill Joynson.

The farm was a spread-out collection of buildings comprising the farmhouse, washhouse and outbuildings all huddled together, next to a large hen house, sitting in the middle of a neat garden surrounded by a carefully clipped hedge. There was a generator for electricity which powered the milking parlour, and it also brought up water from the well, although it was only used in a limited way. At other times water had to be pumped by hand from the well, and oil pressure lamps were the norm for lighting in the house. A copper boiler in the washhouse was lit each Monday for all the washing, but the drying did not only rely on a line, because Lucy regularly draped the hedges and bushes with her sheets.

Not only rats were considered vermin, but also rabbits did a great deal of damage to the crops. When a large field of oats near the farmhouse was being cut with the binder, Wilf, Bill, and the men went into the field to stook the sheaves with guns by their sides. The startled rabbits kept running further into the ever diminishing corn that was still standing, as the binder made inroads into the crop, while the men removed their cover in the laying corn, as they made rows of stooks.

'Can you shoot?' Wilf asked me when I went out to the field with the 'Baggins', a basket full of pasties, pies and cups that Lucy had prepared for the men. She carried the Billie-cans of tea behind me. When I admitted that I could, Wilf said to Lucy, 'Get out that small air rifle and she shall have a go.' So, with strict instructions about aiming directions, I joined their team, keeping up with the men and accurately potting a number of rabbits who had finally scattered in panic. At the day's end, these were either skinned for the evening cooking pot or hung for another day's meal.

There was no sentiment wasted on the rabbits by anyone, because they wasted a great deal of much needed food. I learned to skin a rabbit quite efficiently, and took several back for Mrs. Wrigley to eat, or for her distribution to the needy, while Bill took a few to his

Wilf skinning a rabbit in front of the binder.

mother and older sister Pat who lived in Redcar, during the weekend on his BSA 500 motorbike. They were a very welcome food source.

That summer was magical, riding from Warlaby Lodge and exploring the countryside, or working at Broom Close Farm. Bill missed his sister Mary with whom he had been very close, and to ease his loneliness and make my holiday less full of work, he offered to take me on his motorbike to interesting places in Yorkshire, in his free time.

We went to visit his mother and his sister Pat, in Redcar, a bracing North East coastal town, where it seemed that the north winds blew right through the skins and bones of the hardiest residents to turn their complexions mauve with cold. Then another day we went up to Sutton Bank to watch the gliders soaring high on the rising thermals that swept up from this steep cliff.

I shared my time between Warlaby Lodge and the farm, and helped Mrs. Wrigley with the summer fete on the Green in Ainderby Steeple, where there were fancy stalls of every kind, with colourful flags attached to trees fluttering brightly in the sunshine.

Bill's sister Pat and his mother.

Many children, wearing their party frocks ran about, but at one point they were called to order by the school teacher, who then arranged them around a Maypole which had been erected in the middle of the village green.

With the first chord struck by a small band, the children began skipping in formation, each holding onto the end of a ribbon, some to the left and others to the right, going in and out, in ordered fashion as the ribbons crossed and wound round the pole, becoming ever shorter as they went. At last they all turned round in unison, and retraced their steps, dancing as they went. With twirls and flourishes they bowed to their audience, and repeated the performance another three times before it came to its final conclusion. I had never before seen this kind of country dancing, and was delighted by the patterns created.

As the summer passed, with the ground having been heated by continual sunshine that year, mushrooms started appearing in great profusion in the horse paddock, and I often rose early just as the mists were rising and ran around with a basket to pick the largest white globes before they opened too far. Mushrooms are such a treat when totally fresh, and I often ran in my bare feet through the soft dewy grass, which was kept short by horses, to collect my breakfast for the day, and shared my findings with the rest of the household. There were still many tomatoes in the greenhouse, so I raided them too for the morning feast.

My time at Warlaby was coming to an end, because school started during the last week of September, and soon I had to travel back to London. So I went to say good-bye to all at the farm, driving the trap with Patsy behaving perfectly, and felt very sad at having to go. Wilf put a box, specially made to hold five dozen eggs, in the back of the trap, saying that they knew food was still short in London, and could collect the box when they came down to London for the National Dairy Show held in Olympia in November.

Lucy urged me to visit them again during next year's holiday, because she had enjoyed my company. For me it had been like living in an alien world, so enjoyable, yet so different from home in the south.

IN FRONT OF WARLABY LODGE.

I was now growing up, becoming more mature, and able to take responsibility for tasks given to me. When I returned to Warlaby, I packed up my belongings and loaded the trap in readiness to retrace my steps to meet the bus at Leeming Bar. Mrs. Wrigley took charge of the reins as she tucked the rug round our legs, speaking with her usual economy of words, 'I have enjoyed your stay. Make it longer another year. Give my best regards to your father. You'll be taller by next time.'

She added, 'here's a parcel of mushrooms. Bring some riding breeks that fit you on your next visit.'

All this was said as we rode out of Warlaby, briskly trotting towards Leeming Bar, while I sat ruminating on my new friends – old Henry, Emily Wrigley, then Wilf and Lucy McLaughlin, Jennifer and Bill at Broom Close, and worlds away from my usual life. As I finally boarded the bus that had arrived from Scotland, I felt that the long summer was ended. I was now returning to my other world in London. I did not know then that I had met my future husband.

BANISHING BWANA DEVILS

The memories of my summer break in Yorkshire sustained me with happy thoughts and fed my imagination during my last year at school. I felt as if I had two personalities – one which enjoyed the noise and bustle of a busy town life, peppered with exciting activities, along with the variety of southern accents (still strange to me), and a different one which preferred the slower-paced existence, learnt and absorbed from childhood in Ireland, then in Lancashire, and now the familiarity of life in the north eastern counties.

By the time I returned home with my five dozen eggs in the wooden box, it brought home to me the seriousness of food shortages still prevalent in London, where racketeering in ration books and coupons for basic foodstuffs were rife, although petrol was now plentiful and had been de-rationed in 1950. However, petrol for agricultural use, which was dyed red and much cheaper, was still a 'currency' for some unscrupulous people. Strangely, rationing became a lot worse for a time after the war than during the hostilities. In my case, the food rationing only affected me consciously because of my sweet ration, a mere two ounces a week, (sugar being rationed still for another year or two) therefore most young people chose their sweets very carefully, to ensure they lasted as long as possible.

I often went to the grocers where our ration books had been registered, to collect our meagre weekly portions per person, such as the 2ozs of butter (about 60 grams), 2oz lard, 4oz margarine and 2oz bacon to add to two eggs and the small, blue 3oz bag of sugar to match the weighed-out flour in the same blue 'sugar-paper' bags. I hesitate to imagine what had been added to our foodstuffs to bulk out our meals, but few of us were really short, and as a result we probably ate a great deal healthier than people do today.

The local butchers shop offered cheap 'flavoured' sausages for fewer coupons, but the greatest savings were to be found at fishmongers, where unrationed, beautifully coloured and strange fish were offered to any adventurous cook, sometimes with cooking instructions. I soon became a devotee of fish in all its strange guises. I brought home some snook, a strange imported American fish, jellied eels and winkles, which only my father and I delighted in eating. The 'catfish' soon became 'rock salmon', being a more acceptable name for it. By the end of 1951 once the government had changed to the conservatives, the moderate increase in food imports started to make a difference, but relatively normal supplies of food was only achieved by around mid-1954 when rationing was finally relaxed.

I set to work with a will at school, and also enjoyed going regularly to the swimming baths with my father. He kept up my rowing training, but could not persuade me into ball games of any kind, because I still could not judge the speed or distance of approach of the darned balls.

An American snook fish.

Sometimes we went to the theatre in London, and watched the current musical in one of the theatres such as *Carousel, The King and I* and *Oklahoma*, then seeing the opening performance of *South*

Pacific, a new musical with Mary Martin playing the lead role.

Going to the pictures was a weekly treat for everybody because, apart from usually having a good story, it allowed us to experience the world, not least from the newsreels which continued to run. It broadened our knowledge, particularly of America, from where most films came, showing the dances, music crazes and clothes that were the latest coupon-free American fashions of the time.

The end of my time at St Paul's School came in 1952, with GCE examinations taken, end of term concerts performed and good-byes said to my form mates. I would long remember my good friend Penelope Frith, a Baron's Court dweller, Ann John, my painting friend, tall and stately Caroline Crawley, and fun loving Jill Martin. Not least, I said a heartfelt thank you to my lovely form teacher, Miss Higginson, who had seen me though some tough times at school. Now it was time to move on. My godmother Aunt Daisy had paved the way for this transition, but not as she had planned.

She had arranged an entrance to St. Martins Art College in London for me, where painting was the main discipline. However, the education authorities, noticing that I now lived in Isleworth, Middlesex, and not at the address given in Holland Park, transferred my bursary to the Twickenham Art College, a seat of learning which was more commercially orientated. This change of venue was not to my liking, but it did wonders for my drawing skills, painting methods and graphics, and in fact gave me a good groundwork for future art work.

This modern, purpose-built building overlooked Twickenham Rugby ground. This was a bonus because whenever any major matches were being played, not a single space could be seen along the window sills, and viewing was at a premium.

I cycled from home every day, through Mogden Sewage Treatment Works with its gyrating, spraying arms which travelled around the cinder beds, creating soap suds due to the surfactants in the water. This blew around in the wind, catching in the tall trees surrounding the place, miles of lacy foam traceries, hung up like fine Brussels lace, fit to sew on the hem of a petticoat.

From St Pauls, I maintained just one friendship with Jill Martin, which lasted for many years, but now at Twickenham Art college, I had the opportunity to meet new people. One of these was a girl called Cynthia, whose great talent was the ability to draw portraits. She had drawn several small pictures of Herbert Lom, the film actor, with whom she had a 'crush'. I learned a lot from her about portrait painting, but had great difficulty in understanding what she said, with her true Cockney rhyming slang and accent.

There is a great deal in this year which I cannot recall, however two teachers spring to mind: Mr Gould for technical drawing, and Mr Bottomley for fine art drawing, as broadly spoken a Yorkshireman as Cynthia was a Cockney.

Mr. Bottomley was very interested in illusions, and the workings of optical illusory art work. One day, he took a group of us to see *Bwana Devil* which was showing in a Leicester Square cinema, because he wanted to show us the new developments in the Natural Vision 3D System. When we arrived at the cinema we were given a pair of cardboard spectacles, fitted with green and red lenses, and labelled left and right. Intrigued by it all, we put them on and settled down to watch the film.

It was a true story about the 'Tsau man eaters', or man-eating lions in Uganda. While the actor Robert Stack manfully dealt with the situation on the silver screen, these terrifying lions seemed to leap out at us and over our shoulders from their 2D settings with the help of the spectacles, and amidst a great many screams, most of us found ourselves in frightened heaps on the cinema floor. When Father, knowing he had missed something spectacular, offered to take me again, I flatly refused his offer.

The group of young people I was friendly with were from our local choir, whose ages ranged widely and who were from several different schools. At one time, Anthea and I both vied for the attention of the same choirboy, Herbert Davis, whose Irish mother, Clara, invited us both to see *The Quiet Man*, the latest John Wayne film starring Maureen O'Hara. There-

after we went again several times to re-watch the film and bought records of the music to play on our small record players, unfortunately sickening any sundry listeners with the oft played repeats. Herbert confounded us both by taking up with another Maureen, whom he eventually married.

The music of my teenage years was very much influenced by the 'trad Jazz' era. We bought records of Acker Bilk playing *Petit Fleur* and *Stranger on the Shore*, and Eddie Calvert's golden trumpet could be heard for some years with *Oh Mine Papa*. The Jazz scene was very much alive with Kenny Ball and His Jazzmen, and Chris Barber with his trombone.

Whenever I hear the music of that period, it takes me back immediately to that time of my life, listening to the songs of Vera Lynn, Bob Hope, Bing Crosby and Dean Martin. With a host of others like Johnny Cash and Rosemary Clooney, my musical memories are extensive, because Mother and her housekeeper, Mrs Hart, nearly always had the wireless playing the latest music.

It was the kind of music favoured by local bands at Saturday night dances, where a strict kind of unwritten segregation occurred, when the boys lined one side of the hall, while the girls sat down the other, and only moved into the middle to dance together when the music began to play. By this time our fashions had changed from war time economy of materials to fuller skirts, many petticoats and tight wide belts.

I had hoarded many cast-offs from Jane, and amongst her clothes found some of her shoes that I could wear, previously known as 'coupon busters', a three-in-one piece of footwear. Ladies shoes required seven coupons per year, taken out of one's meagre clothing allocation – interestingly, it was a very long time before we stopped measuring our shopping in these terms. The shoes were patent leather with Cuban heels, which, when detached, revealed thinner ones for evening wear inside the originals. They even became party shoes when the fake diamond studded bows were attached at the front. The 'make-do and mend' slogan had obviously been in the designer's mind when creating these clever shoes. I loved wearing them.

In February 1952 King George VI died of lung cancer at Sandringham, at the age of only 56. He had succeeded his elder brother Edward VIII, whose reign lasted only one year in 1937 through abdication to marry the American divorcée, Wallis Simpson. Various members of his family were recalled from all over the world, and particularly his daughter, Elizabeth with her husband Philip from Kenya. They had been on a world tour of the Commonwealth, but now she returned as our new Queen Elizabeth II, for the funeral and eventual coronation ceremony, which was held the following year.

We had been awash with rain since the beginning of the year, when a terrible storm on 31 January 1953 hit Britain's eastern coastlines. This was caused by very high tides and surges of water from a low depression which travelled fast down the coastline of the North Sea, thus being forced ahead of the hurricane strength winds. The lower reaches of London suffered a great deal of flooding. Shortly after, we received a card from Jeannie, who had taken over running the café in Fleet Street, to tell us that Lil, the café owner, had been drowned while visiting her mother at Canvey.

The fearsome water had swept over low lying Canvey Island in the Thames Estuary during the night with no warning, and 59 people there were drowned. They were living in holiday chalets and little prefabs which had been built after the war to house bombed out Londoners.

Nearly 1,000 people were killed along the east coast during that night, yet they were not headline news for weeks, because our communication systems were so poor, relying on an indifferent or non-existent telephone service at that time. The daily newspapers were asked not to create horrific headlines about the event, so soon after the horrors of the war. However, news of the great tragedy gradually filtered through, when questions were being asked about the poor maintenance or absence of sea defences, especially when it was revealed that the sea swept through Kings Lynn unimpeded, killing hundreds. We heard eventually that over 2,000 people had been drowned on the same night in the Netherlands.

It seemed that 1953 was turning into a momentous year. Like all Londoners at that time, we lined the streets and attended the processions, be it funerals, weddings or state occasions. In March 1953 only ten weeks before the grand coronation celebrations, came the death of old Queen Mary (still known as May of Teck), the wife of George V, who lived to the ripe old age of 85.

Memories of the funeral of the old Queen was brought back by this photograph taken of Queen Mary with my Aunt Daisy and some wounded ex-soldiers – a half-hidden memory, like a shadow flitting through one's mind. It included our meeting some years before at the 'sale of work' in Knightsbridge, of her wearing a toque like a crown on her white hair, and sporting many rows of pearls across her bosom.

Now we attended her funeral, as a mark of respect, all dressed in dark coats and hats, lining the streets in the rain as her coffin, laid on a gun carriage, was pulled slowly past, by eight black plumed horses, to the mournful strains of funeral music, played by the band of the Scots Greys. I marvelled yet again at the precision of the arrangements for this and other such occasions as the cortège passed by. I realised then that I was witnessing another historical moment. It was an extremely long procession, a great many carriages, many horses and so much rain.

The arrangements for the Coronation of Elizabeth II took over a year to organise, because it was a state occasion for the crowned heads of Europe, with guests from all over the world. It was probably the largest ever royal gathering to be organised.

Finally in the summer of 1953 the coronation took place. Towns throughout the country held street parties, and we, in Isleworth, staged a Masque entitled 'Merrie England' in Osterley Park, in which everybody took part. Shops were ablaze with bunting, and goods relating to the festivities were offered for sale.

I was looking forward to seeing the magnificent and very old Gold State Coach carrying the Queen, in the long parade, winding its way through London. In great contrast, well before the event, my father finally had had enough.

'We will go to see your Great Aunt Evelyn in Dorset, who is feeling a bit low. Uncle Brownlow has recently died, and I believe my cousin John is staying at present, so I'd like to see him. She has a new large television, so you will not miss a thing. In fact you are likely to see more than the people standing in the crowds.'

Father would not be persuaded by Mother to alter his plans to suit her wishes. The probability of yet another session of cold camping on the Mall to watch the procession loomed large on the horizon, as she fully intended to go with Jim and a group of friends. Jane was with her friends in London, so Father and I travelled a few days before down to Dorset in his small car, packing a few presents for his aunt. His Uncle Brownlow, who had lost an

Letton, Blanford Forum, Dorset.

arm in the First World War, had been my grandfather Stuart's brother. This was a part of my Stuart family whom I had never met.

I was not sure where we were going, but as we approached the town of Blanford Forum in Dorset, the countryside around it had a clean and invigorating feel to it. Numerous sheep meandered over grassy fields, while the Red Devon dairy cows were much in evidence, contentedly grazing. We turned towards Pimperne, a village in the locality, travelling a few miles before reaching the entrance to Letton. This turned out to be a long tree-lined gravel driveway, only revealing the house itself when driving round an enormous cedar tree with low-sweeping branches and onto the circular driveway in front of the house.

It was an impressive sight. Constructed of red brickwork and Portland stone, it was a square Georgian mansion with a great many tall windows, topped by a carved stone balustrade around the rooftop. Some very tall red-brick chimneys peeped out into the sky, like stairways into heaven, piercing the clouds which became staging platforms for rooks flying to and fro to the nearby rookery, in the tall trees at the end of the front lawn.

Entering through a stone portico into a spacious hall, we were met by Aunt

Evelyn, a slim, well-dressed woman with an autocratic bearing and kindly eyes. She settled us both in the bedrooms for our stay, before sweeping us down the wide staircase again.

'Goff, my dear boy, how good it is to see you again. John is on leave at present – will be coming home tomorrow, but Burleigh, having just got married, has left for Africa now. They've only electrified the ground floor, so you'll have to manage with candles upstairs. I'll leave the oil lamp on the landing table which I've lit for safety.'

Oil lamps? Candles? I thought I had left this out-dated methods of lighting with Mrs Wrigley in Yorkshire, but now realised that any house set deep in the countryside lacked electrical power lines, the laying of which had to be organised by the owners when funds permitted. I remember feeling so sad that here was yet another beautiful house, bereft of people, as the size of the family dwindled, and almost nobody now lived permanently there to appreciate or care for it.

Aunt Evelyn threw out short sentences, a little like Mrs Wrigley had done, as she walked purposefully to the dining room, which had been laid up with polished silver and cut class goblets for a meal which had a nineteenth century style to it. After the meal, which had been served by an unobtrusive and silent manservant, we moved on to the drawing-room with elegant long windows, the curtains undrawn to allow a view of sloping lawns and tall trees with trunks which cut the red dying sunset into stripes. The trees were full of birds, whose noise subsided into silence as they settled to roost. I was handed a polished wooden box with a mysterious mechanism.

'You can amuse yourself with this whilst you are here,' said Aunt Evelyn. It was an old musical box. Aunt Evelyn showed me its workings, which when wound up, played about ten tunes, with beautiful clarity and perfect timing. This one item left

my strongest memory of Letton, as I recollect sitting in the elegant drawing-room in the evening. When hearing these sounds, I am again transported back to that time.

Cousin John Stuart, an officer in the army, arrived the following day. He and my father had an excellent rapport, and would take long talks together around the grounds. He was a tall man, about ten years younger than my father, with a military bearing, good looking, good natured, and quick with his repartee. We all watched the Coronation together on my

My painting of Letton, 1953.

aunt's television, and as predicted by father, saw more of the action than the waiting crowds, but I remember it less than the place in which I now found myself staying.

I explored the grounds and surrounding fields, taking delight in investigating the walled vegetable gardens, greenhouses and potting sheds, all overgrown and crumbling away for lack of care and a gardener. The peach trees fastened against the old brick walls were still fruiting heavily, and the onions and other vegetables were thriving amongst the various weeds.

Great aunt Evelyn Stuart and my cousin John.

We went to Pimperne Church with Aunt Evelyn on Sunday, staying for a meal after the service at the vicarage, with the Rev Foxall-Smedley with his wife and daughter Diane. They had an exchange student from Paris staying with them, Jean Dupont. It was then that I saw the value of learning French at school, because I found that I could converse reasonably with this lively young man in his own tongue. He certainly spoke no English. Diane and I worked in the garden with Jean for the afternoon, making a big bonfire, laughing at each other's jokes, and by the end of the day we all promised to be pen pals when we left. I met him the following year in France.

It was decided by Aunt Daisy that it would benefit me if I went to a domestic science college. She chose a residential course for one year at Cuckfield Park in Sussex. My aunt, also being my godmother, paid for the course, feeling that she would take a hand in my upbringing, because I had no clear idea of what I wanted to do – even after a year at the art college, which had not greatly inspired me.

The Old Rectory at Pimperne, 1953.

Before attending the new college, Father persuaded me into going with him to that cinema again – Bwana Devils.

'You should never let anything frighten you so much that you cannot face it. You must study how it was made, and ask, can it actually hurt you? And why were you frightened? Enjoy the cleverness of it. Always remember that you can face anything you choose, with more understanding and the right frame of mind.'

So Father set the seeds for a new way of thinking, as we talked. Eventually I walked into the cinema with more confidence beside him, as I remembered his every word. Now I could enjoy the thrill of pretending I was with those large Ugandan lions as the film-makers had intended. I had banished the 'Bwana Devils' for ever.

CUCKFIELD PARK

Cuckfield Park is situated in the village of Cuckfield, near Hayward's Heath, Sussex. Spending a year there was a little like being sent to a 'finishing school', as my mother had been in the late 1920s.

Cuckfield Park.

There was an important intent from the teachers to teach as many useful domestic skills to girls who had hitherto been in a non-home environment or a somewhat cloistered existence at a boarding-school. I was a year older than the majority of the other girls, and had gained from the freedoms of the previous five years since the war ended, so viewed the whole process a little differently.

Known as a Domestic Science College, it was housed in the most romantic of buildings, a sixteenth century Elizabethan manor house, built in a square with an inner courtyard, with beautiful designs within its brickwork and barley twist shaped chimneys. The wide oak floorboards creaked when crossed, however so lightly, and the panelled walls echoed the colour of the highly polished floor and broad stairways, gleaming and reflecting the shine of the ever present bowl of flowers in the ancient hall.

Large carved wooden fireplaces by Grinling Gibbons, a sculptor of great renown, born in Rotterdam in 1598, were in the main rooms. The house was built in 1574 by the ironmaster, Henry Bowyer, with his wife Elizabeth, who used their wealth to show off their growing position in society, carving their initials in the stone chimney piece in the dining room.

My inquiring mind gathered these facts as I looked around the house, marvelling at the old beams and carved ceilings between them. My room was a small one for two at the top of the house, and I, being senior by at least a year, had a room to myself, leaving the lower floor of larger dormitories for the younger girls.

From this position I could view the countryside around, but soon I shared my well-being in this eagles' eyrie with a new room-mate, Phillida Goring. She was also an older girl, who had travelled from Trinidad, daughter of a well known film star Marius Goring. She sang strange songs, dressed flamboyantly, and entertained everyone at times with shadow plays behind a sheet with a powerful lamp rigged up precariously behind her.

The view from my bedroom.

I was dragged in to be the 'fall guy' in these plays, and we had enormous fun, bringing a tropical element and strange animals to the proceedings.

Having previously housed many members of staff to run the large kitchens, the building was ideal for domestic science teaching, and had been converted with the latest fixtures and fittings to suit the purpose. We were all there to work hard, at learning to run a successful house, and work we did.

I still have my copious notes written in neat hand-writing, on each subject. Not only did we have tuition on all forms of cookery, but also lessons on fancy cake making, housewifery, with advice about repairs and renewals, dressmaking, tailoring, household furnishings, household money management, setting out banquets – this last subject included the planning required, as well as training on buying and storage of food for these occasions.

Not content with that, we had to learn how to interview prospective employees, how to deal with the problems of staff, and develop planting lists for a gardener to grow vegetables the year round. We were young and energetic – we woke at seven to start our tasks, often finishing the day, finally, with sewing in one of the two drawing rooms.

In the sewing room with a cat on my shoulder and, right the ballgown I made.

We had to learn to dance and entertain graciously, and to this end, small groups of young men were invited to be guinea-pig guests for this purpose. The drawing-rooms were interconnected with each other, together creating a 'ballroom', once the dividing wall was folded back. At the end of each term, this was where we tried out our skills at being hostess of the evening. We made ourselves ball gowns, and learned how to make various soft furnishings.

In my free time I roamed the grounds, which contained a beautiful lake, and acres of mature ornamental trees. For this purpose, I usually offered to take the spaniel Timmy, belonging to the two head teachers, Miss France and Miss Black, for a walk. This

Walking with Timmy the spaniel.

gave me the excuse and the freedom to be out when the younger girls were confined to the house, and Phillida often accompanied me.

We walked one Saturday into Cuckfield, the nearby village, to browse among the treasures in the antique shop, where I bought an Italian glass vase and a green pot. Pleased with my purchases we then wandered further up the winding village. It was a warm, sunny autumn day, with the insects humming among perfumed flowers in the cottage gardens as we slowly sauntered back down the hill again. Phillida stopped to tie up her shoe, lifting her head to listen to a voice on the other side of the hedge.

'Listen … do you recognise that voice? I do. Just pause for a moment – I'm sure

I'm right.' She poked about in the hedge to see if she could discover whether she was right. Unfortunately, her rough handling of the growth on our side of this screen resulted in giving us away to the watcher on the other side. With a swift swipe of the far-side branches, a face now appeared.

'Good afternoon, young ladies, do introduce yourselves. In fact, come round through the gate, do it properly and in comfort, and have a cup of tea.' Was this voice being sarcastic? I rather

Robert Morley.

think it was. With that command from such a fruity baritone voice, we hastened through the gate and into a well-kept garden with a manicured lawn, which had been laid out for playing croquet. We were ushered to sit at a tea table laden with cakes and strawberries under a large sun umbrella. I was soon left in no doubt as to whom our host was, Robert Morley, because I had seen him in many well-known films.

Robert Morley was a versatile and witty actor in

The Ghost of Berkley Square in 1947 and more recently *The African Queen* in 1951, both of which I had seen; I also remembered *The Little Hut* a stage play in 1950, that I went to see in London with Mother, remembering its very clever staging. Now here we were doing our best to hold an intelligent conversation with this suave and well-mannered actor, while eying the strawberries in a bowl, the fine bone china and silver teapot.

He was somewhat portly, wobbled like a jelly when he laughed loudly with deep rolling sounds like thunder reverberating round the clouds, and although rotund, had an aristocratic bearing, and was kind to his gate-crashers. There had been three other people having tea, and were on the point of leaving when we entered, but whether it was his house, or he was just another visitor there we never knew.

'Would you both care for a cup of tea? I only drink china, but it is most refreshing on such a hot day. May I be so bold as to ask you what you were doing behind the hedge, and where have you popped up from?'

We had to ad-lib a little, saying that we recognised his voice, and wanted to meet him, next we told him of the college. He asked us to join him in a game of croquet, and for the first time I learned a few elementary rules of the game, and a few of the less scrupulous ones for determined winners.

The afternoon turned out to be very pleasant on such a warm day, and at the end

of this unexpected tea he insisted on escorting us both down the long driveway and back to the college door in a very gentlemanly manner, walking sedately and swinging an ivory dog-headed walking stick in time to his steps.

He suddenly put a hand in his pocket and offered as a parting gift two tickets to see *The Final Test* soon to be released. We left him with the autumn sun shining on his bald head, his broad smile and those twinkling eyes, and with many thanks for his kindness to us both, we watched him walk back through the ancient gates and down the long driveway to his home. The Italian vase now sitting in my china cabinet reminds me of that day so long ago.

During the autumn my parents drove down to see me, and brought with them the latest news of home, including the accumulated letters. Thus I received an early invitation to a relative's wedding to be held in London. Weddings always need forward planning, not least in our scattered family so it was necessary for invitations to be sent to distant relatives at least three to four months in advance.

When my cousin Robert Hamilton-Riche, then living in central London, became engaged to his fiancée, a wealthy heiress, I received my invitation to his wedding from his mother several months before the event, which was to be held at St. Martins-in-the-Fields, Trafalgar Square. It was to be a grand society wedding.

During the Easter holidays Mother offered to take me to London to buy a dress for the event. Robert's mother had met me briefly after the Chelsea Arts Ball, and advised me firmly to ensure that I was suitably dressed – I was not to turn up like a hippie, thus embarrassing her in front of her new 'in laws' in one of my flower-power outfits or a skirt which was the wrong length. Knowing of my straitened financial circumstances as a student, Mother offered to buy a suitable dress.

Fashions in the 1950s were beginning to be influenced by the 'up and coming' Kings Road groups, who encouraged shorter skirts. This

Mother, Aunt Lucy and I.

mimicked the latest new look fashions from Paris, and represented a rebellious statement by emerging fashion conscious and earning teenagers who now had money to spend on themselves. When I travelled into London, I saw that the fashion shops were beginning to follow this trend. I looked around the stores with my mother and her good friend, Aunt Lucy, known since our Northern Irish days. Her Major husband had been in father's regiment, and had a calming influence on mother.

A fairly long and beautiful shantung shot-silk creation caught my eye, which was not of the newer length. The shimmering colours of shot-silk, turquoise, greens and blues, was like the action of moving and rolling waves, breaking at the edge of the sea. It would set off beautifully the shocking pink hat, with gloves to match, which I had acquired, and I was really excited by the find. I had experimented with my hair colour, and decided that I was going to be copper-coloured. Now I thought that I had a new image.

In the family, we were aware that my mother had a strong will. She could be extremely kind and generous, but with an overwhelming and imperious manner, was known to brook no argument. She also had the money to bribe obedience from her less fortunate relatives. We all knew that, provided we agreed with Mother's wishes, life would be more peaceful, and certainly easier to avoid constant rows. I knew that this was how my father had survived over the years, developing the greatest of skills at 'playing' her game.

I had been quite ill with pneumonia, losing a great deal of weight to just seven stone. I was still very thin, having the body of an under-developed teenage girl. I was at the point of gaining a womanly shape, and looked forward to a new dress.

After working so hard, a visit to the shops in London was a great treat. Dresses are normally made for the average woman of 5 feet 6 inches, however I was only 5 feet 3 inches tall, so when trying on the dress it kept catching my heel in the hem.

I made a mild remark to Aunt Lucy, while Mother was paying for it. 'It is a trifle too long, but I could easily put a small hem on it.' Unfortunately, Mother had rotating, radar ears.

'Stuff and nonsense, these modern fashions here are ridiculous. You'll wear it as it is,' my mother retorted firmly. And when I picked up my parcel to take home, she said, 'I'll take it with me, because I won't have you altering it. You can change here in London before the wedding.' When I pointed out that I would be arriving on the train in time only for the ceremony, she stoutly said, without thinking of train times,

'You will be attending the pre-wedding drinks at the hotel and can change then.' From long experience of the consequences, I did not argue with her. After my shopping excursion with Mother, I returned to work at my studies, and certainly in better health, now fully recovered from the effects of pneumonia. I had filled out a bit and was at last endowed with bust and hips as nature intended.

As the months progressed, and the wedding day approached, I found and wrapped up a suitable gift which I could easily transport on the train. I had to make another decision too, namely, to buy a suitable alternative dress, in case Mother forgot to bring the one bought originally, so I chose to complement my wide brimmed shocking pink felt hat with a cream coloured coat, which covered a fashionable silk plum coloured dress to travel in, and certainly long enough to avoid confrontation with my mother if she noticed it.

My pink hat and new copper-coloured hair.

The running of a train service is not an exact science, certainly not in those days. Trains often paused for unexpected line repairs, and although I had made seemingly fool-proof plans, and taking journey times into consideration, I was fairly late in arriving at the London terminal. This allowed me time to take a taxi, arrive at the Church of St Martins-in-the-Fields and find a seat near my parents and Aunt Lucy before the ceremony began.

It was not long before Mother berated me audibly in the church, while heads started turning around to look at her with frowns on their faces. Mother had a penetrating and rising tone to her voice.

'Oh. There you are, late as usual,' she exploded. 'Why do you always have to be the awkward one?' The guests in adjacent seats started to glower at her, but mother was oblivious to their annoyance.

'Now you have no time to dress. You will insist upon spoiling my plans.' My long suffering Aunt Lucy with many years of practice quietened her down.

'Before the start of the wedding breakfast will be soon enough to change at the hotel.' Aunt Lucy privately assured me that I looked fine, and anyway, my alternative dress was a good colour and the right length, while Father smiled at Aunt Lucy and murmured 'Quite so.' Mrs Hamilton-Riche, as the groom's mother, sat on the front family pew, and thankfully missed all this unnecessary fuss.

The service proceeded with all pomp and ceremony, and the bride looked stunning in her gown, hopefully having acquired it with less drama than for me with my dress. Eventually we all left the church after a lengthy photographic session, the taxis taking us to the Savoy Hotel nearby for the wedding breakfast. I was immediately whisked off to the beautifully appointed and very large ladies rest room by my mother and my aunt, followed by half the lady guests who had 'retired to powder their noses.'

'Be quick now, take off that dress, and put this on.' Mother demanded instant obedience, regardless of how many people were there who happened to be watching, and there were a lot. With impatient hands my beautiful plum coloured dress was pulled off and dumped unceremoniously on the floor. I was handed the turquoise silk dress to replace it, pulled out of Mother's large bag.

This was the terrible moment of truth. Opening the long zip up the back, I started to ease myself in, but soon realized that four months since originally buying the dress, I had put on weight again, being now in better health and was now far too large even to contemplate wearing it. My mother pushed me, heaved and squeezed me, imploring others to help with the task, even though the errant gap was at least three inches wide of the mark, a strip of flesh showing beside the zip. She leapt around with frustration and anger, in a noisy frenzy of rage, being thus thwarted in the end, not realising how unreasonable it all sounded to the puzzled onlookers.

'I know you have done this on purpose to spite me, because I wouldn't let you shorten the dress.' She shrieked at me, her voice rising to such decibels, that it attracted some passing staff, who were placated only by comments of 'Some little wedding hysterics from a guest.' Finally, not liking to be thwarted, and unable to control her fury and temper, my mother took hold of the dress, ripped the delicate material off my half-dressed back, and tore it apart, dropping the pieces into the waste bin, saying as she did so, 'Now you cannot attend the wedding party in your underclothes.'

She swept out of the room, totally forgetting that I had arrived in another very presentable dress. The guests in the powder room, who had never met my mother, were absolutely horrified, but those of us who knew of her terrible temper, melted away as soon as possible. Aunt Lucy hastily retrieved all of the dress pieces, which she put into my bag.

Aunt Lucy in her wedding outfit.

'Waste not, want not – this will make a lovely skirt. I know you enjoy sewing. Go and greet your cousin to give him your gift, and say nothing of this incident. Some gossipmonger will be sure to tell him sooner or later.'

So I joined the guests for a celebratory couple of hours, carefully avoiding one angry parent, but spoke to the other, who was propping up the bar with the men. I told my laughing father the correct version; he showed absolutely no surprise. Then I slipped away to catch my late evening train.

Sometime later, I saw my dress in another shop, with a range of sizes, and on a whim, bought a larger well-fitting one of the same colour and design. I travelled again to London to attend my mother's birthday the following November, and wore the new dress specially to show that I had appreciated her original gift. However, the gesture backfired on me, because as soon as Mother saw what I was wearing, she went into the attack, without waiting for my explanations.

'There, you see, you could get into that dress after all. You should not have made such a fuss and embarrass me at Robert's wedding. I was most put out by your behaviour and your selfishness. You horrify me.' She had forgotten that she had ripped the original dress into pieces. How I hated her at that moment for belittling me, however hard I tried to please her. Any future explanations of my adult weight and new purchase were useless, so as usual I kept my own council, but earned a broad smile of understanding from my father. We were both good at keeping silent for the sake of peace.

THE FRENCH CONNECTION

My stay at Cuckfield Park was a happy one, and I gained confidence from the experience. I enjoyed this kind of practical course, learning many new skills which I had hitherto not imagined. I also received a 'Distinction' for my cookery, which resulted in being offered a place in Paris for one month at the Cordon Bleu School of Cookery, which I felt was a great honour. Here I topped up my knowledge of culinary skills, and honed my French language.

There were no frills in this place. It was crowded with around nine other would-be young chefs, all working hard to master a great many culinary techniques, and in a different language. We worked at long tables in an underground kitchen, where it was extremely hot, with a variety of different chefs. They showed us how to perfect strange but exciting ways to prepare the food, all tasted by the masters upstairs, who reported their judgements, the successes and the flops. Failures were only tolerated once.

I had written to Jean-Paul Dupont telling him of my stay in Paris, and he now called at my hotel to see me. He kissed me on both cheeks, clearly enthusiastic about sharing a little time with me.

'Let us have a day out and I will show you the sights of Paris. Your French has improved remarkably since last we met at Pimperne. How long ago it all seems.'

He had grown into a dapper well-dressed young man of nineteen with no trace of the unruly schoolboy, who had played in the vicarage garden with Diane and myself. Now he had an air of self-assurance which had been lacking when younger. We decided upon a weekend, when I was free and at the appointed hour, Jean called at the hotel, well dressed in grey chalk-striped trousers and navy blazer with brass buttons. His colourful tie was as bright and wide as his smile, and his new moustache complemented his wavy fair hair. He was full of bounce and keen to be off.

After standing under the Eiffel Tower, peering up the inside and experiencing the enormity of its height, we took a boat up the Seine, gazing at the passing buildings. Eventually we set off to walk through the area of Montmartre, built on a large hill, topped by the gleaming Sacre Coeur Church, its spires reaching up into the velvet of the deep blue sky. Adjacent to its façade was a pleasant tree-lined square, the Place du Tertre. Here a large group of painters were working diligently upon easels, each with their own styles, and producing colourful work, using a brush or palette knife, and working under the plane trees through which the sunshine created a dappled pattern on the flagstones beneath.

At each corner sat customers at tables under twirling umbrellas, where musicians played a range of accordion music, strangely complementary to each other. We sat with a glass of wine apiece, soaking up the atmosphere and smells of an endless, warm summer day, with insects creating a soft drone in the background. Whenever I hear strains of accordion music playing the various French melodies during this time, I am reminded of the Place du Tertre.

We went into a small restaurant for an evening meal, full of mouth-watering aromas. In the lowly lit interior, with small table lamps glowing, we were surprised to find a monkey, attached to a long sliding chain, running back and forth between the tables, begging for titbits. He

The Sacré Coeur Church, Paris.

seemed so appealing to the customers, that he easily gained his supper without much trouble, during which time we enjoyed a typically French meal of Langoustines, dressed with a white mayonnaise, green beans and fried artichokes

While strolling back to the hotel that evening, we discussed plans to visit the art

The Place du Tertre.

galleries the next day. Then Jean pulled me into an off street alley for a romantic kiss – at first. But it soon became clear that he had further things on his mind.

'No. Please don't. Just let go of me. You are spoiling the day. It's been so pleasant up to now.' Eventually, after ignoring my pleas, it took a really hard slap from me to bring him to a halt. I was absolutely horrified to realise how far he was hoping to go. I was certainly not going to tolerate this.

'All girls expect it when taken out for the day, and the chaps have to get their practice in somehow,' he said. This was a very new discovery to me and quite unexpected. This brought a completely new dimension to the interactions I had hitherto experienced with men – until this time, I had assumed all my friends of either sex were just that – good friends, with no hidden agendas.

'Well, not with me, you don't, so keep your distance. Don't touch me again.'

216

I started to retreat swiftly towards my hotel with a very red face. How could I have been so stupid? Now I began to see also the cockiness of this young Frenchman, who viewed any unwary girls merely as playthings. Foolishly I had been flattered by his attentions, but it didn't help that my French was only in its infancy. I needed some remark to burst his inflated ego.

'And you smell of garlic too.' I added while trotting up the street. This silly remark was just thrown in, because it had nothing to do with the matter in hand, but Jean persisted and said hopefully, 'I can soon cure that. Well, what about tomorrow then? What about our plans? Shall we go to the galleries and the Louvre, and then have a meal?'

My intentions had obviously not yet been understood, but it only took ten seconds for me to refuse any more outings or contact with him. I had obviously been treading in dangerous water, and had no idea how to deal with the possible consequences. I went to bed resolved to avoid trouble like that again. For the next few weeks I threw myself into my work in the cookery centre in Paris to finish the course. Nevertheless, at a later date I was able to take a trip to this lovely city, during which time I was able to enjoy some of the famous galleries that I had read so much about.

Soon my stay at Cuckfield Park in Sussex had come to a close, with end of term prize-giving day, after which came the Grand Ball organised by all of us. Our parents and special guests were invited. We wore the new ball gowns which we had made in the needlework department. Mrs. Hilder, our long-suffering and kindly teacher, who lived in the grounds of Cuckfield Park at The Red House with her seven year old son, spent many hours with us in her garden when the weather was fine, to perfect these creations, which were then pressed and hung up in our workroom ready for the occasion. The ball proved to be a great occasion as a befitting the end to a marvellous year. Afterwards, future employment was the main topic of discussion with the head teachers before I left finally.

The two heads, proud of my culinary success, were eager to help me find work. To this end, as a temporary post, asked if I was willing to look after eight girls, who lodged at Homme House in Much Marcle near Ledbury, in Shropshire. Their parents were in the diplomatic service living abroad, and these youngsters were destined to attend university in the autumn. But during the early part of their holiday period someone was needed to oversee their meals and entertainment. I accepted.

The house in Ledbury, like many old establishments, was used for a while during the war as a hospital. Now it was run by an efficient, elderly Scotswoman, plainly dressed in tweeds, with Calvinistic views and a clipped Scottish accent, which cut through the

Homme House, Ledbury, Shropshire.

merry chatter of her young charges. They were the liveliest, most self-opinionated and well-dressed group of girls that I had met, who needed an older girl as a chaperone for their activities, but I soon felt that the difference between our ages was not great enough.

I was out of my depth with them, and had to keep my wits about me. Endless hours were spent occupying these energetic girls, walking around the district, and playing tennis or croquet with them. The old house was equipped with two tennis courts and large lawns, which reminded me of Aunt Evelyn's house in Dorset. Unlike hers, this old Georgian Mansion was having a new lease of life as a 'private hotel' for young ladies.

Sometimes, we went into nearby Ledbury for shopping sprees. The girls had access to large amounts of their spending money from the headmistress, Mrs. Ferguson, who expected me to ensure that these excitable teenagers spent their money wisely. Interestingly, the stipend for my job was far less than their over-generous allowances.

One trip into the village of Ledbury caused some problems, because the girls wanted to go to the Saturday dance, held weekly in the village hall. Permission was refused by Mrs. Ferguson, thinking it was too dangerous for them to mix with the local boys. The leader of the girls decided to walk there anyway and the rest were happy to follow her. I had no power to stop them, so promptly approached Mrs. Ferguson, well before she discovered the fact, to explain where they had all disappeared to during the late afternoon.

'This is intolerable. You are supposed to look after them. Go down to the village and stay with them, then walk back as a group. They are not old enough to be out by themselves. You must get them back by eleven.' She rolled her Scottish 'r's querulously when angered.

The more agitated she became, the broader her Scottish accent. Being strong-minded sixteen and seventeen year olds, they were far too modern for Mrs. Ferguson's puritanical, almost Edwardian attitudes. I had the dubious advantage of being only a couple of years older. By now, based upon my own experiences, I really did understand her fears. So I walked down to the village, about two miles away, as fast as I could, realising the un-lit, winding country road was somewhat hazardous for the unwary. The dusk was deepening into a starry night. The edges of the road were black under the evergreen trees which lined the half-hidden kerb stones. This area never felt the warmth of sun, so hidden leaves were very slippery.

I was not able to catch up with them until I had reached the village hall grounds, where I could hear the happy strains of 'First you put your two knees close up tight...' being sung with great gusto as I walked up the pathway. 'You swing them to the left, and swing them to the right...' was accompanied by the heavy beats of a loud and tuneful country band.

With an enthusiastic singer, we were invited to 'Step around the floor, kind of nice and light, then twist around, an' twist around with all your might.' More flourishes with a drum roll heralded the next call, 'Spread your loving arms way out in space...' followed by the instructions to 'You do the Eagle Rock with such style and grace' with everybody singing lustily...' Swing your foot way round, then bring it back,' matching actions with the words.

The Gatehouse at Homme House.

By the time I had got to the hall, very much out of breath to the strains of, 'That's what I call Balling the Jack', I saw that no harm had come to my little group, because they were enjoying the old dancing steps made popular by Danny Kaye, and then Dean Martin in his 1951 film *That's My Boy.*

I recall this occasion very well because of the following incident, which hindered the task of trying to get them back to the house on time. The consumption of alcohol at any dance for teenage girls was then unheard of, but I suspect that one of the local lads had laced the soft drinks a little, because they became tipsy, so more difficult to control. It was becoming increasingly obvious that I would have some difficulty to extricate my group before 10.30 without any major arguments – this was a worry because we had at least two miles to walk.

Nevertheless, I had enough authority over the merry 'leader' to get her moving, even at a slow pace, and fears of the dark motivated the rest. With a couple of torches to light our way, we progressed through the night, holding on to each other as their fear of the darkness became more evident. It was pitch-black and we walked as if we were blindfolded. Then suddenly one of the girls shrieked.

'I've twisted my ankle. I cannot put any weight down on my foot – I can't walk.' They tried a variety of ways to help the sobbing girl. Two of the tallest in the group, supporting the injured teenager on either side, made slow but steady progress along the road, fearful now of speeding traffic approaching us, so the two torches were deployed, at either end of the rows of threesomes, as 'safety lights'. One girl sug-

gested that she go on ahead to warn of our late arrival. However, I could see that this suggestion had hidden dangers, therefore I insisted we should stick together.

Then a motorist stopped to offer a lift to the injured girl, but this plan was also fraught with danger, due to the risk of a complete stranger taking the injured girl away from the safety of the group. At that moment I felt the heavy weight of responsibility for their safety.

Then I had an inspired thought, and said to the driver: 'You could help us all by driving to Homme House and warn Mrs. Ferguson of our slow progress. Tell her what has happened; we're all keeping together and are OK,' I replied. I asked him if he would take my message quickly because I knew she would be very worried, the time being well after midnight by now, and we were all very cold.

Fortunately, help soon arrived again, in the form of a large car owned by one of the staff from Homme House, and the shivering travellers were quickly taken back, the strained ankle was bandaged, and all the tired girls put to bed. Mrs. Ferguson with pursed lips and angry in a controlled manner, said she would discuss their behaviour in the morning. So I suspect that new ground rules were being formulated.

'The head at Cuckfield Park spoke very highly of you, as one of the two senior girls, but you really are not old enough for this job.' Mrs. Ferguson was almost accusing me of lacking maturity, then said as an afterthought, 'I hadn't realised that you were as young as you are, but you showed great sense and responsibility in keeping the group together, and for that I thank you.'

Mrs. Ferguson inclined her head to me regally as she spoke and was gracious with her praise. Thankfully the time had come for me to move on, leaving her to revise her rules, and train a new recruit. I headed for home and my holidays. The memories of this incident were etched in my mind for a long time.

Pauline Moran, who had been my sister's friend at the secretarial college, now had a job with a manufacturer, Weatherdair Ltd, designing all kinds of high-fashion summer and winter clothing. My sister had gone to her nursing training, but I had continued our friendship, although Pauline was in her early thirties. Knowing I had arrived home, she came over to see if I was interested in working for her firm briefly.

'Hello, Pauline, what can I do for you? Father said you needed me.'

'Yes, your Father says you speak French, you seem to have a photographic memory, and are not afraid to travel. Will you come with me to Paris to a fashion show for the coming spring fashions? I've seen you drawing from memory, so come with me for this purpose. You can be my camera.' Then she added, 'I've got two tickets to see Dior's collection, and there will be over 200 outfits to see over two days.' This was too good an opportunity to miss, so I was delighted to accept her offer, not really knowing precisely what she wanted of me.

While we crossed over to France on the ferry, Pauline told me that in order to compete with the designs coming out of France, British fashion houses needed to spot where the new lines of the latest creations were heading. She was good at this, but cameras were banned at the shows, so she had decided to take me as a 'walking camera' and advised me what I should concentrate on remembering.

A kind of espionage, I thought. How exciting. Her firm provided us with tickets for the train and boat travel, funds for our stay for three days, with enough for taxi fares as well. We had travelled early and planned to explore the city on our first day, before attending one of the shows the following morning, and similarly the same time the next day. This would make the best use of our time.

Paintings by Pissarro, above, and Marc Chagall, below.

We booked in to a modest 'Pension' on the edge of the Montmartre area where prices were within reason, then headed off to look at a group of art galleries. Many were showing Post-Impressionist work, with well-known works by Monet, Pissarro, Klein and Cézanne, whose strong lines and colours appealed to me, while another gallery exhibited the work of Jean Dubuffet, with his child-like drawings, juxtaposed with works of Marc Chagall from Belarusa, colourful paintings depicting the folklore of his homely village of Vitebsk.

They spoke to me in an illustrative way which had great appeal. It was also the first time that I saw the cubist influence in the colourful works of Robert Delaunay and the muted tones of Fernand Léger. I was pleased with this unexpected chance to see for myself some of the paintings which I had studied when at art school, depicted in many of the books given out for study.

We slept well, and were woken very early by smells wafting up from several little bakeries, producing fresh French loaves, croissants and strange cakes. The clattering of vehicles on the French cobbles, and the chimes of numerous church tower clocks, which had gone unnoticed the previous evening, along with the bustle of the street cleaners, added to the morning sounds typical of this French environment.

The men were brushing water along the gullies, where spouts rose up from openings along the pavement edges, devouring the rubbish swiftly, before disappearing into 'sink holes' in the bowels of the steep roads. Within half an hour the streets were clean again. Hastily dressing in our latest fashionable, full-skirted dresses and nipped-in waists, with matching saucer-like hats, gloves and bags, we breakfasted

221

the French way on croissants and coffee, before setting off to the Avenue Montaigne, clutching our entry tickets for the Christian Dior Salon. The show was to be in two halves that day, with a light lunch sometime after midday.

La Place de Tertre

Now assured of our seats, we could relax sufficiently to admire the superb creations strutting before and above us on the catwalk. The models looked extremely thin, like sapling trees swaying in a gentle breeze, seemingly extremely bored with their role, exhibiting not once the slightest fleeting smile, across pale and haughty faces, with black outlined eyes. As Pauline pointed out items of interest to her, I marked my catalogue with personal hieroglyphs of my own.

Pauline Moran (extreme right) at the fashion show.

Since most of the audience were already scribbling notes, like dedicated reporters, I did not feel out of place. When we stood up for our lunch, we strolled around a myriad of animated and superbly dressed women, and talked to several interesting buyers. One man hovered beside us to chat, and seemed to be more interested in Pauline herself, than the firm she represented. Named Pierre Lacroix, he exuded charm as only a practised 28 year old could. He was well dressed, well-mannered and could compete with any film star for his looks. A bit like Gregory Peck, I thought.

'Would you care to join me for dinner tonight? We could go up the Eiffel Tour, because they have an excellent restaurant at the top. As you are both only here for three days, it is a must.' I was included in the invitation, but I doubt that I was the prize he was aiming for. With that, our evening was organised. Although on this occasion I felt that I was the gooseberry, I didn't care, being far too excited by the proposed trip up this famous landmark.

It was fortunate that Pauline had insisted we both wear our best cocktail dresses, because, as we eventually ascended this famous tower by lift, we stepped out onto a very salubrious environment. The restaurant had an extremely plush, plum carpet and décor which instantly created a feeling of being transported into a film set of well-dressed film stars. All was glitter, with polished crystal glasses and silverware, reflecting the fabulous jewellery which enhanced the colourful silks, blue and green satins and the rich red and gold brocades of the evening wear. I was absolutely speechless.

'I am so glad you were able to attend this gathering. It is given yearly for those attending the fashion show, as a kind of thank you, but I expect for them it extends the moments of deliberation of whether to buy some creation or not, this one or that one.' Pierre chatted away happily. 'Would you like to meet the creator? He's somewhat shy, but is my friend.' He waved a hand in greeting, to an older man, beautifully dressed, a little heavy, with thinning hair and by now nearly fifty, who strolled in the direction of our table, being greeted by everyone as he passed.

Christian Dior at the dinner.

'These are my English guests for the evening. They were at the show today.'

Pierre introduced us to Christian Dior, who took each of our hands in turn to kiss; he peered into my eyes briefly, murmuring, 'What blue eyes, so deep.' He smiled, chatted for a few moments more, then strolled on to another table where he had a seat. The enormity of meeting such an icon of fashion was not lost on me as a teenager, and was a moment to be savoured for a long time. Thereafter I followed his career until sadly he died in 1957, having influenced the world with his incredible post-war fashions for years to come.

I had mentioned earlier in the day a wish to see the famous Opera House, even from the outside, regretting the seats were invariably booked up for months ahead. Pierre, ever resourceful, showed us Paris and the Opera House from the observatory walk, circling the top of the tower. The panoramic view of Paris showed up for miles in every direction. He said, 'Tomorrow evening after the second fashion show, we shall go to the opera, but I am sorry if it is one you have already seen.' Never having been to an opera at all, I really did not mind, and was delighted to go to the one he had booked, like waving a magical wand to gain the coveted seats.

We were enthralled by the ethereal settings of the scenes, created by clever lighting, netting, drapery, and the superb singers of *Lucia de L'Amore*, having learned that it was an interpretation of Sir Walter Scott's historical book *The Bride of Lammermoor*, with the score written by Donizetti.

The Opera House in Paris.

It was an even more magical experience than being at the top of the Eiffel Tower. After our third day we returned home very tired, burst-

223

ing with experiences, feeling that it had been a job well done.

The 'camera sketches' were quickly organised into colourwash and line drawings, with extra notations, about fourteen of them, 16 inches by 18 inches in size. These were put into a folder which Pauline took to her boss the next day. Pauline told me later, that in his office he spread them out, gave a whistle of approval, and said 'Well worth the money.' before calling in his staff to discuss details and then to get started with creating some variations of the Parisian fashions to be made up in London.

Pauline couldn't contain herself with glee when she came home, then rushed round to see me.

'Here is a packet for you from the boss. He is delighted with all the details that you've managed to capture. He hoped that we enjoyed the show, and were not too bored.;

Bored. He really didn't know. But when I opened the packet, I found my pay for that week's work to be just over £350, which in 1953 was a staggering amount for me. Into the Post Office Savings account it went, for each drawing had netted about £25. This was at least a month's wages for the average person. But it was not only this reward I gained. I had experienced some insights into another world and had a whiff of increasing independence.

BROOM CLOSE AND THE BULL

While I had been travelling to France, Mother had kept herself busy with her usual myriad of interests and friendships. Not least, she offered her help to a close friend, Len, who ran 'Sweet Things', a tobacconist and sweet shop in the high street in Isleworth. Since his wife's death it had become difficult for him to manage his stock control, because he had no great experience, training or knowledge of how to do this.

Len, the sweet shop owner.

With her usual flair for organising, whether people liked it or not, Mother soon had a team of willing volunteers, assisting Len in the administration of his business, spending a lot of time in and out of the shop. By now Len, in his fifties, had become the very life and soul of the group, and his ego was bolstered by her interest in his affairs. Surprisingly for a small, bald-headed and short-sighted man with pebble-glasses, he was for the first time the centre of attention, enjoying the limelight for all it was worth.

Jim was the very antithesis of Len. He was a tall, thin and wiry individual, still fit from years of army training, and always well organised. Regularly, he walked down to Len's shop for his cigarettes. From shear anger, he started an argument one day with Len outside his shop about his growing friendship with Mother, which was directly related to a conversation he had heard whereby Len was suggesting a new cruising holiday which she might care to organise and part finance.

It transpired that Jim was simply trying to protect Mother's interests. 'You are using her good nature to line your own pocket. Why should she pay for it?'

With a few more choice words, he leant over, attempting to grab Len by his lapels and shake him, like a terrier a rabbit. Instantly, avoiding Jim's hands, Len struck Jim in the face, which knocked them both off balance and onto the pavement, grappling with each other furiously. More blows were struck, more blood flowed, and soon many people became embroiled as others tried to separate them. The two bleeding noses were making quite a mess.

I heard of the fight from neighbours and from my father later, so my recollection is really second-hand. Father was walking home when he saw this lengthy affray come to its final conclusion. With glasses broken and a woeful expression, Len was now being ministered to by three women, including my mother, all trying to halt the bleeding from his nose. Ignoring Len completely, my Father spoke quietly and urgently to Jim, as he grabbed the fallen man.

'Come along now, my friend, give me your hand, and let's get you cleaned up. No need for a fuss – we've seen worse. A couple of plasters and a cold pack will do the trick.' With this, he retrieved Jim from the pavement and manoeuvred him out of the way, almost pushing him through the considerable crowd which had gathered, who were left wondering what the fighting had been all about. They arrived home,

Jim was patched up by Father, after which they sat down in leather chairs, placed on either side of the study fireplace, with a whisky apiece.

Both men had nurtured this 'ménage a trois' for years, satisfying the needs of all participants in different ways. Jim had a home, Mother had her liaison with someone she could boss, and Father had his freedom from her temper and from being ruled by her iron rod; but my mother, seeking new pastures had strayed outside this 'silent fence' and had 'broken the rules' according to both men. My father ruminated. He was very philosophical about the situation.

The Winterbournes, Jim, a friend and Len.

'Time has come to move on. Don't you think so, what?'

'No good crying over spilt milk, eh?'

'That man's a 'rum cove' and no mistake.' He did not like Len at all.

'Better not to tangle with that sort, old fruit. No good will come of it.'

'Val's temper is far too unpredictable these days. It's like lighting a touch-paper to a fuse at times.'

'Tell you what, our friend Winterbourne up the road, whom you get on with reasonably well, has a very large spare room to bunk down in, now that his son has left home. We'll ask him,; and with a cool head, Father steered the incident into nothing that could be gossiped about, but said later to Jim, now installed at the Winterbourne's house a half a mile away, 'You really killed the Golden Goose for yourself there, didn't you, old boy,' as they strolled up to the corner pub in St. John's Road for a companionable drink, chuckling at the incident and again the best of friends.

When I returned home, the matter had been concluded. Mother was in a temper. Jim was nowhere to be seen, and I seemed to be in hot water for the minutest thing. I asked Father to tell me the whole story of what had happened. Father believed that Jim, on reflection, was quite glad to be away from an increasingly difficult situation, because the close relationship with Mother had run its course.

We all missed Jim's presence in the house for various reasons, except Jane, who was busy with her work in the hospital and her boyfriend, Rhoddy Barnes, a trainee doctor, to whom she became engaged. It was difficult for me to fully comprehend why Jim had moved away, except that I could understand his anger with Len. He had been a part of my family for about ten years, since the time that we had lived in Clitheroe.

It was a sad time for me, but my father kept in contact with Jim on the quiet. He had acted as a kind of private batman, to my father who said that as a 'casualty of the war' he owed Jim 'care, and a soldier's loyalty'. Obviously, having been concerned that Jim had no home of his own, he felt obliged to support him with sufficient funds to be comfortable.

Rhoddy was much in evidence for a year or so with Jane, until her insistence in having her own way for setting a date to get married. This caused a big row in our kitchen one evening. It was much like one of Mother's tantrums. But Rhoddy was firm in his wishes to continue with his studies to be a doctor and was supported by Father.

Rhoddy, Jane and our parents at a dance.

'I have my own career to think of, and it will take at least another four year's training to reach my goal. I would really prefer to postpone it until I have fully qualified and can earn a good salary.'

'I'm not prepared to wait that long,' she became more voluble and excitable as Rhoddy would not be persuaded to her way of thinking. She finally exploded with, 'You can do what you like. Here's your ring back.'

Jane took off the engagement ring and threw it with some force at the poor man across the room, where it landed hidden behind the gas cooker, beside the Aga range. She picked up her bag and stormed out, slamming the door. A plate crashed down from the plate rack and shattered into a hundred little pieces, followed by a stunned silence. The ring stayed lost for about six years, lodged on a ledge behind the cooker.

Jane at Middlesex Hospital.

'I think that young man has had a lucky escape.' Father chuckled, for he could see the funny side of things, now realising that Jane was showing the embryo of her mother's temper tantrums.

However, Jane benefitted by this turn of events because when she had finished her basic training, she branched out into a midwifery course to continue her training. During those years, I had at last a good relationship with her, and often stayed in the nurses' home in London, going to many shows that were all the rage at that time.

We attended the jazz club in Soho where Acker Bilk was playing nightly. His fame was growing, with his 'Stranger on the Shore' and the much loved 'Petit Fleur'.

We went to films to see our favourite stars such as David Niven, John Mills and Margaret Rutherford. Jane, who loved stylish clothes, made several outfits based on those we saw on the screen. Not having had to contend with clothing coupons, the Americans reflected this with the lavish wardrobes used by the stars in the films.

Before taking up the post which had been offered me at Ellesmere College as a senior training chef, starting in October, I travelled back north to Yorkshire, because it was still only early July. Once again I had received an invitation for a summer holiday, this time at Broom Close Farm. The thought of having some time away from the warring factions at home was particularly attractive to me.

This time, I did not stay with dear Mrs. Wrigley at Warlaby Lodge. I travelled on the coach from London to Leeming Bar again, and this time was met by Lucy Mclaughlan in her car. She was barely five feet tall, hard-working and friendly, with ginger crinkled hair, and always breathless with her asthma. Since the car was a large one, she sat on a pile of cushions to reach a good driving position. She and Wilf had stayed at our house the previous November when they attended the National Dairy Show at Olympia in London, showing their prize Friesian cattle, and had pressed me to make a visit to their farm.

Lucy and baby Geoffrey.

Broom Close was a very old farmhouse, down a long driveway, following a hedge and between the fields, standing in about 250 acres of pasture and arable land. It was not yet modernised with electricity or running water, although both services were planned to be installed shortly from the nearby town of Northallerton. The farm was bounded at one side by a railway branch line, where trains stopped occasionally at a platform near the level crossing of Yaffoth Halt.

At that time, the trains had precedence whereby, if cars required free passage, the barred-gate had to be wheeled across the track by the gate keeper and allow the cars to cross, before closing across the road again. Later, in the 1960s I believe the order of this was reversed, as the line became less important. The permanent Halt Keeper lived in the gatehouse with his family and a few young children, who mingled with the resident hens and a couple of noisy geese.

I had a low-beamed bedroom with a window under the eaves, looking over the yard. It was definitely back to candlelit bedtimes again. The main room, the kitchen, was lit by a pressure paraffin lamp, as were the other main buildings within the farmyard, which was surrounded by dairy and byres or cattle sheds. When switched on, water was pumped by generator from a well in the yard, into the house, the dairy and the wash-house. At other times, water was retrieved, using a hand-operated pump handle, pouring out of a cast-iron spout in the yard.

On washing days the copper boilers and dolly tubs in the wash-house by the back door were well filled and heated with coal fires beneath. I was pleased to see Jennifer, now aged eight, and her baby brother, Geoffrey, now toddling around.

He followed Lucy around into the enclosed garden bordered partly by a close-cropped privet hedge and a stone wall. On washing days, Lucy would drape the pink sheets, yellow towels and blue overalls over this wall to dry in the sunshine and the constant Yorkshire breezes. The colours of mixed washing mingled with the vibrant blues of the delphiniums, the pink peonies, and multi-coloured hollyhocks in the flower beds in front of this elevated washing line, while the smalls were arrayed in rows upon the close-cut lawn, then were turned over.

Broom Close Farm, near Northallerton.

This was an arable and dairy farm, which had Friesian cattle in most of the grassy pastures which surrounded the buildings, when not under cultivation. Some of the thickest grassland fields had been earmarked for hay, which at this time of the year, with the weather fine, was being harvested. So with the  binders at work, the thick grass was soon laid flat to dry in the sunshine.

Once dry on the upper-side, and usually the following day, the grass was 'shaken and stirred' by hand-held pitchforks, or mechanically turned over with a hay turner, which left it all in neat rows in the sunshine again, to dry its underside. Finally the dried grass was made into large, and well-compacted hay bales, collected by tractor and trailer, to be taken to the barn for storage to avoid the threatening and rumbling thunder storms, which might ruin all the work.

Since my last trip to Yorkshire, I had been writing to my friend with the motorbike, Bill Joynson, who had the job of farm foreman, organising the arable side of the farm. The farmer was Wilf Mclaughlan, whose main interest was his accredited herd of Friesian cattle, large black and white cows, who gave copious quantities of milk if managed well. So he milked them three times a day, in fact every eight hours, significantly increasing his yield. He kept careful records in his herd book, and while I was staying there, soon involved me in this record keeping whenever a calf was born.

'I want you to paint in the markings on these four printed 'calf shapes' with this black ink. There's a left, then the right, and one for the front of the head, and lastly one looking from heaven.'

He chuckled delightedly to have gained a helper for this onerous job; keeping records was a reasonable task to undertake, but painting black ink shapes was not. Each new calf was also given its birthday, a name and number, and recorded on the sheet in the Herd Book Records, together with its mother's number. Nowadays, cattle are ear tagged on both ears, and perhaps their hides tattooed, but in the 1950s, the importance of keeping records was only beginning to be recognised by the older farmers.

A Friesian cow with new born calf.

Breeding ever better strains of milk-producing cattle had mushroomed, to increase yields after the war, and Wilf was enthusiastic about his herd. I helped with the milking procedure, switched on the generator and used the new electric milking machines, then cleared up in the dairy, learning the ways of the cattle, as they learned mine. Starting at 5.30am in the summertime did not daunt me then.

Early one morning I saw some of the cows had escaped into a newly-grown ley of grasses and clovers, a field lush and green with tasty offerings. Unfortunately, one of the cows stumbled and rolled over, swelling in size like a barrel with its feet pointing skywards in the bright morning sunshine, and lay still. This was caused by gasses, created from the consumption of a too rich and undigested clover-grassland, trapped inside the cow's stomach, and at this late stage was a killer. It was clear that the animal would soon die, perhaps within fifteen minutes, therefore speedy action was essential.

I called to Wilf, and told him what I had seen. Without a moment's hesitation, he and two others ran to the field carrying a long, thin, sharp kitchen knife, with some tubing and other equipment. Within moments Wilf had carefully placed the point of the knife on the prostrate cow's side and plunged it in, measuring the place and depth carefully as he went. Instantly a rush of foul smelling gas rushed into the air and the ballooned cow subsided to its original shape. As a result, I had my first lesson in the food rationing and management of overly-rich foodstuffs for cows, which knowledge was obviously essential to a cattle farmer. A vet would have used a Trocar (a sharp pointed tool) and a cannula (a hollow thin tube to keep the hole open) but the hastily gathered emergency tools worked. The cow recovered well and 'lived to tell the tale'.

But another cow, which we called the escape artist, nearly did not. She was a restless animal, and was always looking for gaps in a fence or an open gate. Spying a golden opportunity of a thinned hedge and the single bar across the road at Yaffoth Halt, she made her bid for freedom down the railway line at a fair speed. The gate keeper sitting in his 'observation loft', saw the commotion, heard the breaking barricade, and called down the line on his telephone for a blockade to be erected across the track, then put all his signals to Stop.

It was like a 'Wild West' Rodeo, with men waving their hats, trying to lassoo the cow, corner her, head her off or grab her as she ducked and wove her way around them all. It looked like a colourful ballet dance with the black and white cow, expelling clouds of agitated hot breath in the chill early morning air like a steam engine. As we watched, the shrieking gatekeeper's children leapt around, also chasing the hens and noisy geese. Eventually after a great deal of energy was expended by everyone, the cow became tired and was led away gently with a halter back to her field. The hole was well repaired. And so was the road barrier.

The Great Yorkshire Show was a 'must' for farmers. Although having being in existence for many years, and having used various different venues, it finally acquired a permanent site near Harrogate. It was only in its second year there when Lucy and Wilf entered their cows for showing, and the prize bull, named William Marshall, which they had bought recently.

He was a magnificent Friesian animal, with black and white markings, a white triangle in the middle of his black face topped by two wide, short horns jutting out of his head, which contained the curly hair on top, like a fancy hair-do, between his ears. He seemed reasonably docile especially when patrolling his wives. In my case I was not a challenge to his supremacy. Although he wore a deadly-looking bull-ring through his nose, he behaved impeccably when offered food in a bucket.

When I was asked to wash the bull for the show I had mixed feelings of doubt and fear, but I said that I'd give it a go. Wilf was to wash some cows

Wilf and I at the Great Yorkshire Show

in another pen nearby. Dressed appropriately in dungarees and wellington boots, I watched while Wilf tied the bull's head into the corner of the pen on either side, with halters round his head, and also through the ring in his nose. This way the poor creature had no chance of moving far, but when I entered the pen with a large bucket of water, liberally laced with the medicated liquid soap used in the dairy, I was wary, and talked soothingly to him as I started with a scrubbing brush on his head. I felt that if the bull could actually see me with his large brown eyes, he would probably get used to my onslaught on his curly hair which was caked with muck in places, and I wasn't really hurting him.

He was a little restless, answering me with a throaty but somewhat baleful 'moo' repeated every few minutes, switched his tail, and shuffled his feet, but I persevered until the bull was several shades lighter all over, after which I rinsed him off thoroughly. I combed the quiff of hair between his horns, then lacquered them but did not dare do his feet. In the sunshine, he quickly dried off, and I stood back to admire the results of my plait-decking of his tail with coloured ribbons.

William Marshall had finally had enough, kicked over the bucket behind him, swung his powerful hind quarters at me, and knocked me flying, slithering on the pen floor to the other corner. At that distance I was out of his reach, or I think I would have been trampled upon. Since he could not move his head round to see me on the wet floor, I slithered out of sight, out of reach and out of the pen as quickly as possible, a little bruised and angry with myself for being so careless near such a large animal. I should have remembered my previous experience in Garstang with the Jersey cow moving so swiftly, who had thrown me in defence of her calf.

'I've forgotten to lacquer his hoofs, I'm so sorry.' Wilf and Bill had been watching and laughed at my demise, having been careful to keep an eye on the proceedings, for safety's sake.

'Don't worry, I'll do them tomorrow before the show. The rest of him looks great.'

So William Marshall was loaded up with the washed and now impeccable cows, and transported to the Great Yorkshire Show, where we all went the following day. I went with Bill on his motorbike. We viewed all the pens which held sheep, pigs, and cattle of every breed, and also the farming machinery stands, country crafts and flower show. We sat for a while watching the sheep dog trials, where the wily dogs tried manoeuvring their obstinate woolly packs of five sheep to do their bidding.

Rows of beautiful riding horses and shires took their places in the show ring. The best of every category of animal was duly awarded a colourful rosette according to the judges' opinions, with William Marshall collecting two first-class awards. Amongst the stands I spotted a model of a bull which looked remarkably like William Marshall, so bought it to bring home with me to remind me of my efforts to bathe the bull. He had collected his reward. We finished up in the small fairground area towards evening, trying out our hand at the rifle range, before heading home again, tired but content.

Jenny and her son.

As the months progressed through July and August, I joined in with all the farming activities, and visited many places, being taken by Lucy or by Bill on his bike. Lucy came from a large family of Sandersons, who lived in the area of Yarm, where her brother farmed, and also her sister Jenny and husband Tom. The Sanderson family likeness was remarkable between Lucy and Jenny's seventeen year old son. No one lived too far away, making it a closely knit family where many exchange visits were made. By late August as the weather became hotter and sultrier, the harvesting of the barley, oats and wheat took precedence over other activities. Cutting was undertaken with the binder, and was the first activity, allowing stooks to be created and laid-up vertically. Days later, once the stooks were thoroughly dry, they were gathered up and carted off to form corn-stacks.

Bill had an exacting eye for building the corn stacks. While everyone else threw up the sheaves onto the ever-growing stack, he caught these deftly, and placed them with care around the perimeters to make the right shape. The core was in-filled with spare straw, and finally a cone for the top was constructed. The stacks were covered with tarpaulins and weighted down at the corners with bricks. They then awaited the threshing machines at a later date. We had studied the new combined harvesters at the show, and many farms were moving towards these modern methods. Nevertheless, on many farms the older harvesting methods prevailed.

Lucy undertook a weekly bake, feeding all the workers, especially at harvest time, and I soon learned to make large quantities of fruit pies, pasties, teacakes, cakes and tarts, as well as the weekly bread-making. During harvesting, food was taken out to the workers in big baskets, with large billy-cans of tea and cups, at least three times a day so the quantity of food consumed was considerable – fuel for the workers. I was taught how to drive the tractor, and put all the 'baggings' or 'bait' (as this food was sometimes called) onto the trailer when the fields being harvested were beyond the nearby inbye field.

The children begged free rides to and fro from the fields and delightedly helped with collecting up cups and plates in the sunshine. They picked bunches of summer flowers from the boundaries of the fields, bright red poppies, pink campions, and blue cornflowers which showed their heads above the waving stalks of corn. Rabbits still scuttled for cover. If they dared show themselves, they were in great danger of being shot for the pot.

After the hard work of the harvesting, Bill took me on trips to the Yorkshire coast on his motorbike, visiting numerous places, and also to see his mother. I did not want to return to London, because I was becoming acclimatised to the pace of the farming community, and also a deepening friendship with Bill. He caused my pulses to quicken, and I did not want to part company with him. And he seemed to feel the same way. I knew that I needed to return home to my new job, so I agreed to write to him regularly while I thought about my future life.

I felt that I had now reached a crossroads.

*Visiting the North East coast
with Bill.*

THE SHROPSHIRE RAT

Returning home I saw that Jim had settled down well to his new environment, while Father alternated his interests, spending time in his garden, on golf tournaments and running the southern branch of his Regimental Association. He was constantly away at meetings in London, helping resettle former members of his regiment, one job amongst many at the association.

My sister embarked upon a midwifery course, and declared that she was intending to go out to Kenya. She had heard that a maternity hospital was needed there, and proposed starting one, planning to enlist a number of nursing staff. She would be the matron in charge. I was quite impressed when she told me of her plans, but did not doubt for one moment that she would achieve her goals, being the forceful person that she was.

Now tall, slim and good-looking with her bright blue eyes and brown hair, she oozed charm when it suited her. About the same time as she finished her course, Sir John Williamson, a patient in the training hospital, was about to be discharged and sent back to his adopted home town of Nairobi. Being the owner of a diamond mine, and not short of funds, he planned to take with him a private nurse, to help manage the treatment for his terminal throat cancer. Cleverly, Jane applied for this job and was accepted. The stipend was generous and of course she was delighted that she was now travelling to her intended destination free of charge.

In contrast to Father, Mother was now without Jim, her constant companion, so she was footloose, restless, and somewhat sad. She was looking for a new direction, with new challenges and goals. She decided to become more involved in grass-roots politics, supporting the local Conservative Party. Our house now became the committee rooms, during which time she organised dances and socials in Isleworth and nearby districts to generate party funds.

She acquired a small printing press which was installed in the back room called the den, found one or two volunteers for running off posters, not least enlisting the help from the Richmond Theatre group, the Tudor Players. Mother loved being involved with this organisation because it gave her added status.

At one of Father's regimental dances.

Father involved Mother socially with his association, for which I accompanied her on a number of occasions to the dances and gatherings, organised mainly for ex-regimental members. On these occasions, my limited selection of evening wear was greatly enhanced once I took over part of Jane's old wardrobe of dresses. It was rare for me to have new clothes, but I accepted this happened to all younger sisters, who were always referred to as a 'Second-hand Sally' in a family. Like a fledgling bird, I could admire the plumage, before gaining my own plumage as I matured.

Since we had nearly all 'flown the nest' permanently, I think Mother was at last having to think anew of her role in life, trying out 'new hats' for different occasions. Len did not join our household in place of Jim, but nevertheless became one of Mother's close friends, because she discovered that he was easily manoeuvred, manipulated, and willing to do her bidding, while rarely answering back.

My place in the family became less important as I grew older, but I still enjoyed having my home as a 'pit stop'. I could still sit in Father's big armchair in his musty, book-lined study, enjoying numerous conversations with him, or listen to his selection of records: well known classical pieces, light operatic arias, and brass band pieces like 'Bells across the Meadow' by William Ketelebey come instantly to memory, and lovely old songs pulled out from his pile of 78s, wafted out of the open window on the evening breeze, somewhat scratched from age but still playable.

He read me poems from his well loved poetry books or passages from the *Jungle Book*. Occasionally he would re-cite from memory long passages from some poetry, which I would have thought he must have long forgotten. He was becoming older, but those merry blue eyes of his still twinkled. It was not uncommon for him to laugh out aloud at some outrageous story, as he recounted it to me, or aired one of his many risqué limericks collected over the years. He had a wicked sense of humour, and some of his reminisces of incidents about his life gave me an insight into what made him the kind and considerate man that he was.

I was beginning to feel sorry for my parents, who had been married in 1933 before the outbreak of the war. Father went away with his regiment five years later, and did not return until 1948 from India. It was a time when my mother was

My parents on their wedding day in 1933.

235

just coming into maturity, having been a pampered teenager after the death of her mother.

Their marriage, like many other couples at that time, did not have the best chance for happiness in the following ten years. His capacity for understanding her emotional turmoil during those years of separation was always evident in the way he dealt with matters when he eventually returned home.

I still did not have a permanent career in mind, and felt like a will-o-the-wisp at times. I often dropped in to chat to my Aunt Daisy, my godmother, in her little underground flat in Addison Avenue, where she would listen to my uncertain aspirations for the future, always making wise comments to guide me. I told her of Bill's growing attraction to me, and his hint of getting married. I was very much in love with my tall, good looking farmer, and never thought about the ramifications of a change of lifestyle it would create for me. Since I was barely eighteen, I found it difficult to make wise choices – in fact, any choices. My previous role-model and confidant had left for Africa. And I hated being under my mother's feet, because she was still an arch manipulator.

'It would be as well to wait a while; for at least a couple of years. See how you feel about it then,' she counselled me. Old Aunt Daisy had my father's ear, being his aunt and long term 'proxy mother' after my grandmother Stuart had died in my infancy.

'As you've been offered that job in Shropshire, it would be as well to try it out. See a different way of life, meet new people; it will broaden your horizons.' She smiled at me encouragingly to show she approved. I knew that somehow she understood my mixed-up feelings, because I was neither a girl, nor yet a fully-grown woman. I had also told her of my doubts about the offered job, and would have preferred a local appointment. This seemed so very far away. Still, I went off to Shropshire on the appointed day, to Ellesmere College as a lady cook, a job which Miss France from Cuckfield Park College, had found for me, and she had given me a marvellous reference.

Ready to leave for Ellesmere College.

Ellesmere College was a Boys Private Boarding School, housed in an old, large and stylish red-brick building with many tall dormitory windows, an impressive hall and entrance, and a long, wide dining hall. The dark polished wood, which showed years of hard graft that had been administered to ensure that the interior was kept in pristine condition, shone up the wide, ornate

Ellesmere College, Shropshire, 1954.

staircase.

The beautiful chapel near the hall where morning prayers were held, could house the whole school which numbered approximately 500 pupils with about fifty staff. Shafts of sunlight streamed through the coloured glass windows along the sides, illuminating its high rafters, bedecked with many flags and coats of arms which provided an insight into the numerous years of historical events.

The school was founded by Canon Nathaniel Woodard in 1884 on a generous site of 114 acres (46 hectares), in association with the Church of England Authorities, said to be formed for the 'sons of the middle classes'.

I could see the Victorian architectural influences of those whom had built fine churches and cathedrals with carved stone ornamentations. Inside the building the corridors for the kitchen staff were very long and usually cold, their living quarters were cramped, reminscent of the early Victorian era and badly planned.

The kitchens were stone floored with fairly modern equipment, similar to that which had been fitted at Cuckfield Park. These were much larger, with huge cold-store rooms which led off from the main central kitchen, with a great scullery behind it. All the dishes disappeared here, grubby and soiled, to reappear again like shining full moons, ready for restacking on the cavernous shelves.

Wendy, Iris and Sylvia.

'Lady cooks' was the description given to the three of us all trained in cookery, myself, then Sylvia, a quietly spoken gentle soul, with wispy fair hair pulled up into an untidy topknot bun, and Iris, a lively and hard-working Welsh girl with short-cut dark hair, who would break into song unexpectedly at any time – both were about my age.

We were to provide good, nutritious food three times a day for approximately 600 people. There were nine Welsh maids, three for each of us, and four permanent scullery maids, who beetled about, moving piles of dishes and plates off the big lifts, which trundled laboriously from one floor to the next by means of pulleys.

The great oven cooking trays were piled high beside a sink for the attention of a scullery maid assigned to that task. The maids all spoke to each other in Welsh, as well as muttering various negative comments to me, also in Welsh. They appeared to be reluctant to work with an English girl, whom they thought inferior to themselves. Not understanding any Welsh, I asked Iris to explain what they were saying. Iris seemed to think she was in charge of the kitchen, but whether she was or not, she certainly had great authority over the girls.

'They're sniggering about you behind your back, look you. They think you don't understand their chat. And you don't. But I know how to sort them all out. We'll soon cure that.'

As a result, Iris decided to spend some time teaching me a few Welsh phrases, many of them not too polite. We rehearsed these for me to chastise the awkward girls, from time to time, or throw my Welsh comments into the conversation and startle them. Quickly, the kitchen maids started to gawp at some of my comments. As one could imagine, they became quite uncertain of themselves, not knowing what I could and couldn't understand. From then on, their behaviour improved dramatically.

Iris.

The three of us changed our routines of work every month, because there were three different cooking activities; the meats, the vegetables, and breads and pastries, although everyone helped with the breakfasts. A large cauldron of porridge was produced daily, and rows of sausages and rashers of bacon placed on wide trays, which slid into the big ovens like shoals of swimming fish, glistening in the hot fat.

Vast frying pans were soon covered with metal egg rings, into which the 'not so fortunate' operator for that day had to break about 500 eggs. This reminded me of the slippery and moving frogspawn on the surface of a pond. Since then I have never fried an egg without being reminded of this long gone image. The enormous ovens provided great trays of fried bread, and then all was transported by the kitchen porters to the two lifts and hauled up to the next floor.

Cooking may be considered an art, but under the conditions in which we worked, surprisingly the end-results were often masterpieces, coaxed out of a team of quite inexperienced labour. The big food stores were extremely cold in direct contrast to the unbearably hot kitchens, which kept us on the move continually, almost as fast

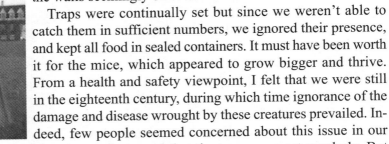

as the very large mice which we saw occasionally fleeing around under the equipment, in and out of the crevices along the walls seemingly on secret missions.

Traps were continually set but since we weren't able to catch them in sufficient numbers, we ignored their presence, and kept all food in sealed containers. It must have been worth it for the mice, which appeared to grow bigger and thrive. From a health and safety viewpoint, I felt that we were still in the eighteenth century, during which time ignorance of the damage and disease wrought by these creatures prevailed. Indeed, few people seemed concerned about this issue in our kitchen. Nevertheless for my part I ensured that the traps were set regularly. But due to the extremely arduous working environment, when ready to retire to our rooms at the end of the day, we were too tired to worry about such trifles, because we had to be up again before five, to start the new day.

The housekeeper at the school, Mrs Stone, was in overall charge of the staff and provisions, with calculating eyes and a reluctant smile on her thin lips. She was a well upholstered and well dressed lady of middle age. With carefully permed hair, rosy cheeks and never, ever seen without her cameo earrings clipped on and matching brooch pinned to her bosom, she sailed into the kitchen domain with great authority, to give orders and sometimes alter the numbers of staff requiring feeding for the day, passing the notes she had made to Iris.

As one of their privileges, the teaching staff had an added tea-time menu of beautifully created cakes and sandwiches, served on silver cake stands, in the comfortable staff room, with special bone china and tea pots, jealously guarded by Mrs. Stone, as she presided over the staff tea.

Mrs. Stone was also responsible for looking after our wages, held in the safe in her room, which were paid monthly in arrears. On one occasion though, I wanted to buy some clothes before the month's end, but had insufficient money to do so. Having asked for, and being granted a loan in advance, both Iris and I went shopping one afternoon to Wrexham. I bought a bottle-green woollen suit for best wear, and a woollen dress, because it was getting colder as the days shortened.

Our trips to Wrexham on our days off were enjoyable, which created a bond of friendship, thus helping me through the unusually hard work and long hours. On her days off, Sylvia often went to her parents' house nearby, which gave her much needed respite from the daily grind.

Iris was the prime mover for free time activities. Quite soon, we had established a weekly routine to walk from the school in the evenings, past the canal, into the village of Ellesmere. On most Saturday nights there was a dance in the Town Hall, where we eagerly learned new dance steps mingled with the old favourites. They were mainly old time dances such as the Valeta, and Military two-step, intermingled with the ever popular Waltz-Country-Dance and the Square Tango. Nevertheless, since the war, many new American favourites had been introduced and were interspersed between the usual ballroom dancing numbers.

We were not short of partners either. On the outskirts of the nearby town of Oswestry was a big Army Basic Training camp. Every Saturday night, the coach from the camp drew up outside the town hall main entrance, while a Sergeant stepped out to count his charges very carefully, as they alighted, announcing very loudly that no alcohol was permitted, before bellowing his evening instructions: 'Be'ave, you 'erberts, I'll be back 'ere at 11.30 sharp, so you'd better be waitin', all present and correct. An' no drinking. An' no fighting. An' no sex. An' no stowaways.'

After leaving all these unattractive instructions for the young soldiers to absorb, off he went with his coach, leaving two sergeants as minders and a coachload of smart, well-polished young men eager to get dancing. There were also a number of musicians, who made their way to the stage to unpack their instruments.

I enjoyed these evenings greatly, quickly learning to dance with a variety of expert

dancers, but was drawn to one of the trumpeters whom I talked to at the break times. I asked him to play some of my favourites, especially the well known Eddie Calvert pieces. However, as a dancing partner I soon found him lacking, because he was always on the stage playing music instead. After the dancing evening had got started, all of a sudden, a series of shouts could be heard, coming from within the dance hall: 'She's mine. You bloody soldiers keep coming here where you're not wanted.'

Soon other angry voices joined in and increased the intensity of the noise. Louder voices became more shouts. Then punches were thrown as the proprietorial rights of the local youth were challenged, while the Redcap soldiers seemed unable to break up the foray. A couple of officers who happened to stroll past from the local pub, stepped in through the door, and instantly the fight subsided to nothing, drying up like a passing storm, leaving puddles of discontented youths to lick their wounded pride and dented manhood.

The whole coach load of soldiers, restricted to their 'glasshouse' for seven days, were banned for at least a month at the dance hall, giving the local dancers time to re-establish their friendships, their partners and their social life.

This suited Iris and I, because we were keen to learn new dances from a dance teacher, Mr Williams, who taught different groups during each evening. We watched him preparing a group of eight couples into a Formation Dancing Team, because this kind of competition had recently become the latest craze.

Originally started in the 1930s at the Astoria Ballroom by Frank and Peggy Spencer in London, Formation Dancing became very popular. By 1949 it was televised as *Come Dancing*, which spawned a host of clubs and teams all over the coun-

The formation dancing team.

try, such as Mr William's little group. Iris was a natural dancer, tall and graceful, so was delighted to be invited by Mr Williams to take part.

Initially left out, my chance to be part of the dance group came about when a girl of about my height became ill with appendicitis. Mr Williams looked around for a replacement. He was very agitated, because he had worked hard on the routine, which we all knew, step-by-step.

'The contest is only six weeks away. How am I to replace Janet at such short notice with this routine? It's quite complicated. And someone who fits the costume.

They have already been made.'

'Please put Wendy in Janet's place as she is the right height and knows the routine well,' Iris had chipped in hastily in front of another dancer, who was offering her services as well. Clearly, because his teams were so popular, several girls now wanted to join.

Afterwards, we walked back in the dark, both happy – I was content to be in the team that evening. It was a frosty and a clear moonlit night as we listened to the rhythmic hoot of the barn owl flying silently through the tree tops to its nest, where it folded its wide, white wings neatly before entering the hole sheltering its hidden bed of dried grass and feathers, carrying a mouse, to consume in peace.

So it was that I joined the Formation Dancing Troupe, and spent many hours of rehearsals to improve the timing of the routines. Normally, I went down to the village on the bus, which was always a little early for the dancing class. On an impulse one evening, having arrived, I walked a little further along the street and called in to one of the two public houses, to speak to Jack, my partner, a young man of about 26, who ran the premises. As I walked into the bar to ask him what time he would be finished, the air was electrified instantly.

Total silence. You could have heard a pin drop. Not a word was spoken by the men inside. Within seconds, Jack came from behind the bar, and grabbed me by my arm, propelling me outside onto the pavement.

'What d' you think you were doing, going in there? Have you no shame, woman?' And he strode off back into the bar, slamming the door. Whatever was wrong? I was soon made aware of my mistake when I told Iris, who laughed long and loud at me. 'Women are not allowed to enter public houses or even the bars in hotels, in Wales.'

'But we're in Shropshire.'

'Near enough, this is border country,' was her only explanation. So I had to apologise to Jack when he arrived, explaining my lack of understanding of the rules of gender separation in the Welsh borders. I rehearsed whenever I could but still had my work to do at the school. One day, Mrs Stone noticed that I had started to slow down during my work, and asked me whether I was ill?

'No, but I am a little tired. I've been chosen for the Ellesmere Formation Team, and we've been practising for the contest, at the end of the year in a big hall in London, and I still have my dress to alter.'

Mrs Stone was quite surprised to hear of my participation, but also interested enough to suggest that I bring the dress back to her room for inspection. She asked me to put it on. It was a white satin dress with miles of tulle and organza covering it, with touches of plum-coloured trimmings at the neck, with three large plum-coloured roses placed strategically on the hips.

'It needs taking in quite a bit; the other girl must have been larger than you. Leave it with me while you are working and I will adjust it for you.'

She was as good as her word, showing an unexpected and

kindly side to her nature. I was given a packet of shining sequins and a container of plum-coloured dye to alter the white satin dancing shoes which I had bought. When work for the day was finished, she showed me how to make up the dye with boiling water, in the echoing and empty kitchen.

At this time of the day, the kitchen was an eerie place, with strange rustling noises and gurgling pipes around us, as if all the equipment was having a whispered argument, adding to the noises of the almost invisible mice. I offered to dye Iris's shoes, but she joined us to do her own, and soon we were both correctly shod. Mrs Stone then spent some hours altering the dresses for us. Finally she announced that she would hang them in her sitting-room – for safekeeping, she said, but I believe she wanted to ensure that we both went to bed in good time, ready for the start of work the next day.

As the days shortened into starlit evenings, our excitement rose, and nervousness increased until the great day arrived. Term time had just finished, and the pupils streamed home for their month long Christmas holidays. In contrast, the school kitchen staff were given just ten days, because preparations for the new term were required, including stores to organise and spring cleaning had to be started.

The day arrived – having loaded the beautiful dresses into the coach, the team along with its luggage was soon off to London for the contest. I was quite familiar with London, but now saw a different side to my home town. We all stayed for two nights in a guest house in Kensington, which my mother would have called 'somewhat seedy'.

The following day, we arrived in good time at a vast dance hall, teeming with beautifully dressed dancers, with glittering lights reflecting in the mirrors on the walls, and rows of seats surrounding a highly-polished sprung dance floor. The five judges sat on a raised platform behind a table laden with certificates, prizes and cups.

The competition was divided into different categories, so we had to wait until our slot for the 'Old Time Dance Medley' was announced. Finally we were called up. We glided onto the shining floor, taking up our positions. Once the music started,

we forgot the watching crowds completely, while we performed as the well rehearsed team that we were. There were cheers from the crowds around the hall as we completed our routine and eventually left the floor. To our great delight, the final results justified all our hard work, because we won the third prize cup, along with a present and certificate for each dancer, presented with words of congratulation by Peggy Spencer.

The journey back to Ellesmere the following day was a merry one. Singing on the coach accompanied by the opening of many presents, which were beautifully packaged, including expensive chocolates for all the girls. I was determined to keep mine for Christmas, so put the box in my holdall, together with my new certificate. When we arrived back at the village, the driver took Iris and I to the school gates. We showed Mrs Stone our certificates, and presents, explaining to her in detail the events of the last few days. She noticed how late it was, and pressed us to go to bed.

'You must be very tired, repack the rest of your things tomorrow for your Christmas holiday.'

So, with no more urging, off I went to my room, scattering my clothes about, and climbed into bed, dropping into a deep sleep. During the night I awoke, uneasy and aware of something not quite right. I opened my eyes cautiously because I thought somebody was sitting on my bed. Fear made the hairs rise on the back of my neck. I lay still, thinking whether I had imagined it, but no, there was certainly an alien movement on my bed. I swivelled my head round fractionally, because I could feel a hand, perhaps, on my stomach. My heart started racing, and my fear reached such a fever pitch that I could not scream.

Then I saw two large black eyes like round shiny shoe buttons, watching me, right in front of my face! In that instant I realised that a large brown rat with a twitching, bewhiskered nose was perched on my chest. Its tail was extremely long, helping it to balance carefully on my sleeping torso. It also made me realise that many of those big mice I had seen in the kitchens were probably rats, living in close proximity to us all.

With great haste I sat up as the rat retreated across the bed, down to the floor, scuttling away to the corner of the room, and finally slithering out of sight. It was then that I noticed the rat had decimated my box of chocolates, now completely ruined. Belatedly I realised that the chocolates had attracted the creature in the first place. That was the end of any further sleep for me that night. I needed to think out my next move.

The following morning, without further hesitation I packed all my belongings, then went to the telephone in the hallway and ordered a taxi. I told Iris what had happened, gave her my beautiful dress to return with hers to the Ellesmere Dancing Group, and asked her to give my message of regret to Mrs Stone. When I arrived home, I wrote to her formally to tender my resignation, saying I was not prepared to compete with rats in my living quarters.

BUSBY STOOP

When I arrived home from Shropshire, I felt quite exhausted from the long hours of work at the school, and the strenuous practice for the dancing competition, so I spent a lot of time sleeping to recover my energy levels. From the episode in Shropshire, it took quite a while to calm my fear of rats. Having never been a squeamish person, I had to reason with myself that they were surviving the only way they knew how, ensuring that they were close to their food supply, provided courtesy of the human occupants of the school.

My parents and I.

Once I was comfortable with this explanation, I was able to put the incident out of my mind and move on, because I did not have to deal with the problem face to face; but my father corresponded with the school authorities about the 'rodent looters'. The deputy head informed him tersely that 'the matter was now in hand and being dealt with.'

I joined an Old Time Dancing club, going once a week to nearby Hounslow for some light relief, during which time I heard of a job from one of my dancing friends. I desperately needed a job because I had not settled upon a permanent career. As it turned out, I secured a place in the design department of Pattinsons, a machinery components factory.

Whether installed in cars, trucks or planes, or other mechanical equipment, most engines require dials to indicate all manner of speed, times, revolutions, heat, pressure or other measurable information. At Pattinsons, I designed the dials from specifications, provided to me by the manager, which gave me guidance on what was to be measured, their shape and sizes, divisions, lines, and inscriptions. Once finished, my blueprints were sent down to the shop floor and laid onto aluminium, printed, cut out and finished off with a silicon coat. I worked in an office together with a young myopic girl called Mavis. She was a chatterbox with fair, frizzy hair and clumsy enough to continually knock things off my desk.

Initially, I enjoyed the job, being quite easy, especially through my technical drawing skills learned at Twickenham Art School. Nevertheless, due to coming from a different background, I felt like an alien amongst the factory workers in the canteen. They reciprocated the feelings, making fun of me by imitating the way I spoke to my face – I was the 'la-de-da' lady. I was at a loss to know how to improve matters. The kindly foreman with a keen eye for atmosphere, and a stopwatch for a brain noticed this. I wondered which of these two attributes prompted his next move.

'I've brought you a kettle for break times. You don't need to go all that way down to the canteen. It's such a trip to get there – a waste of time.'

He then produced out of his cavernous overall pockets, like a conjurer pulling several rabbits out of a hat, two beakers and three tins containing tea, sugar and biscuits for the two of us. 'Mavis can look after you here,' was his parting comment as he glanced at Mavis and carefully put a bottle of milk on the desk. So now I had my little empire and was earning my keep in this strange job.

A few houses along our road lived a Polish photographer who strolled down to chat with Father at times, from time to time exchanging war stories while they trimmed the front hedges, neatening those parts that were out of reach of the milk-float horse, who had left corners uncropped while the milkman was delivering his wares. The horse enjoyed the fresh shoots of our privet hedge, usually standing there for a longer period of time because our house was at the bend of the road, and within easy walking distance of several houses.

Mr. Lewsey's photograph of the author.

'Wendy has a job at Pattinsons now, in the design department,' Father chatted away to Len Lewsey as he worked. 'She'd do those colour pictures for you, that you mentioned, if you asked her. She goes to Hounslow on her bike for the early shift, so returns home fairly early.'

Colour photography was still in its infancy as far as automatic colour was concerned, and to produce fine photographs with subtle hints of colour needed a delicate touch from the bottles of photographic inks. Now I was working in my spare time for Mr Lewsey tinting fashionable portraits, which were often rosy-cheeked babies or extravagantly clothed wedding couples, and occasionally pets.

Father asked him if he had enough work to keep me occupied full time, because after a couple of months at the factory I was extremely bored with the job. It proved to be repetitive and did not stretch my imagination much, so I was relieved to find

that the photographer needed a full-time keen eyed artist, so I changed jobs again. Black and white studio photographs came rolling in fast, to be given the colouring treatment, with hardly a pause for some weeks, as his imaginative work as a photographer became more widely known.

Mr Lewsey was asked to photograph some packages for Coty's perfume and accessories, which were intended to be used for advertising purposes in the local chemist's shop. He had discovered that Coty at their Kent factory in Ashford was running a competition for new packaging designs. Coty perfumes, created in France at the turn of the century, were now much in demand. Having been bought out by an American firm, their products were marketed in beautifully designed Rene Lalique bottles, which I really admired.

'Can you design a fancy box for a set – the perfume, talc powder, soap and spray?' he asked. 'We could enter it for the competition. You could make that beautiful bottle the main feature.'

'How long have I got to do it? Will you photo the items? Can I use your photographic inks?' My fertile imagination was instantly seeding ideas for this interesting project.

'I'll have to send in photos of our entry by next month.'

Accepting the challenge, I designed and made five boxes out of fine card which I painted, one each for the separate items, and then a group package. The photographs were sent by registered mail, after which we waited for what seemed like an eternity for news of the outcome – we were convinced that the designs were good. After repeated phone calls and letters, Mr Lewsey was informed that we had not won, but all the designs were now the property of the company and would not be returned.

'You should have read the small print. We can now use any of the designs in future sales drives,' was the brusque reply. About a year later, I saw my designs being shown off for an 'autumn promotion' by the firm. There was absolutely nothing I could do about it.

One day Mother invited her classroom friend from St Paul's for tea – Joyce Grenfell. Since she was an old 'Paulina' of the school, we had all been entertained by her on the school stage on several occasions when she had been invited back to give talks about the art of acting. She exuded jolliness and confidence, and was an observant and spirited lady. Now she commiserated with us on the crafty tricks used in business.

Joyce Grenfell.

She laughed a great deal when she heard of the roaming rat on my bed in Ellesmere College. I was still a bit upset by this horrible incident when I recounted the story to her. As a way of simulating the situation, and with such realism, she pretended to be The Rat, and created a world in which the rat visited its friends in 'a kitchen', looking for food.

Her acting was so convincing that it transported me into a different world. As a result, my negative experience was altered to such an extent that I never thought of the creature with such fear again. She had turned that incident into such a comedy that it helped me to apply Father's maxim: 'Know your enemy well', reducing my fears into a *Wind in the Willows* kind of scenario, full of little creatures. As is well known, Joyce went on to become one of the most successful comedy actresses in the country.

I had been writing regularly to Bill in Yorkshire, and also had lengthy and loving conversations with him on the antiquated telephone system. Through this, I learned that the McLaughlans had sold Broom Close and moved to a new farm not so far away, called Skipton Hall Farm, near Thirsk. As a result, they had expanded their acreage, which included the buildings left by the RAF in 1946, plus the usual farm buildings, as well as land for arable and dairy use.

'Come for a little holiday and see for yourself. Bill wants to show you something here.' Lucy Mclaughlan also chatted to me on the phone and was a persuasive hostess. I needed little persuasion to visit them at the new farm. I knew that Bill was also as keen to see me, as I was to see him again. So now I felt welcomed and wanted for myself, not just as a spare member of my family in London. The spring rush of wedding photographs had slackened off, so there was not as much demand for my work at that time of the year, so I told Mr Lewsey I was going for a summer holiday. I explained all this to my father, who was in the middle of a series of golf tournaments so it was not the ideal moment to broach the subject to him.

'Fine, fine, you go and enjoy yourself, your Mother won't be back from her trip for at least another three weeks.' He said vaguely, smiling to me as he was thinking

Thirsk clock tower

of other things. Mother had gone cruising with her friends.

'They do not really care what I choose to do with myself; I could have announced that I was taking a trip to the moon, or China.' I thought to myself, while busily packing my small case, which still included Piglet and my small travel worn envelope of fairy pictures. I had the unshakeable belief in fairies riding on the rainbows to land on any place that I happened to be. Since we had all travelled a long way together, their once vivid colours were now faint through constant handling over the years.

I returned to Yorkshire in the early summer sunshine, this time arriving at the McLaughlan's new farm, travelling up the A1 on the bus to Thirsk. I arrived on a Monday, one of the weekly market days. Thirsk is an ancient town with cobbled streets and a clock tower in the centre of the square. The market trading took place there, colourful stalls overflowed into the surrounding streets like the lava flow from a volcano, teeming with activity and noise. It was late afternoon and The Black Lion was doing a roaring trade with the local farmers and traders who had spilled out with some chairs into the sunshine with their pints, closely shadowed by their ever faithful working dogs, while their bartering continued good-naturedly.

Bill met me in Thirsk, with smiles and questions as to what I had been doing during the past months. We drove towards Skipton-on-Swale on the Ripon road, past the 200 year old left-handed oval racecourse, through well-tended fields and on to the hamlet of Skipton, which straddled the River Swale by an ancient bridge beside an equally ancient church.

The flag on the top of St John's Church peeped through the trees lending a little coloured relief to the hazy summer sunshine. At this point we turned into the entrance to Skipton Hall Farm, parked up and went into the farm kitchen to greet the family, where they were gathered for tea. Wilf, Lucy, and her two children, Jennifer and little Geoffrey, were joined by Lucy's sister, Jenny who was keen to meet me again. Both sisters came from a large farming family, the Sandersons, who were all remarkably alike – of small stature and auburn colouring. However, in contrast to the rest of the family, Jenny was tall and dark, yet probably the closest emotionally and looks to Lucy.

Bill Joynson.

After tea, Lucy wanted to show me around the new farm – what a difference to the other one. Vast acres of land, and partly covered by strange and curious-shaped buildings – since 1940, the flat area around this district of Yorkshire had been used for several British airfields. When I delved into the history of the area it became clearer. The No. 6 (Royal Canadian Air Force) Bomber Group officially assumed operational status on 1st January 1943 when for the next three days the RAF handed over to the Group six stations. These were Leeming , Middleton St. George, Dishforth , Croft, Dalton and, lastly, Skipton-on-Swale, which was then still under construction. All these squadrons were flying Wellingtons and Halifax IIs or Vs.

It was not surprising that the farm was littered with many Nissen huts, and giant corrugated half-coconut shaped sheds. There were two tall derelict concrete control towers and a now defunct runway lay abandoned, growing tufts of casual grasses and creeping convolvulus in the crazy-paving cracks streaking across the concrete.

The airfield had been decommissioned in 1946 and nature had soon returned, quickly disguising the ugly concrete structures once all human activity had ceased. It amazed me to think that all these Nissen huts had been occupied by the Canadian Air Force detachments as recently as only eight years previously. In many of the now unused sleeping quarters, scribbled messages could still be seen, and I could imagine the aircraft taking off over the towers, en route to Europe.

Amongst this patchwork of different-sized, round and square buildings was a large house, Skipton Hall, which was standing within its own garden. The farmhouse was a late seventeenth century red brick Georgian mansion, built with three floors on an elevated site, with windows which decreased in size, from floor to floor. There was a walled garden at the back, and extensive lawns at the front, with peacocks roaming around beneath the shrubbery, their calls like lonely demented souls in a wilderness.

Having now said hello to the family, and played with the children, Lucy showed me around their new farmhouse with its large kitchen, solid fuel stove and stone floors. The family occupied the ground and first floor, which seemed very large, after which we progressed to the top floor, where another six rooms appeared unused. From these smaller windows the view was extensive, and the window seats very broad.

'Bill now has the job of farm manager, and these top rooms are for him to turn into a self-contained flat if he wishes.' I think she had visions of their farm manager moving on to a more lucrative job with accommodation, but her alternative plan was well thought out.

'We have a cowman, Joe Maltby, living in the tied cottage there and we've started a new venture, making use of some of the buildings to rear turkeys. It seems a very profitable line.' Wilf McLaughlan had moved on happily to this change of livestock, when he found out how efficient and knowledgeable his new cowman was with the herd and new milking procedures.

Joe and Bill.

She chatted on in her husky voice, with her red, wavy hair, now cut short and her four foot six inch frame bobbing up and down to keep up with me as we walked among the buildings. We strolled past a small cottage on the roadside, enclosed by a stone wall, where Joe, the cowman lived with his young wife and six small children. It was close to the dairy for organising the daily milking of the herd of pedigree Friesians. These were the direct descendants of the Broom Close herd, brought with them when they moved farms.

Bill's role now encompassed managing all the arable land, rotating the crops and organising the machinery required for this task. He was assisted by a variety of farm labourers. One seemingly very ancient farm worker with very long finger nails, George, was known as 'Bill's lad', because he stayed very close to him, doing whatever he was requested to do. He was full of stories of the recent past which made the war years seem as if it was only yesterday.

'I mind a time before't end ot' war, 'n airplane took off wi' seven men in it, just o'er theer,' waving his arm to indicate a field, he paused for dramatic effect before continuing, 'It was treetop high, when it fell oot t' sky and landed on anuther 'un, causin' a big explosion, an' a fire yu cud see in York. All those Canadians were killed. Seven of 'em fell oot t' sky, and seven were on't ground.' He repeated his story with embellishments like a practised storyteller, but it was based on the truth.

This tragic accident happened in 1943, when one of the bombers, a Halifax Mk11, fully laden for its journey to Germany, suddenly stalled after taking off and crashed onto another waiting bomber which was also fully laden.

'It blew 'owt a fair few winders hereabouts, tha' knows.' He ruminated on the consequences of the crash to the district, while he was

Old George and Bill.

working. He enjoyed working for a new and younger manager and was keen to do what he could despite his increasing arthritis.

I stayed with the McLaughlans and Bill in the farmhouse for a warm summer that year. It was long and sultry, producing a good harvest. There were two extra girls now to help Lucy indoors and also for tending the rearing of the poultry, as the business was growing.

During this time my relationship with Bill blossomed, so that we decided we would get married the following spring. In the 1950s there were no thoughts of co-habiting, for all desires were kept until after the wedding, so it was a case of taking ones life's partner on trust. I sat on the broad window seat in the upper floor room staring out at the view, and wondered whether I should be able to manage this new life so far away from all that I had previously known. But 'hope often overcomes caution' when in one's teens. The fact

Nissen huts at Skipton Hall Farm.

that Bill was about nine years older gave me the confidence to lean on his wisdom, for although fairly shy he was well educated, well-intentioned and knowledgeable.

He took me to meet his sister Pat, and his mother, who lived in the shop they owned in Redcar, on the North Eastern coastline. Unfortunately, the weather was raw and bracing on that day, and I thought what a hard life they lived in their newsagent's shop, crammed with nick nacks, haberdashery, toys and cigarettes. They would be up before dawn to receive bundles of newspapers, and late to bed long after the latest returning workers had called in for their cigarettes and evening papers.

They had taken the shop on after Bill's father, who had been an engineer in Manchester, had died during The Depression. The shop and house were occupied

Bill and I at Whitby.

by his mother, his two sisters, Pat and Mary, and his Grandmother Dresser. The view from their first floor sitting room window showed the vast expanse of the North

Woodbastwick Hall, Norfolk, demolished in 1971.

Sea, and glancing left along the shoreline the perpetual lights from the mighty steelworks of Dorman Long.

It was a household full of women during the time when Bill attended Sir William Turner's Grammar School in Coatham, Redcar. After returning from his spell in the army, he attended Woodbastwick Hall (demolished in 1971), an agricultural college in Norfolk, where he studied for a new career in farming.

I never knew his Grandma, or his sister Mary who had died at nineteen, but often met his mother with her friend Mary Hawkins, when we took shopping trips into Harrogate, during which time his sister Pat would look after the busy shop. She was full of fun, and had a very kindly disposition.

We thought it a good idea to take up the offer of the flat at the farm. It required plumbing for a kitchen and bathroom, and we spent time decorating and furnishing the place. There was now a proliferation of new designs in materials and furniture which we made use of to create a welcoming home. It had its own entrance at the back of the house, which led up the stairs to a sitting-room and two bedrooms with windows overlooking the front of the

Bill's sister Pat.

251

house. The kitchen and bathroom faced the back with another room for further development. Who could possibly object to our plans?

The farming calendar continued, because harvesting of wheat and barley from the large fields took precedence, followed by potato lifting. Most children in Yorkshire had a half-term two weeks 'potato-lifting' holiday, timed to coincide with the readiness of the crop. Lastly the sugar beet needed gathering before the winter frosts.

Mary Hawkins and I with Bill's mother in Harrogate.

In order to spread out delivery to the sugar beet factory, the beet was stored in clamps, huge mounds of beet blanketed with straw, then covered over with a thick layer of earth. All over Yorkshire, many tons of beet was lifted for processing at the same time.

Bill on his BSA500 motorbike with young Geoffrey.

Sugar beet had grown in importance during the war with an absence of cane sugar from overseas. A sugar beet factory, opened in 1924 near York, had mushroomed into a huge processing complex. Working there was a 'reserved occupation' for men, similar to the coal miners' jobs, because we were still not out of the woods as far as feeding the British population was concerned. Bill and I went round the factory on an organized tour, but the smell of the boiling beet and the intensity of heat generated, made the trip to be remembered for its unpleasantness.

We often went into Thirsk to the picture house called The Ritz in the evenings, making a welcome break from work. It was particularly memorable to me because this little old-fashioned building with a balcony, built originally in 1912, had the two back rows of seats which were double width for the courting couples, something that I had never seen in London. With 100 seats on the ground floor and the same number on the balcony, it seemed to be always packed with cinema-goers.

We also strolled down to the nearest hostelry in Skipton-on-Swale, the Busby Stoop Inn, which was an old coaching inn at a crossroads, a mile nearer towards Thirsk. It was a convenient distance for a stroll after Bill's work. We often went there to warm our toes by the large open fire, beneath the low wooden

beams that straddled the room. On occasions, we would go for a drink, and joined the local enthusiasts to play dominoes, who congregated most evenings for a game or two, while others played darts.

'Don't, for goodness sake, sit in that theer chair. It'll bring thee bad luck.' One old farmer pointed to an old wooden chair in the corner, which was the only vacant seat in the crowded room.

'Why not? I can't see another.' But nevertheless I continued standing up leaning against the wall nursing my drink instead, for the man's comment sounded urgent and caused a creepy feeling to run up my spine.

'It's 'aunted (haunted), and ought to be burned. Does tha know why this place gits its weird name? – bin called t' Busby Stoop for many a year, tha knows.' The old man was enjoying frightening me with his ghost tales.

The story gradually leaked out like the slow drip of reluctant bathwater, as the three men continued their game of dominoes, and taking it in turns they continued the story, which was based on a true tale.

The gist of it was that a Thomas Busby married the innkeeper's daughter, Elizabeth Auty and took up residence in her home. He tried throwing his weight about and upset the innkeeper, Daniel Auty, by sitting in the old man's favourite wooden chair by the fire. In a temper one day, while trying to grab the chair for himself, he stuck a knife in the old man, killing him, and was tried and hanged at York Assizes in 1702. Before he died, he cursed old Auty and all who sat in his chair. Eventually, the corpse was suspended in chains from the stump (called a stoop) of the old tree outside the inn, where it hung for some years as a warning to other miscreants to keep away.

A much later incident led credence to this tale, when two airmen in the late 1940s, having sat there all evening in the chair, started for home and were killed in a car crash. Not long after this, a local cabinet maker, Carlo Pagnani, befell the same fate, adding fuel to the superstition in the early 1950s during the time I was there. Some years later in 1972, in desperation to kill off the fears of locals, the chair was donated to the Thirsk Museum, which displayed it suspended in the air to prevent anybody sitting in it.

Front view of Skipton Hall from the farm buildings.

We were wrapped up in the practicalities of furnishing the flat once the alterations had been carried out, while I rang home several times to tell my mother excitedly of our progress. Suddenly the penny dropped, and she started questioning me closely.

'When and where do you think you will get married? You are too young yet. You don't have our permission. I'd better come to see this flat you are furnishing. What about your job here and what will you tell Mr. Lewsey? Have you spoken to your father?'

Her comments and questions came thick and fast; like an express train gathering speed at every turn until it eventually ran out of control, she spluttered out her thoughts, until she finally crashed into the reality of the developing situation.

THE 1854 WEDDING DRESS

Bill and I decided to travel to London in the late autumn to tell my parents of our decision to get married, explain our plans and to invite them to visit the new flat. Unfortunately, it was like dropping a bombshell on them, because it was certainly not what they had anticipated for me at all.

Rather too late, they had woken up to the fact that I was now a grown up young woman, and no longer to be treated as a child. They had neglected to socialise me amongst their pick of young men whom they considered right for me in their eyes, and were horrified that I had chosen a farmer, a profession they considered completely unsuitable.

My painting of the view from the flat in Skipton Hall.

Patiently Bill explained that we had been given a large six-roomed flat, that he had a good job, and in time intended to acquire a farm of his own. Pursed lips and angry exchanges on their part did not alter our resolve, instead only strengthened our desire to go ahead with the plans. The more they found fault in our intentions, the more I dug my toes in.

Visiting the Dairy Show at Olympia, London

We argued that the new job coupled with the delightful flat was an opportunity not to be missed. It must be admitted that their arguments were also fairly sound, because I was only nineteen years old, and my future life was likely to be quite alien to what I was accustomed. Critically, the fact that I was so tired of Mother being such a constant 'control freak' in my life fuelled the rebellious fire in me.

We took a day to visit the Dairy Show in Olympia, where we met up with some other Yorkshire Friesian breeders who had also been at the Great Yorkshire Show. This was a welcome break from the ongoing arguments with my parents. Soon, Bill had to return to work, having only taken a few days off, while I battled on at home.

Aunt Daisy talked to me at length, but while saying the same thing about waiting until I was a year older, could not answer my question, when I said, 'What for? What am I waiting a year for? Another boyfriend? Another job?'

Jane was recalled from Kenya to talk to me. She appeared to be angry about this turn of events. I suspect that she did not relish the thought that her younger sister was getting married before her, and stuck to the old Victorian 'precedence' procedure held in old families. As a means of applying pressure, she slyly told Mother she thought that I was probably expecting a child. I was appalled by this suggestion. This piece of slander was in complete contradiction to my steadfast view of maintaining sexual abstinence before marriage. Nevertheless, it resulted in Mother insisting on the indignity of me having a doctors' examination to prove otherwise.

Eventually Father capitulated, and Mother followed suit. I was under age and needed their permission, so as soon as this was given a date was set for the following June by Mother, and she decided that it would be in London. Now the full strength of her organisational prowess came into force, with some decisions being made without my consent. She treated me as if I was in disgrace, and was not prepared to listen to my proposals for my own wedding. 'You don't need bridesmaids, and my old wedding dress, altered to fit you, will do very well,' she told me, her steely-blue eyes glinting menacingly and daring me to argue.

However, I had allies to hand, with an interest in the action. These were mainly my Aunt Lucy and my sister Jane. Jane had now realised that the occasion was to go ahead, so wasn't going to give up her chance of being a bridesmaid. My father, now reconciled to ensuring that this would be a proper occasion, for once stepped in and argued with my mother, which eventually silenced her.

'That won't do at all. We will have a proper family gathering. And I'll pay for whatever dress you choose. And of course you must have bridesmaids.' So the matter was settled.

Invitation lists were drawn up, and Bill was consulted initially about the suitability of a date. Mother's choice was not convenient for the farming community because it was right in the middle of the haymaking season, which meant that many of our friends could not attend. She insisted on this date, duly asking Bill which members of his family would be attending – this caused more consternation for them. Bill's mother could not face a London wedding, and Pat would not leave her Mother, who was not in the best of health but she suggested a compromise. Bill's youngest uncle and aunt, Sidney and Rene Joynson offered to come and stand in as 'substitute parents' for Bill.

A large variety of parcels started arriving, these being wedding gifts. My mother had the sense to organise the dispatch of many of them to our new flat, before they arrived to our family house in Isleworth. Bill, Lucy and Wilf made sure of their safe arrival in our new home. Even a beautiful red Wilton carpet was sent by Great Aunt Evelyn, and boxes of china,

Bill's uncle and aunt, Sid and Rene Joynson.

glassware and linen all accumulated in our flat, awaiting unpacking, including a bookcase, a mirror and a
'Vono' couch, which caused some consternation getting it up the stairs.

Having looked around the dress shops, and considered various advertisements for having a dress made,
I decided upon an alternative idea. Rather than buy a
new dress, I persuaded Mother's dressmaker of old,
Mrs Tighe, to alter the crinoline dress, which Grandfather had given to me in the 1940s. I knew that it had
been worn by his Grandmother in 1854 and probably
trimmed a few times for different occasions.

Betty Ryde, John Harald and Jane.

Mrs Tighe set to work, taking off the pink ball-
gown trimmings, and adding the same coloured satin sleeves to match the design,
because sleeves were an essential feature in the 1950s. Next, she inserted a long zip
between the lace holes, which were then filled with seed pearls, and added Brussels
lace over any alterations. The dress was beautiful, and I was delighted.

I sat with Father in his study whilst Jane and Betty Ryde, daughter of our near
neighbour, who was the other bridesmaid, discussed with Mother what they should
wear and studied patterns in the other room. Flocked organdie I heard mentioned
several times, as Jane chose lemon yellow, which was to contrast with the pale blue
chosen by Betty. My preferences were not consulted, as the final stage was being
set for my OWN wedding day. I was now getting cold feet.

'I'm not sure if I'm doing the right thing.' I said and confided some of my fears
to my father that I hadn't voiced before. 'Well, cancel it then, if you can. Your
Mother is in full swing.
Nothing would change
her plans now. But
maybe it's just nerves.'
So I kept quiet, because
I was so in love with
my kindly man from
Yorkshire, and believed
in my inner strength to
cope with the great
changes that faced me.
It seemed exciting and
adventurous but I also
craved a more peaceful
home life.

At Christmas Bill re-
turned to meet some of
my family, during
which time we held a

*Left to right, back: Len, friend, Mother, Uncle Barney, Uncle John and
Tony Hargreaves. Middle: Aunt Daisy, Dad, Aunt Evelyn, Libsie Hargreaves, Aunte Melene. Front: Bill, Wendy and Jane.*

The 1854 wedding dress.

Christmas party where he met many of my aunts, uncles and friends. This was the first opportunity for him to meet a few more of them.

I took him to meet the new vicar of St John's church, the Rev. Kelso and my friends in the choir, where Anthea and I still sang, albeit occasionally now. The vicar read our banns, and the choir agreed to sing at my wedding. John and David Harold from next door, came in to join us during the Christmas festivities. They took Bill out to the pub, which culminated in John offering to be the best man. No-one had thought of this detail!

Mr Winterbourne, whose house was at the end of our road, had a remarkable wife. Mrs Winterbourne, with her lovely clothes and regularly waved hair, like the film star Marilyn Monroe, was the thinnest person I had ever encountered, in contrast to her husband's corpulent frame.

One of her great talents was to bake beautiful cakes for all occasions, which had provided private 'pin money' for some years. My father called in to the Winterbourne's occasionally to chinwag with Jim, and had witnessed her undoubted skills. He suggested she made me a wedding cake.

'You cannot ask her; Jim lives there,' was my mother's unreasonable comment which caused ribald laughter from Father, and from a few others present. He went ahead and ordered a two tier cake to be made, without Mother's consent, causing another outburst of anger – poor Mother, how she did like being in the driving seat. She was even angrier when I went to help ice it, an activity I had done many times before.

During the cake icing session, Jim gave me a little trinket box as a wedding present, which had belonged to his mother. I showed it to Father. It was old, delicately carved with a filigree design, and had fancy brass hinges and an unusual clasp on its side. While offering the present, Jim said, 'This box came from China many moons ago. I bought it while abroad with the band. As I've no family now, I want you to have it. Perhaps it will remind you of the musical times we had together.'

But Father gave me a warning of possible stormy moments

The wedding cake.

ahead... 'I shouldn't flash that in front of your Mother, if I were you. She had always coveted it during the time when it sat on the chest in Jim's room. She will hide it away for her own use or smash it in temper, for sure,' he said, and with those warning words I hid the parcel in my luggage.

Mother finally took overall charge again of organising a lavish wedding breakfast for about 60 guests, provided by caterers. This was laid out as a buffet in our drawing room, supplemented by staff who would walk discretely around the room to pour drinks and serve the many and varied delicacies.

Mother had realised her ambitions for at least one of her daughters to have a wedding and social occasion to be proud of. She sent out invitations to all our many relatives, her friends, and as many of mine whom I could persuade her to include. The cake was to be cut in the garden with the speech making, later in the afternoon, at the conclusion of the reception. Nothing was left to chance, except dealing with potential bad weather, although an alternative venue was planned for, proving her undoubted and extensive organisational skills. She would never lose her touch for organising any occasion.

When June finally arrived, the weather was kind, with a deep blue sky heralding a spell of

Betty, John, Bill, Wendy and Jane.

259

sunshine and warmth, while the early grasses were by now parched into many hues of brown.

The garden had been carefully tended for weeks by Father and his gardening friend, resulting in a magnificent show of sweet scented and colourful summer blooms, love-lies-bleeding, dahlias, tall yellow lilies, sweet peas, and carnations. There was a good choice to make creative flower displays around the house, and Jane took charge of this activity, because she had an inspired eye for flower arrangements.

Our wedding finally took place in St John's Church in Isleworth, beautifully decorated with scented and colourful flowers, which were arranged up the aisle, and lit up by the sunshine as it shone through the upper windows. This reminded me of the shafts of light seen in St Pauls Cathedral years ago.

My mother at the wedding.

With a full choir of my friends attending, and my bridegroom, Bill, tall and handsome in the sunshine standing by my side, our musical wedding took place. As far as I was concerned, my dress, made in 1854, was more beautiful than any new creation, set off by my new necklace of pink amethysts. I carried a posy of pink and white roses to complete my ensemble.

Many unexpected guests were present: my dear old aunts Nona and Gee, had arrived from Egypt and were staying at

William Goodair making a speech.

the Sesame Club in London. Now very old and even more wizened like polished walnuts, they were brought by Grandfather's friend, William Goodair, his visitor to Bowerswood, who still managed to look debonair despite his advancing age. He wanted to take part, and offered to be 'toastmaster' of the proceedings before the cake cutting event, so unexpectedly made the opening speech.

'I have decided to represent the old order, Wendy's grandfather's generation, for I see there are one or two still here. Her

The furs of the 1950s.

grandfather would have loved this occasion. He has watched her grow from birth to womanhood with pride, but sadly he died five years ago. So I am opening the speeches and ask you to raise your glasses to those that have gone before, and to the happy future of those here today.' This was followed by my father, who was witty, by John who was nervous and Bill who was pleased to to be done with the speeches on such a hot day.

My other younger aunts were at the wedding resplendent in colourful silk dresses and fox fur capes draped over their shoulders, as was the fashion then, which they finally abandoned in the late afternoon when the weather became too hot to wear.

Uncle Barney and Aunt Melene, also complete with fox cape, who had been strongly opposed to the wedding, now came with big smiles and a big present. Uncle Stephen with his friend Daphne and Justin O'Sullivan appeared, and our friend Evelyn, who worked for the McLaughlans, came to represent those at Skipton Hall, because the farming calendar was in full swing in June – hay making time. The mixture of guests was so diverse that it represented the various layers of our lives in a curious way.

I hoped that Grandfather was looking down upon me with a smile on his face, because I was sure that he would have approved of this day – and also my wedding dress, into which I had sewn 'something old'. I would like to think he would have been proud of me, because I knew that my father was. There was no going back now.

The 'something old' was a folded piece of paper from my old envelope, a faded fairy and the leader of the troupe, to guide her fairy band down the rainbows to my new home.

This was the first day of my new life, a new beginning, a new reality.

EPILOGUE

The first quarter of my life up until getting married in 1955 has been extremely varied, exciting and momentous – nevertheless, the latter three quarters have been equally so.

The year 1955 was an obvious and natural time to conclude my recollections. Now that I was married, my way of life shifted into new environments, and relationships, of which I had a better control. The turbulent wartime years receded in my mind and became a personal history.

We did eventually move to our own mixed farm in Cumberland, and also were lucky enough to have four sons, Tim, Nick, Jerry and Andy, who were as tall as their father. All engineers in different disciplines, they have travelled the world and in turn have produced the next generation of six young people, who now appear to be as good looking, artistic and clever as I had hoped they would be, but of course any Grandmother would say that. So I continue to watch the future with anticipation.

While travelling around Britain over the years, I have made a point of visiting many of the places which once had an important or interesting meaning in my life. But one thing has become clear as I started to look back at previous times. The aura surrounding a beloved place also needed the characters themselves who lived there, because without them, the magic spell is somewhat shattered, instead there is only a hint, or a vague perfume of bygone moments to tease one's memory.

In 2009 I took a holiday in Northern Ireland, revisiting my childhood haunts, and eventually found my original home, now renamed and extended, with the drive and entrance repositioned on the roadway. I had walked up the old familiar road, watched over by the monkey puzzle tree, still surviving in the same place, but now enormous, and could smell the familiar seaweeds of low tide, while the seabirds cried out, searching for food on the uncovered seabed of little rocks and sands.

I hesitated at the unfamiliar new gate, but remembered, when peering in, the five steps up to the front door. I rang the doorbell, and was answered with the query, 'Can I help you?'

'I used to live here over seventy years ago, and wondered if I may step in for a moment to see again my old home?' I asked an efficient looking young lady.

'You're very welcome to come in. Do sit down, and have some tea and freshly baked soda bread with us. I can see that your wee dander has tired you out.' She led me into her sitting room, which I recognised as our dining room, remembering the fire sprites of long ago. She brought in the aforementioned refreshments.

'I've often wondered who used to live here, for although a very comfortable house, it is a strange place.' She began to talk of her family and of their move to this house from Newry.

'My family have loved it here. The children took over the top floor for themselves. My son had the front room and my two daughters the big room at the back where the sunlight streams in. There was a big doll's house, which delighted the girls.'

We chatted thus, as I recounted to her the sad moments of our final exit to England at the start of the war. Having finished tea, I rose to leave, thanking her for such an unexpected meal, then she said, 'The house is blessed with fairies.'

I stopped in my tracks, 'Oh, really?' My heart started racing with past memories, for I knew it had been true. I remembered my dear Father and his kindness in allaying my very real fears of those far off days.

She continued, 'Yes, when we arrived, we colour washed all the rooms to freshen up the place and make it less dusty, until we had decided upon more permanent decoration, then furnished the top floor for the children. The first night that they slept there, they saw fairies all around, but when they put the light on, nothing could be found.'

She led me out of the house, adding, 'This happens despite repainting the room several times over the years. They are still there. Strange, is it not?'

It was my turn to smile now, with memories still fresh in my mind, after over 70 years, of the excitement of seeing the fairies. I did not bother to explain how they had flown in.

In the 1970s I continued to explore those half-remembered Irish corners of my early childhood. How short the distances between places now seem compared to the perceptions of distance as a child. The smells of the seaweed along the shore and the continuous cries of the seabirds brought back memories and a sigh for times past. But the docksides have been sanitised, with new harbours and shiny 'yuppy' boats to colour the coastline, and of course many areas of once pure countryside, now sprout houses.

My visits to Bowerswood over the years had been more frequent, because in later years I lived in Lancashire, so was continually drawn to visiting my much loved home. I would drive down the long driveway, in through the gates, round the great ash tree in front of the house on the crunching yellow stones, and away again without ever advertising my presence,

Bowerswood, painting from 1980.

like a sneak-thief in the night. Stealing memories. It was like a kind of compulsion, with car windows open, breathing in the scents of the tall pines in the changing seasons.

Eventually I did announce myself to the owners and was invited in. Once inside I was slightly taken aback – the panelled doors had been made flush, the beautiful Edwardian tiles in the hallway covered with wooden flooring and the carved staircase spindles had been encased with panelling. All was painted white and flattened to suit the modern style, hiding the old grandeur that, which was sleeping under this newer suit of clothes.

The house suffered a fire in 1980, started from a chip pan in the kitchen. Very fortunately the fire only damaged the centre of the house so that, when the firemen eventually pulled away the waterlogged and burned out materials, the original construction remained intact, just as I had remembered it, well-protected from the heat of the flames. Over the following months the house was restored to its original charm with the undamaged Edwardian tiles and carved stair spindles still firmly in place.

The property has changed hands a few times, and the land has been broken up into smaller parcels. Various changes have been made to the house which has culminated in new owners establishing a nursing home, with rooms added at the back, and deciding to knock down the east wing. I did not like the changes much, although the entrance and front reception rooms remained the same. After this experience, it eventually cured me of my visits. But the strong aroma of the trees will always be there, despite the loss of some of the pines, decimated by two severe storms.

Nostalgia for seeing the ruins of The Biggins, my burned-out boarding school sitting in beautiful parkland, took me to investigate the site, while in the vicinity of Kirkby Lonsdale one day. I was rather shocked to discover that the ruins had been removed, and was now covered with a new housing estate – there was no point returning there again, all traces of the past having been removed. The building of Nunk Knowles, into which Moreland School had moved in Clitheroe after the great fire of 1943, has continued to be a thriving, mixed Independent School, overlooking the River Ribble.

Naturally enough, I was attracted to taking a walk around the town of Clitheroe again. The building of Barton's Drapers shop is still there, with the narrow ginnel into the back garden, after which I found the Park Road cul-de-sac where the small playground was situated. It was as if time had stood still – I could readily recall echoes of the children calling out from the tent-door of their home-made zoo, 'Only one penny to come inside.' I saw that the Kings Lane Theatre had been pulled down for redevelopment, and much of Clitheroe had marched forwards to the end of the twentieth century by building into every spare corner of land.

I took a trip to Yorkshire with some friends in the 1990s, and stayed in Northallerton to tour the northern parts of the county. Whilst visiting the famous High Force waterfalls, I was drawn to see Ettersgill Farm, where I had learned so much about the hardy sheep living there. Walking along the road, I saw two men who were treating a barn full of sheep, with a blur of numerous black noses, yellow eyes and a sea of grey wool in motion. One man in his seventies paused, and came over to the gate where I was leaning.

'How do then, can I 'elp thee? he smiled encouragingly. 'I know that smile. It's Wendy, isn't it?' and in that instant we recognised each other, as he smiled with his broad grin, and of course I noticed Ian look at me once again with those brilliant orange eyes. He told me of his mother's death, and also of my dear friend Helen, who had died the previous year in Darlington. The caravan was still in one of his sheds. He seemed to have weathered, shrunk and aged, yet the farm, the sheep and the scenery remained, quite unchanged and timeless. I realised that in 40 years I must have changed greatly too. Now he lived down the valley in Middleton-in-Teesdale, and let out the farmhouse as a holiday let, but still farmed the land around it. When we parted again, he kissed me on both cheeks in salutation, as old friends do. If he had done that when I was a teenager, I would have flushed with embarrassment – times change with age.

During this holiday we passed by Mrs Wrigley's grand Georgian mansion, Warlaby Lodge, but now without the enormous copper beech tree defending its entrance. It was still a large private house, no doubt remodelled to fit modern criteria. I drove in through the entrance to the drive and, finding the owners, explained my intentions. I realised that every place has a unique smell associated with it, created by the surrounding vegetation or buildings, and this was one occasion where I could almost recreate the ghost of the wiry Mrs Wrigley, leaning on the fence of the horses' field and talking to me in her staccato voice, 'Bring your own riding breeks next time.'

I was not too far from Thirsk at that time, so went the extra few miles to Skipton on Swale, where I pulled into the middle of the hamlet, and walked around. This had been the first home of my own. Many changes had taken place, for example, the farm buildings had been re-configured and extended, but the main house was still standing proudly upon the hill, well kept and subtly altered to fit the passing of time, with the top floors having been made into holiday lets. It was warm and the summer smells of harvesting took my mind straight back to those farming days in the 1950s.

Driveway to Cuckfield Park.

Travelling around the south west counties around London in 1990, we went to stay for a couple of nights with my mother's sister, Aunt Melene, who lived in a delightful old half-timbered house, near Farnham in Surrey. We were keen to see my cousin (her son), by travelling to Sussex for a brief visit to where he lived. Melene declined to accompany us, having explained that she had quarrelled with him recently – and we assured her that we would return by suppertime.

On our return journey taking a cross country route back to Farnham, we noticed the village of Cuckfield on the map and decided to make a slight detour to visit Cuckfield Park. It was a

Aunt Melene's house, Outmoor, in Churt.

delightful moment to drive up the long tree-lined entrance to Cuckfield Park, and remember that walk so long ago with Robert Morley in the evening sunshine – such moments have been jewels in my memory. The large old house had reverted to being a private residence once more.

After satisfying my curiosity there, we set off to return to Farnham. Unfortunately, we were a little later than anticipated in arriving back at Melene's house, having travelled cross-country through unfamiliar areas of Sussex and Surrey, and had made a couple of wrong turns. Our lateness caused such a scene. As a young person, wrapped up in my own family problems, I had never realised until now just how very alike in temperament were Uncle Stephen, Aunt Melene and Mother. In different ways, they all had obsessive-compulsive personalities, although often, extremely kind and generous, nevertheless all had terrible tempers. As we entered my aunt's house, we were met with a torrent of angry words.

'How could you be so late? You promised to be back for teatime. Why have you been so long? What can you have been talking about? I thought you were supposed to be visiting me.'

At the same time as being angry, she lifted out from the embers of the fire several aluminium-foil wrapped baked potatoes she had been preparing.

'They will be over-cooked now.' Then she proceeded to hurl them one at a time at us with devastating accuracy, before storming out with the parting words, 'I don't care if you never eat again.'

Now many years later, I remember the pleasure of finding Cuckfield Park still intact, but I remember the pain from those hot potatoes more.

When I think of another house which I visited only briefly in 1953, during the Coronation period, I was really saddened to see that it had been pulled down. This was Letton, which had belonged to my Great Aunt Evelyn, near Blanford Forum. As a reminder of such a magnificent, unwanted house, I produced a painting of it – looking at the picture will always make me think of the rooks, in my mind's eye, gathering in the evening twilight and grumbling as they settled down for the night.

As for London, St Paul's Girls' School in Hammersmith, has gone from strength to strength, changing, expanding, modernising and still producing extraordinary and individual pupils. I have learned over these past 60 years of the abolition of uniforms, the creation of a new library, and other new buildings, as well as a theatre suite for all the pupils to be proud of.

Schools need to be forward looking, and I noticed that Ellesmere College in Shropshire has changed to cater for both boys and girls. I wondered whether the mice or rats ever put in an appearance now, because old, rural houses with little cracks and corners will always be a target for such creatures. When revisiting those old haunts, in my mind I am able to reconstruct the atmosphere of those early days, along with the many people, now long gone, who remain forever in my memory.

In later years my parents settled down to an acceptable co-existence. Len died of cancer. Jim continued to drink in the local hostelry in St John's Road with my father for many years, passing away just before him.

As time has moved on, I now look back with much more affection on my lively mother who, in her late eighties became a gentler, sweet character towards the end. This part of her personality must have been hidden all the time under the energetic and forceful exterior she often showed when I was young, but basically she was an extremely kind person to everybody, whether you wanted her ministrations or not.

Finally I think of my dearest father, who filled me with his homespun wisdom and kindness, which shaped quite a lot of my early, and indeed my later attitudes in life. He lasted for nearly a century with his faculties intact until his final demise, much loved and greatly missed by many, including his regiment, proud to have given him a military funeral.

Many wept as the bugler played *The Last Post*. I am sure that he had been able to hear it.

My father's Rowan Tree

We went to Talkin Tarn one day
To walk in woods, sweet smell of spring
Mixed in with graceful native trees
White blossoms sway with teasing breeze.
Underfoot twigs snapped and cracked,
Hides translucent toadstool ring.
Found mountain ash, now seeking light.
Stem fine, green shoot, twin beetle-wing,
The cotyledon, promising a future height,
A four inch embryo seedling.

Long tap-root winding, guiding down,
Determined searches leaf-mould ground.

RAINBOWS, RECOLLECTIONS AND REALITY

'We'll plant it in this old grey pot',
My father said, 'for it will grow.'
In time the little mountain ash
Became my rowan tree. Like Bonsai of old,
Restricted by its small glazed cache,
With roots curled round, curtailed its size,
Yet flourished in miniature, controlled,
Now formed its ancient compromise.

My father aged and shrank in size,
but kept the tree by his creaking bed.
In nursing home he watered it.
'This little tree will outlive me,' he said.
'My Buddha calls me to a higher plane,
A wondrous state to see.'
His wise blue eyes foretold his end, so old, so cold.
Tears flowed. I planted deep our rowan tree.
From sapling to maturity, it spread its roots
Beneath old ground – now safe, so cool, so free.

New branches sway to passing breeze,
White fairy flowers catch daylong sun
Metamorphose into seeds soon gone.
Red tasselled berries, seen throughout the trees,
Iridescent blackbirds swoop down one-by-one,
Sharp beaks now pluck the ripest fruit they see
So I sit here, watch timeless clouds drift by
Where flocks of wild birds now feed free,
I remember time with Dad at Talkin Tarn,
Who somehow lives forever in that tree.

AFTERWORD

This book is a kaleidoscope of Wendy Stuart's life from early childhood through to the age of twenty when she married in 1955. The writing of it took her two years to organise, research and eventually to set down on paper, done for different reasons not least being a sudden realisation that even her own family is not familiar with her early life – for example, '…but I thought that you were born and brought up in London', an assumption which is very far from the truth.

By making reference to diaries and visitors books kept by her mother, Wendy has augmented her memory, deciding to be selective in choosing specific events which were appealing or of interest to her. As the reader will start to appreciate, each chapter can be read on its own merit, each representing short episodes in her life, which she recounts with an interesting clarity of recollection. From an early age she had a natural instinct for visual memory. In this book we experience the world very much through her eyes, a skill demonstrated through many of the vivid and sometimes quite unusual observations.

Born in 1935 in Lancashire, Wendy is taken to live in Northern Ireland in a peaceful pre-war home with her family, only to move house at the start of World War II, and then move again around the country over the next fifteen years. Throughout this time, one is reminded of the difficulties she experienced in making the transition from childhood through to eventual womanhood.

A key figure in her life was her father whom she adored from her earliest memories. He served in the army as a regular soldier, going to war initially with the British Expeditionary Force in 1939, but is absent from home for a long time until the conflicts in India are settled in 1947. Upon his return home he is confronted with marital problems caused by long separation, but which he overcomes admirably.

For Wendy, her mother was temperamental and 'had to be obeyed', whilst on the other hand, her gentle father seemed to be full of wisdom and good advice. Her sister Jane was mostly to be 'admired', although she had quite a complex personality. Wendy was often the quiet observer of family life, learning to keep out of trouble as she saw it. Throughout the early period of her life, Wendy is supported by the firm belief that her father, an Irishman with a creative spirit for storytelling, controls 'fairyland' for the good of people, who ride on the rainbows to achieve this end. Armed with this belief, along with a handful of tiny paintings of the fairy folk which he crafted, she manages to hold on to her beliefs and her pictures, throughout the war and eventually into peacetime.

From a Victorian household near Garstang, she moves to Kirkby Lonsdale, then Clitheroe, and finally at the end of the war to London, where the bombed out areas were shocking to behold. Coming to London was a wrench, taking Wendy from a place of safety and mainly solitude, to one of bustle, risk and uncertainty. Nevertheless, this is a spur for new opportunities, adventures, and experiences, needed to help draw her out of a world of fantasy and sometimes isolation into the real world. A family house is bought in West London, and after studying at a prep school, leading on to public school for girls, and then to art college and a spell at a domestic science college insisted upon by her godmother. She tries her hand at working in Herefordshire, also travelling to France to work briefly as a clothes designer, which all lead to interesting encounters along the way. Always a restless spirit and unsure of a settled career, she finds a variety of occupations for short periods, but is never completely satisfied with any of them.

Slowly Wendy weakens her reliance upon her parents and life in London. Her love of the northern counties prevail, and having kept in touch with northern friends, she makes several visits to the farming communities which appeal to her, working briefly on a sheep farm in Teasdale, then a mixed farm in North Yorkshire. This finally gives her the freedom to take responsibility for the direction and development of her own life, whilst coping with the emotions of being a naive teenager with little parental guidance. Eventually she meets her husband in Yorkshire and creates her own family.

The research for this book was quite an adventure, with Wendy visiting places where she either lived or visited around Britain and Ireland, often welcomed by strangers with an interest in her task, and occasionally meeting people from the past, after a break of over 50 years. Perhaps fascinating is the very large quantity of photographs included. Wendy's mother was an avid collector of photographs all her life, and also recorded many events and persons with her own camera.

One of the trickier aspects of this book has been to mimic dialect in words, therefore it is to be hoped that the flavour of the speakers shine through, by using some of the 'constructed' words which may be wrong or inaccurate. This book has provided a good balance in portraying some of Wendy's personality, along with life in the country at the time, and interspersed with a good selection of interesting stories and events which she experienced.

Nicholas Joynson, (Wendy's son), September 2015.

My son Nicholas Joynson deserves a big 'thank you' for spending time on the exacting task of proof reading this manuscript, and sometimes advising me on my old fashioned language, my friend Susanne Holt for great encouragement, and Dawn Robertson for patiently waiting till I had finished!

Wendy M. Stuart, October 2015

More books by Wendy M. Stuart also published by Hayloft:

A Lakeland Paintbook
Lakeland in the 1830s

all Wendy's books available at: www.hayloft.eu